GOVERNANCE AT WORK

The **European Science Foundation** is an association of its 56 member research councils, academies and institutions devoted to basic scientific research in 20 countries. The ESF assists its Member Organizations in two main ways: by bringing scientists together in its Scientific Programmes, Networks, and European Research Conferences, to work on topics of common concern; and through the joint study of issues of strategic importance in European science policy.

The scientific work sponsored by ESF includes basic research in the natural and technical sciences, the medical and biosciences, the humanities and social sciences.

The ESF maintains close relations with other scientific institutions within and outside Europe. By its activities, ESF adds value by cooperation and coordination across national frontiers and endeavours, offers expert scientific advice on strategic issues, and provides the European forum for fundamental science.

This volume arises from the work of the ESF Scientific Programme on European Management and Organizations in Transition (EMOT).

Further information on ESF activities can be obtained from:

European Science Foundation
1 quai Lezay-Marnésia
F-67080 Strasbourg Cedex
France
Tel. (+33) 88 76 71 00
Fax (+33) 88 37 05 32

GOVERNANCE AT WORK

The Social Regulation of Economic Relations

Edited by

Richard Whitley and Peer Hull Kristensen

OXFORD UNIVERSITY PRESS
1997

Oxford University Press, Great Clarendon Street, Oxford OX2 6DP

Oxford New York
Athens Auckland Bangkok Bogota Bombay
Buenos Aires Calcutta Cape Town Dar es Salaam
Delhi Florence Hong Kong Istanbul Karachi
Kuala Lumpur Madras Madrid Melbourne
Mexico City Nairobi Paris Singapore
Taipei Tokyo Toronto
and associated companies in
Berlin Ibadan

Oxford is a trade mark of Oxford University Press

Published in the United States by
Oxford University Press Inc., New York

British Library Cataloguing in Publication Data
Data available

Library of Congress Cataloging in Publication Data
Governance at work: the social regulation of economic relations / edited by Richard Whitley and
Peer Hull Kristensen.
Rev. papers from two workshops held in Helsinki in 1995 and Barcelona in 1996.
Includes bibliographical references (p.   ).
1. Industrial management—Europe—Congresses. 2. Industrial organization—Europe—Congresses.
3. Corporate governance—Europe—Congresses. I. Whitley, Richard. II. Kristensen, Peer Hull.
HD70.E8G68 1997 388.94—dc21 97-466
ISBN 0-19-829248-1

1 3 5 7 9 10 8 6 4 2

Typeset by Best-set Typesetter Ltd., Hong Kong
Printed in Great Britain by
Biddles Ltd., Guildford & King's Lynn

PREFACE

This book resulted from two workshops organized as part of the series of European collaborative meetings planned as Theme A on Changing Forms of Economic Organizations of the European Science Foundation's Programme on European Management and Organizations in Transition. This series of workshops focuses on how different systems of economic coordination and control developed, and are changing, interdependently with key institutional sectors, such as political, financial, labour, and cultural systems, across Europe. The first workshop, held in Berlin in 1994, concentrated on the changing nature of the firm in Europe and resulted in the publication of *The Changing European Firm: Limits to Convergence* (London: Routledge, 1996), edited by R. Whitley and P. H. Kristensen. The next two, held in Helsinki in 1995 and Barcelona in 1996, were concerned with the relationships between deep-seated cultural conventions, often institutionalized before or during industrialization in many European societies, more formally established 'rules of the game', and patterns of work organization and control as developed by competing social groups within and between organizations. The present volume brings together some of the extensively revised contributions to these workshops which seek to understand the complex connections between institutions, groups, and work systems in different European countries in a comparative and historical perspective, as well as going beyond earlier, rather sweeping, analyses of Fordism, Post-Fordism, etc. Together these papers both develop a comparative framework for analysing these interconnections and show how particular systems of normative regulation—or governance structures— developed in different societies and continue to influence the constitution and actions of collective actors in the workplace and resultant patterns of work organization. It is clear from these analyses that such patterns remain quite distinctive between countries despite the common belief in the standardizing effects of 'globalization', and that these variations are closely linked to different institutional legacies and structures.

CONTENTS

LIST OF CONTRIBUTORS

Mme E. Campagnac
École Nationale des Ponts et Chausses
LATTS-CERTES
Central IV,
1, avenue Montaigne
93167 Noisy-le-Grande
France

Dr Barbara Hibino
4310 Albany Drive, K204
San Jose, CA 95129

or

Corporate Asset Specialist
Anthem Electronics Inc.
1160 Ridden Park Drive
San Jose, CA 95131

Dr Ad van Iterson
Faculty of Economics & Business Administration
University of Limburg
Postbus 616
NL-6200 Maastricht
THE NETHERLANDS

Dr Marko Jaklic
University of Ljubljana
Faculty of Economics
Kardeljeva pl. 17
61000 Ljubljana
SLOVENIA

Dr Peer Hull Kristensen
Copenhagen Business School
IOA
Blågårdsgade 23 B
DK-2200 Copenhagen N
DENMARK

Dr Christel Lane
Faculty of Social and Political Science
Free School Lane
Cambridge
CB2 3RQ

Professor Kari Lilja
Helsinki School of Economics
Management & Organization
Runeberginkatu 14-16
SU-00100 Helsinki
FINLAND

Professor Ray Loveridge
Aston Business School
Aston University
Aston Triangle
Birmingham
B4 7ET

Mr Glenn Morgan
Manchester Business School
Booth Street West
Manchester
M15 6PB

Dr Frank Mueller
Aston Business School
Aston University
Aston Triangle
Birmingham
B4 7ET

Dr Gerd Schienstock
Research Institute for Social Science
Work Research Centre
University of Tampere
PO Box 607
Fin-33101 Tampere
FINLAND

Ms Diana Sharpe
Department of Commerce
Birmingham Business School
Birmingham University
Edgbaston
Birmingham, B15 2TT

Professor Richard Whitley
Manchester Business School
Booth Street West
Manchester
M15 6PB

Dr Graham Winch
Barlett School of Graduate Studies
University College London
Philipps House
Gower Street
London WC1E 6BT

PART 1

Introduction

1

National Systems of Governance and Managerial Prerogatives in the Evolution of Work Systems
England, Germany, and Denmark Compared

PEER HULL KRISTENSEN

1. INTRODUCTION

When it became clear, more than a decade ago, that the 'Fordist' system of work organization and control was not a universal template for organizing production and exchange throughout capitalist economies for all times, and that other work systems, i.e. 'flexible specialization' (Sabel 1982; Piore and Sabel 1984) and 'diversified quality production' (Streeck 1992) even challenged the competitive superiority of Fordist mass production under 'the new competition' (Best 1990), both managerial ideas and the science of industrial organization changed rapidly. According to Mueller and Loveridge in this volume, managers of multinational corporations, be they British, German, or American, are now adopting policies affected by these new ideas and are trying to enforce new designs of work systems, of corporate governance, and of supplier and customer relations on their business units across the world. A new universal template for the design of work systems is seemingly being adopted, imitated, and implemented in a world where the rhetoric of globalization helps to legitimize managerial changes.

Moreover, business managers throughout the world seem increasingly to be chasing their own tail. Whereas 'the new competition' saw Fordism and 'flexible specialization' as engaged in two very diverse competitive games, the first chasing low costs for standardized products of humble quality, the other chasing such customized variants for which customers would pay a premium for 'difference' and high quality, in the game now evolving the players have to comply with the rules of both games simultaneously. Mercedes Benz is illustrative of this point. Until recently, it was celebrated by itself and numerous observers for its capability in 'diversified quality production'. Recently, Mercedes Benz has engaged in a seemingly chaotic stream of actions (see Mueller and Loveridge in this volume) being convinced that its serious crisis was caused by its inability to meet the criteria of 'lean production'. Moreover, this identity crisis seems to have spread to the entire Baden-Württemberg region, which was originally seen as a 'model society', capable of embedding an advanced form of flexible specialization. Gerd Schienstock in this volume shows how a whole range of manufacturing principles, formerly claimed to be constitutive of Baden-Württemberg's competitive success, are now being questioned in favour of principles connected to the Japanese form of 'lean production'.

Paradoxically, these new managerial ideas, prerogatives, and actions are in sharp contrast to the lessons learned by the science of industrial organization from the debate which made it clear that Fordism was only one of many possible work systems. It became clear that there are many different kinds of capitalism, or forms of economic organization, the evolutions of which take quite different routes and become efficient to varying degrees in terms of world competition at different points in history. If not, the peculiar way of organizing firms and interfirm networks in 'Third Italy', Baden-Württemberg, or Japan would simply not have been capable of challenging the American mode of organizing work after the first oil crisis. It was demonstrated how, for example, Japanese firms had become less rigid and could allow for larger flexibility in production than their American sisters, because they could rely on horizontal communication on the shop-floor and a system of close cooperation with subcontractors, conditioned by a different institutional, social, and cultural matrix than that found in the USA. Equally, the forms of capitalism developing in Eastern Europe bear the marks of their state socialist predecessors, and consequently vary, as Jaklic points out in his contribution to this book.

What seemed significant in comparison with the USA was that some societies embedded economic transactions in different social relations so that they found another balance between competition and cooperation than that prevalent in the USA. Two issues seemed crucial in some of these divergent industrial societies. First, owners and managers had, deliberately or forced by historical circumstances, accepted high discretion and skills among their workers, enabling them to adapt continuously or innovate in terms of products. Second, managers and owners had learned to consider other firms not only as potential competitors, but also as colleagues, the cooperation of which allowed them to achieve their own goals easier and in a less risky way. In short, in some societies institutions and trust allowed the social groups involved in production to play different games from those connected with opportunistic behaviour, shirking, and free-riderism said to be the reasons for choosing efficient forms of economic organization in the USA (Williamson 1975).

In this view, societal institutions affect how work systems are organized. This has led to a continual revision of the original contingency theory by, for example, the 'societal effect approach' (Maurice *et al.* 1986; Sorge and Warner 1986; Sorge 1996). In this volume, Richard Whitley offers a synthesis of numerous studies of how a number of societal factors conditioned different types of work systems. He identifies five major kinds of work system. The focus of his typification is how collective actors are constituted, and how different types of institutions enable different groups to influence how work is organized and how, in effect, discretion and responsibility are distributed among them. This synthesis and the work it draws upon emphasize that a mixture of interwoven societal factors condition social groups' responses to managerial actions and lead to varied outcomes. As was the case during the reign of the Fordist template, managerial practices find a number of distinct compromises, depending on differences between national work systems and their associated institutions.

This volume attempts to explore how deliberate managerial action and the institutional conditioning of organizational behaviour interact, creating distinct national trajectories for how and which changes can be evoked by managers concerning the reorganization of work, which is specified in Whitley's contribution, and in the transactional patterns among firms, which is the focus of Lanes's contribution. From this view managers act within the framework of an already established distinct 'national governance system', which conditions different groups to act and interact in certain ways, in providing them with distinct institutional resources if they evoke strategic actions according to certain pre-established rules for structuring their mutual game (Crozier and Friedberg 1977).

For example, both Hibino's study of the transfer of American and Japanese human resource management principles to Mexican subsidiaries, and Sharpe's study of workers' and lower management's half-hearted 'acceptance' of Japanese managerial principles in an English manufacturing plant in this volume, illustrate the process of adapting a distinct national behaviour to imported principles of management. Changes are imposed, but their outcome is neither easy to predict nor close to intended templates.

The situation resembles the introduction of Fordism in many western European countries half a century ago, where half-hearted acceptance was reflected in growing absenteeism and high turnover of employees, itself again evoking, in some countries, the search for new work systems of which Volvoism and Toyotaism became the most well known. It is worthwhile reminding ourselves that by studying how different groups of workers with different 'world views' and 'careers at work' united in a common strategy against Fiat managers' attempt to modernize along Fordist patterns, Sabel (1982) initially discovered an alternative division of labour, and that politics had a say in the process.

Current experiments take place within a different economic climate, and high unemployment rates put pressure on social groups to accept individually, or as groups, a much stronger hand from managers than was the case in the late 1960s. However, both Sharpe's and Hibino's studies show that even in depressed labour markets, the introduction of alien managerial ideas is not easily achieved.

To the new science of industrial organization, these observations are not surprising. Individual firms operate within a larger context. The work system they operate recruits employees from a formation of social groups which at any point of time are given and embedded in a complex institutional setting. On the other hand, the work system operates *vis-à-vis* a formation of firms, which cooperate and compete on the basis of customs and rules evolved over more than a century of experimentation with industrial development, manifest in the establishment of national institutions. In this complex fabric, social groupings are both constituted as social actors and given the institutional instruments to evoke action. Dependent on their situation, their sense of honour, and their ability to fight for social space, they will develop strategies *vis-à-vis* each other and managers who act according to the new prerogatives (Kristensen 1996*b*). In this dynamic, managers may act in a way which may make their potential opponents consider them an interest group. They will discover that work systems are dependent on which social groups can be recruited from the labour market, and how social institutions within a country either help or restrict them in achieving their goals.

This perspective has been explored in an earlier volume (Whitley and Kristensen 1996). In the present book we enquire about the dynamics of industrial adaptation and change from the starting-point that managers have to act in social formations which have already developed distinctive ways of governing work and firms. These governance principles have been created through centuries of institutional experiments during which social groups both affected and were themselves affected by the social space these institutions helped provide. The nature of firms is an outcome of this social process, which embeds them in social relations, enabling them to interact with other firms in fairly predictable ways facilitating transactions, hiring workers from the conviction that they will provide a fair day's work for a fair wage, engaging in risky projects believing that financial institutions, public R&D, professional groups from educational institutions, etc., will share these risks by engaging in these projects, given that the firm acts according to the rules of the game established by the distinct nation's 'system of governance'.

With the concept 'national systems of governance', we do not suggest a systematic theoretical framework. Rather, the contributions to this volume were written originally as preliminary attempts to identify the elements, aspects, and mechanisms of such governance systems in order to improve our understanding of how processes of organizational change and adaptation would proceed in various countries. Thus, we employ this concept for heuristic reasons and the entire volume is an invitation for such an academic search rather than an end-product. National systems of governance are an outcome of a continuous historical process in which social groups, economic actors, etc. jointly or through the state have attempted to influence each other by trying to 'order' their own situation and influence their opponents. They are the unintended outcomes of such mutually deliberate attempts at 'ordering'. Thus, current managerial strategies may be seen as just another set of deliberate attempts at such ordering which then enter into experiments with and become moulded through the already established national system of governance. This historical process, which follows a distinct route for each country, is the focus of this introductory chapter.

Section 2 is devoted to an elaboration of the concept of 'national systems of governance', attempting to identify the process of their social construction and suggest some conclusions to be drawn from other contributions to this volume. Section 3 discusses how managerial strategies entered into the game of natural governance systems during the post-war period, how this process created distinct problems in the countries compared, and how the situation now seems more or less prepared for managerial interventions of the new type. In both sections, comparisons between England, Germany, and Denmark help us further develop the heuristic concept of national governance systems, whereas conversely the concept helps us identify the different effects which current managerial actions will initiate within these three countries.

2. NATIONAL SYSTEMS OF GOVERNANCE

National systems of governance refer to phenomena which have often played a significant role in theories of organization and management science, though these theories have seldom analysed the systems in their own right. For example, Chester Barnard (1968: 163) suggests that it is crucial for managers to learn, through experience, their subordinates' 'zone of indifference', i.e. the type of orders which are 'unquestionably acceptable'. Without obeying such a zone of indifference, managers simply risk destroying their own authority. Though Barnard thinks the zone of indifference is determined by individuals comparing inducements and contributions (ibid. 169), he is quite explicit that social relations maintain authority of all orders which are considered the zone of indifference to 'most of the contributors'. This maintenance 'is largely a function of informal organization. Its expression goes under the names of "public opinion", "organization opinion", "feeling in the ranks", "group attitude", etc. Thus the common sense of the community informally arrived at affects the attitude of individuals, and makes them, as individuals, loath to question authority that is within or near the zone of indifference' (ibid. 169).

Similarly, Nelson and Winter (1982: 110) suggest that

routine operation involves a comprehensive truce in intraorganizational conflict. There is a truce between the supervisor and those supervised at every level of the organizational hierarchy: the usual amount of work gets done, reprimands and compliments are delivered with the usual frequency, and no demands are presented for major modifications in the terms of the relationship. There is similarly a truce in the struggle for advancement, power, and perquisites among high-level executives. Nobody is trying to steer the organizational ship into a sharp turn in the hope of throwing a rival overboard—or if someone is trying, he correctly expects to be thwarted.

Truces enable organizational members to observe traditions, though not determine what proper actions are, but certainly make it possible to identify, at least *post festum*, what lies outside truces, and only few choose deliberately to be thwarted continuously. 'The result may be that the routines of the organization as a whole are confined to extremely narrow channels by the dikes of vested interest. Adaptations that appear "obvious" and "easy" to an external observer may be foreclosed because they involve a perceived threat to internal political equilibrium' (ibid. 111).

These suggestions were echoed by Granovetter's (1985) insistence that economic transactions are embedded in social relations. This means that social relations may 'govern' behaviour and strategic interaction both within markets and hierarchies, perhaps even facilitate the governance principles of these two ideal-type governance forms to function effectively and smoothly by regulating, through 'criss-cross controls' in social relations (Crozier and Friedberg 1977), the behaviour of individuals and social groups. Such a view can also find support in the 'social interactionist' standpoint (Mead 1967; Blumer 1990).

Having accepted the invitation to examine how strategic action is regulated through social relations, the following chapters provide us with an overwhelming number of observations as to how social relations affect economic relations and patterns of action. Many of these were far from anticipated when we initiated this search. Four contributions illustrate the scope of this book.

First, Hibino shows how social relations between teacher and student in the American and the Japanese educational systems are carried over to the human resource management of firms in the two countries. US teachers adhere to the philosophy that students are 'talented' individuals who need little guidance, only the opportunity to flourish. This implies that instruction becomes very dependent on persons, both in public education and on the factory floors, since both teachers and line managers leave interpretations to students/workers. In contrast, Japan works from an 'experience' model, anticipating learning to be based on guidance by a more experienced party, and individuals are considered helpless without such guidance. Thus, here the burden of learning is placed on the teacher as he or she is considered responsible for the student's success or failure. Similarly, Japan's HRM (human resource management) system emphasizes that line managers are trained through years of experience and guidance by their seniors. Japan's system of job placement is based on more system-wide considerations and focuses on repetition and problem solving. Obviously, social relations between teacher and student socialize the individual to take on responsibility, primarily for his own conduct in the USA. Failure or success is not shared by the two. In contrast, in Japan the student and worker cannot fail without causing problems for the teacher/manager. Conversely, teachers/managers and students/workers expect each other to contribute when meeting challenges.

This makes it understandable why managers in the USA carefully define job contents and establish measures and incentives enabling the individual worker to evaluate if his or her 'talent' fits the scale and scope of the defined task. The employees experience a structured game, already experienced in the school's socialization of the individual. If the employee gets 'opportunity to flourish' inducements in the USA will typically be in terms of a career allowing the talent to be tested yet another time at a higher step of the ladder. If he or she fails, the employee will most often choose 'exit' and find a more proper place to have his or her talent tested. Neither 'voice' nor 'loyalty' (Hirschman 1970) seems to be part of the game in the USA. However, it is fairly understandable that both these behavioural attributes are associated with the nature of the game in Japan, where student and teachers and employees and managers are in the game 'together' and dependent on each other. Hibino inspires us to see how workers' socialization, like students', may also be a matter of getting used to particular forms of authority, and that 'zones of indifference' are constructed in highly different ways in various national systems. Hibino thus stresses new causal factors within the stream of comparative studies which have emphasized the different roles of managers in various countries (Maurice *et al.* 1986; Hickson 1993; Stewart *et al.* 1994).

Second, in Sharpe's contribution we learn that English workers only reluctantly accept the flexible job structure which Japanese-style management tries to impose on them. We could add that they probably do this for good reasons. As long as the British job market in general is dominated by workers with focused skills, it will probably not improve the chances of getting a new job for the worker in question, if he or she agrees, for instance, to do cleaning. Thus, workers' pre-established career systems and mobility patterns make them look for ways of improving their skills, which do not easily comply with managerial job flexibility.

Third, Morgan shows how the possibilities for employees' social action
are dependent on how they, as individuals or groups, provide for financial
security. Whether this is achieved through collective self-help, employer
sponsorship, or through the state, significantly affects the structuring of relationships among managers and workers. Morgan shows how under different conditions workers develop their strategies and behaviour toward
managerial action, dependent on whether they are living in a social democratic, a liberal, or a conservative, corporatist welfare state. Whereas the
social democratic welfare state, in providing financial security as an universal right, enables workers to create solidarity across groups and institutionalize collective bargaining with managers, the situation is very different
in, for example, a conservative corporatist welfare state. Here, individuals
depend both on their employment within a firm and their professional position on the labour market for their financial security. Thus, solidarity of
a wider scope is structurally destroyed among the different layers of
employees.

A worker living in a conservative corporatist welfare state will no doubt
accept a more narrow 'zone of indifference', more humble terms when
truces are institutionalized, and have a much more limited range of 'structured games' to evoke strategies from than workers in social democratic
welfare states. Conversely, professionals from elite associations in conservative, corporatist states will be less inclined to consider their own interests
in the light of others when preparing their group action *vis-à-vis* other
groups. For instance, they may more easily adopt new ideas and managerial strategies, if these serve their own interest. The structure of such a society
means that a dominant coalition can be build among a narrow range of
groups belonging to the elite. This being in place, managerial action can be
imposed by fiat and tight control over work.

The nature of this process stands in sharp contrast to how Lilja models
the game between shop stewards (the trusted person) and managers in
Finland as an example of micro-politics within a social democratic welfare
state. By exercising the legal rights associated with such a position, shop
stewards and managers synchronize their actions. This process helps the
firm mobilize political and institutional resources while simultaneously
forcing the firm to incorporate wider social considerations into its alloca-
tive decisions. In contrast to widely held beliefs, workers through their representative trusted person do not entirely focus on short-term benefits but
are able to incorporate strategic and long-term views due to the careful way
they prepare and select their shop stewards. In this way, the structure of the
game between the opponents turns into a mutual learning process by which
initial managerial prerogatives are improved, while simultaneously creating an atmosphere in which decisions become authorized. If we learn from
Morgan's contribution that it is difficult for managers to establish the 'zone

of indifference' within a social democratic welfare state, Lilja shows how this zone becomes established through participative negotiations.

Both Morgan and Lilja consider how it effects the historical dynamics that different social groups can act on distinct institutional foundations. These institutional foundations make it possible for certain groups to influence the ordering of work systems differently in various countries as highly different strategies become efficient in the mutual game played by different groups. Obviously, these institutional foundations are themselves outcomes of distinct historical processes in different nations. Through the state or their indigenous organizing capability various groups have gained a social space which enables them to influence the organization of work and transactional patterns among firms, so as to secure their future role within economic agencies.

In particular, Campagnac and Winch show how contrasting state policies and practices in Britain and France during the early industrialization period resulted in quite different systems for developing and organizing high-level expertise in these countries. These systems continue to vary and to affect both patterns of group formation and work organization such that important differences in sectoral structures remain. Additionally, the behaviour of the state—and indeed its organization—reflect earlier political and social developments in these two long-established European societies.

Together with the chapters by Morgan and Lilja, this contribution shows that social groups are affected by and able to affect a much larger part of society than immediately associated with the 'economic sphere'. Their ability to fight for social space in that realm is dependent on their ability to engage individuals in associated strategies where group identities can be maintained. No doubt, individuals' loyalty to groups will be an effect of the space already occupied, the sense of honour it gives the individuals, and the resources in terms of institutions and career opportunities of which they, as a group, are in command. But of similar importance is also how this 'group existence', of, for instance, British engineers, has been defined against other groups, whether some groups have made truces with other groups enabling them to cooperate and compete in mutually reinforcing ways.

However, these considerations make it clear that, when looking at how authority is exercised, truces established and maintained, and games structured within the 'economic sphere' by addressing the 'sphere of social relations', a number of new questions arise: how did the social groups emerge at first? How did they regulate their mutual competition and cooperation within and between firms and how was the state and the wider society mobilized in order for these groups to maintain and develop their identity? Our discussion so far indicates that answers to these questions must be based on and understood through the historical processes by which social groups emerge within a larger social system already populated by other social groups. Thus, rather than anticipating national systems of governance as the 'structure of relations' which may impose a 'social order' on society, we may expect an ongoing process of ordering, involving a larger or smaller number of groups trying to influence mutually each other's actions. The structuring of this game is what we consider to be at the root of national systems of governance.

Dewey (1927) has suggested a general framework for how this dialectical process of experimentation operates within a democracy. Whereas the life of given groups is institutionalized as a set of occupations (ibid. 44–5), new groups are formed in response to the joint activities of these former groups. They shape their identity by fighting for ways of regulating the consequences of the traditional groups on themselves. At first new groups emerge as new publics. Such publics will try to make the state an agency for organizing, or institutionalizing, viewing regulations to be necessary. However, the state, being constituted by agencies created as a result of the successful organization of past publics, tends to obstruct such new publics, and to form itself; the publics have to break existing political forms (ibid. 31).

In Europe, this experimental process took a particularly intensive form during the industrial revolution because of changes in constitutional orders paving the way for parliamentary reforms and freedom of association. In other regions the state was given such political forms that this dynamic never succeeded in establishing itself. In e.g. tsarist Russia conversely rights and obligations for and the very definition of social groups as well as the authority relations among groups working within enterprises were established autocratically by the tsar (Bendix 1974).

We shall elaborate this view by making first a hypothetical sketch of how this dialectical experimental process unfolded within the classic example of the English industrial revolution to give the social relations there a distinct form of governance, which could be termed 'market'. Subsequently, we shall compare how in the German and the Danish case this dialectic combined different forces and led to other principles for ordering social relations (legal-professional bureaucracy and reputational relations).

*The dialectics between social groups and publics in constructing
national governance systems in industry: England, Germany, and
Denmark compared*

The industrial revolution and the birth of capitalism is a particularly intensive period during which publics throughout Europe revolted against conditions created by transacting parties in the previous, mainly feudal period. The success of these publics in establishing themselves led to new forms of transaction among the newly created groups who achieved certain new identities and roles in society. Their new forms of transactions in turn affected large numbers of groups within the body of the old order. Thus, while new group identities were established, former groups rediscovered their identity by having to create publics that could fight for state regulation of the effects of these newly established groups and their transaction patterns. As indicated already, in taking these first two steps into a circular dynamic of cumulative causation, such dialectics will depend much on how new and old groups are organized, which resources and institutions they can draw on when communicating their voice to those in command of the state and other agencies. This process suggests a period of European history in which old and new social groups could no longer take for granted the protection of their social identities and therefore experienced a great need for forming publics. And yet, the society in which they tried to give voice to their problems had not yet prepared the political forms enabling them to do so in an easy way. Thus, in many European countries, the need to fight for social space among both new and old societal groups also implied fighting for the right to constitute themselves as a public and to be represented within the constitutional order of the emerging national states. The French Revolution in 1790 was a turning-point in this process, when the Jacobins established citizenship 'as the dominant identity against alternative identities of religion, estate, family and region' (March and Olsen 1995: 64).

As will be clear from the following, this socio-historical process has no determinate outcome as it will depend on distinct conditions for forming groups and publics within or over against the state. Yet we will try to show that it is through this experimental historical process that the fundamental principles of national governance systems are established or socially constructed to structure the game among strategic actors during the following maturing industrial period. We shall try to outline the specifics of this dynamic and its resulting governance principles for England, Germany, and Denmark, whereas Ad van Iterson in his contribution outlines the contours of the comparable process for the Netherlands. In our comparison we focus on the historical dialectic between the emerging new bourgeois class, the traditional class of craftsmen, and the working class, whereas van Iterson focuses on the emerging relations established between *Burghers* and *Heeren*, which organized cooperation among the 'cities' of Holland through a very elaborated form of peer control. This system of governance enabled the cities to engage in high-risk large-scale projects that gave Holland its peculiar position in overseas trade and an ability to engage in reclaiming land from the sea constructing dikes and dams, i.e. activities that have strongly influenced the continuation of Netherlands economic development.

Establishing 'markets' as the national governance system in England
In 1790, Adam Smith died, fourteen years after his book, *The Wealth of Nations*, was published and received by large groups of English society as

a prospect of prosperity in which the market would take over the role of governance from the governing mercantilist state. Why not then just anticipate that the 'market' would become established as a national system of governance as effected by the successful formation of a bourgeois public? There are two reasons for not just aligning ourselves to this explanation. First, we would not get a glimpse of the dialectical process which instituted this system as a governance system. Second, and more importantly, we would be unable to understand what this system of governance implied at the level of social relations.

The aristocracy and the emerging entrepreneurial class in England were much more successful than the 'working classes' in affecting public opinion and getting the state to change its administrative practices. The reform of Speenhamland Law (Bendix 1974: 42ff.; Polanyi 1957: 79) with the Poor Law of 1834 was one outcome of this process. This transformation also reflects a change in the self-conception and identity of the English aristocracy toward their subjects. From having acted with an adult's sense of responsibility for his dependent children, whom he, of course, has to discipline and punish but also to secure a place in life, the aristocracy and the emerging entrepreneurial class started to believe 'that people must depend on themselves' and 'that the "higher classes" are not and, in fact, cannot be responsible for the employment of the people or for the relief of the poor' (Bendix 1974: 73). This change in public opinion was effected by an ideology formulated with scrupulous clarity in Malthus's *Essay on Population* (first published in 1798). From his perspective, the poor were victimized due to their habits of marrying too early and therefore having too many children. Only if the poor could show moral restraint would they be able change the 'law of nature that population always tended to increase faster than subsistence' (ibid. 78–9). Thus, poverty and starvation were the outcome of the masses' behaviour. Starvation, then, was the only effective regulatory mechanism, given their moral state.

The Poor Law of 1834 implied that all relief to able-bodied persons and their families was to be administered in a 'well-regulated workhouse'. In Bendix's view, the unintended effect of merging the aristocratic and the entrepreneurial publics was that the entrepreneurial class established authority over their factories:

Though not intended for this purpose, the 'well managed work-house' appeared to give added justification to the manufacturers' exercise of iron discipline in their enterprises. And under these conditions it appeared as if the spokesmen for the industrial order made their claim to authority by attributing the responsibility for economic progress to the manufacturers and the responsibility for all distress and poverty to the people at large. (Bendix 1974: 99)

If direct starvation was made an 'incentive' for the lowest of the paupers to look for work, fear of starvation, or the 'well-managed work-house', made the journeyman accept conditions of work in factories or cottage industries, even though his tradition might tell him that he was working in the 'dishonourable' parts of his trade and was not acting in keeping with his sense of honour, which used to govern his work. Both Bendix and Thompson (1968) support the view that the English artisan, as well as the journeyman, through these reforms, had his 'zone of indifference' toward entrepreneurial masters' authority greatly expanded. If the choice was between obeying orders and being laid off, and if unemployment meant becoming a subject in the well-ordered workhouses, craftsmen did not have much of a choice. In effect, the new capitalists could command, coordinate, and combine an immense number of skills during the industrial revolution without having to strike a delicate balance between groups with strong codes of moral obligations in exercising their skills. Nor did entrepreneurs or managers have to organize an order within the firm sensitive to the different identities of various craft groups.

In England, as in many continental countries, property was used to discriminate between those with constitutional rights and those without, but in England much more effectively than in other countries, smallholders partly working as artisans etc. suddenly lost their means of subsistence from the commons and the forests. Morgan informs us in his contribution to this volume how importantly this affected the workers' anticipation of their situation, being purely dependent on selling their labour to achieve financial security.

In our view, the socially constructed financial insecurity among people of 'humble stations' made the managerial job easy for English owners. It allowed them to leave the art of organizing industrial activities to a mere continuation of traditions established under the putting-out system. Typically, English merchants had appointed middlemen among artisans and journeymen to act as organizers of work teams, or cottage production. Simply by exercising pressure on these middlemen when settling the terms of trades, entrepreneurs could leave it to them to exercise pressure on the members of teams or cottagers they organized. Of course, the increase in population and migrating Irishmen intensified the competitive pressure on journeymen for being included into such teams, and among middlemen of being granted the 'privilege' to organize such teams. However, in the end this authority structure also depended on the disciplinary socialization closely tied to the identity of roles through which apprentices were socialized by journeymen to become journeymen. The basic social divide, which Lazonick (1991: 43–58) has showed to be between top and middle management in England, stems from the institutionalization of the 'market' as the firm's internal disciplinary mechanisms.

This system of governance is very distinct. It both constituted a specific structuration of individual and group life, and regulated the collective actions which could be initiated. With 'market relations' also penetrating the internal organizing of firms, there was no pressure to develop toward the ideal type of bureaucracy. Compared to the USA, the family firm played a much more important role, and as the need for managerial skills was low, it was perfectly legitimate for owners to ignore rules of meritocracy and to be openly nepotistic (Chandler 1990: 292). The professionalization of managerial roles in the USA, with the rise of modern engineering and business schools, had few 'pull-mechanisms' in England. While managers in the top apex were often family members, the traditional patterns of craft-organized factory production ruled in the lower stratum, according to Tolliday and Zeitlin (1991: 279).

Before the Second World War, labour management in much of British manufacturing industry was based on an indigenous variant of craft production which exhibited little tendency towards the assertion of direct control through deskilling technology or bureaucratic method. Among the central features of this system of production was a heavy reliance on skilled, autonomous workers for the performance of a varied range of tasks that required considerable know how and discretion. ... At the same time, however, most British employers remained intensively cost conscious, constantly seeking to cheapen and intensify skilled labour within the existing craft organization of production by a variety of methods from the extension of the working day and the manipulation of incentive payment systems to the multiplication of apprentices and the substitution of boys or 'handymen' for adult tradesmen on simpler and more repetitive tasks.

This factory governance system was also applied to subcontractors and competitors. It is a recurrent theme in debates on the peculiarity of British capitalism that owners were perfectly able to join a common front when identifying, for instance, the common enemy as the English working class. On the other hand, employers' associations were much less successful in establishing common codes to regulate their members' mutual behaviour (Tolliday and Zeitlin 1991: 296ff.). Lane stresses and analyses this theme in her contribution to this volume. She shows that even at the level of employers' interest associations there was a tendency to institutionalize a 'market principle' in the mutual competition for membership with the implication that employers lacked the means to influence the state. The effects were many, showing in the deficient ability to institutionalize enduring relations between suppliers and customers and even to take common action toward the state to evoke regulations and services that might have strengthened entire industries. Even relations to, and participation in, negotiations with the state have become an individualized relationship for the single firm. Compared to the Netherlands, where the very identity of a capitalist enterprise, according to van Iterson, was a collaborative effort monitored by peer control, the English case stands out as strikingly distinct, though it has often been interpreted as an example of universal principles of capitalism.

The same phenomenon also helps explain why relations between employers' associations and labour unions are basically a history of endless conflicts, rather than a complicated pattern of interacting strategies, sometimes leading to conflicts, while in other situations, where the interests of a united trade are at issue, could lead to cooperation. The sense of trade honour, which could have provided the means for employers and employees to evoke a common public against the state, financial institutions, and other interest groups, had simply been destroyed, not least because the authority of English employers rested on the 'contractual acquisition of property', and Bendix (1974) suggests that with the social construction of such a divide it is simply not possible to take on the roles of others (in Mead's (1967) sense) across this divide.

Equally, the craft-workers in English manufacturing industry could only fight for their space as journeymen, apprentices, and masters by destroying their sense of honour, being forced to think in terms of earnings rather than new ways of using and improving their skills. This increasingly determined the unions' agenda, and subsequently destroyed artisanal aspirations. No wonder, then, that industry was considered to be a monstrous alienating force, even during the most prosperous period of its machinery. Having lost most of the public fights for what might have prevented the degradation of the sense of honour for different groups of artisans, the basic problem became to defend themselves against the worst effects of 'free competition' among themselves when entering into contracts with employers. Group identities were changed into class identity, and such issues as the Standard Rate, the Normal Day, and Sanitation and Safety, achieved through general agreements, became key issues for the emerging unions. This forced employers to organize associations in response to such demands, which again helped workers unite so as to engage in more offensive struggles for social space through the state (Webb and Webb 1919).

The Webbs (1919), however, claim that unions worked simultaneously on the three assumptions (ibid. 562 ff.): the Doctrine of Vested Interests, the Doctrine of Supply and Demand, and the Doctrine of a Living Wage. Whereas the latter two doctrines may be interpreted in line with 'class solidarity', the first doctrine implied 'that the wages and other conditions of employment hitherto enjoyed by any section of workmen ought under no circumstances to be interfered with for the worse', and therefore constituted a paradoxical solidarity principle. This doctrine had developed during the period when some crafts were fighting against machinery and other innovations, but it gave the whole British union movement a tendency to fight rather for the social distribution of social space already achieved in factories than more offensively to compete for occupying the spaces that would arise through industrial development. For instance, the establishment of formal industrial educations not controlled entirely by apprenticeships was seen as a threat to the protection of such stations in life. The Webbs demonstrate that by tradition 'right of property' and 'right to a trade' are closely interwoven (ibid. 565). Thus, the working class fought united for the privileges achieved by some of its members and eventually the above-mentioned divide among master and servant was to a lesser degree reproduced at a lower level among workers with different privileges.

No doubt, this peculiar way of organizing English unions was an effect of trades succeeding in getting their social place and privileges regulated through parliamentary reforms. Thus, an unsuccessful would-be middle-class public continued to live through a certain type of unionization. It also gave English unions a permanent organizational problem, which could not easily be reconciled: should they try to amalgamate in order to achieve common ends, or should they try to maintain the highest degree of freedom to act for diverse trades and then try to federate across many different trades and groups in order to form publics for specific issues of a broader interest? Being never reconciled, this dilemma introduced 'market relations' into inter-union relations, as 'mushroom unions' would pop up to contest old unions, and try to compete for members by offering lower fees and promising higher benefit schemes, thereby eroding the finan-cial strength of the union movement in general (Webb and Webb 1919: 114–15).

Contrasting cases: Germany and Denmark
In contrast to the English case, social group formation, reproduction of identities, cooperation, and competition with other groups took a very dif-ferent dynamic in Germany. As pointed out by Maurice, Sellier, and Silvestre (1979), the German working class came into being during a period when the population expanded rapidly, as in England, but the working class grew even faster and more suddenly. As an effect of this development the German working class was much more homogeneous, and less divided by artisanal divisions, according to Maurice *et al*. Emerging half a century later, free trade in agricultural products helped lower living expenses to the effect that proletarization was less a feeling associated with starvation. Probably, the German working class had learned from the experience of their English colleagues and had found inspiration in the early history of the socialist movement, which made them at first form a single party and later trade unions (ibid. 5). Thus, the German workers were less occupied with depend-ing on their former stations in life than engaged in having a say about the space they were going to occupy.

What is remarkable about the German development, and which at first helps it to become a less heterogeneous class, is that while industrialization was associated with a sharp reduction in independent artisans both in Britain and France, the decline of the German *Handwerker* was very limited between 1882 and 1907 (ibid. 5). Streeck (1992: 112) offers an explanation of this distinct situation, referring to Bismarck's countermove against the then public offensive created by the German Social Democratic Party:

Especially in the 1870s and 1890s, when modern industry increasingly entered the traditional markets of the small artisans, free trade began by these to be perceived as a threat to their independence and as a first step towards their being absorbed by the new, large-scale factories. Fortunately from their perspective, their growing concerns were shared by the Bismarck government, for which the proletarization of a group which was one of its staunchest allies presented a formidable political threat. Offering the independent artisans legal and economic support was seen by Bismarck as an ideal opportunity to cultivate a *Mittelstand* constituency that would for a long time be immune to the lures of Social Democracy and provide a stable base of support for conservative governments. It was this specific political exchange which started the legal institutionalization of *Handwerk*. While regimes changed frequently in the twentieth century, none of them could or would afford seriously to antagonize the *Mittelstand*, and this made it possible for the artisanal lobby to win and consolidate step by step its two central institutional privileges— the *Handwerksprivileg* and, fully formalized for the first time in 1935, the *Meisterprivileg*.

The effect of this institutionalization process was twofold. On the one hand, it prevented the dynamic of low-quality/low-price competition within trades, which the governance system in England instituted, while simulta- neously limiting the access of large firms to have small firms organize sweat- work for them. More important, even, for the group dynamics involved, it did not force unions to be concerned with defending continuously the 'right to a trade'. Thus, German unions could afford to organize along divisions of industry rather than trades, while the middle classes simultaneously nour- ished the idea of *Beruf*. Together these effects created a readiness for invest- ing in and cultivating qualifications, rather than purely defending them as vested interests.

They were in part the reasons why German industrialization developed along two polar trajectories: small artisanal sectors protected institutional- ly and the establishment of large firms supported by offensive Credit- Mobilier-type banks. Germany thus developed two very different types of society:

Large firms were primarily a regional phenomenon in fin de siecle Germany, and they were located in the Ruhr Valley, central Prussia, old court and trading cities (such as Hannover, Kassel Augsburg, and Munich), and the Saarland. Firms were large in these regions because they could draw on very little preindustrial infra- structure of artisans or home producers as suppliers. They were forced to produce everything that went into their product themselves (Kocka 1980). In regions where there was a rich preindustrial infrastructure—for example, Wurttemberg, the Kingdom of Saxony, southern Hesse, or Baden—industrialization occurred within that structure, and the size of firms continued to be quite small. Moreover, most of the regions of small firms, with the exception of Rhineland, were located outside of Prussia in states that entered the German Reich beginning only after 1866. One of the conditions of entry was that these regions retain sovereignty over their tax, education, and industrial policies. This structure effectively blocked all important background framework changes that could have made large and small producers play by the same rules. (Herrigel 1994: 114)

Though the different types of actors were not playing by the same rules, the two systems of governance did not coexist without influencing one another.

Whereas English firms gradually growing in size could build on the self-organized exploitative competition among journeymen and middlemen as a principle of organizing, the large-firm sector in Germany took its template from the public bureaucracy and Prussian military, which at that time had no counterpart, neither in England nor in the USA. White-collar employees, initially known as *Privatbeamte* (i.e. private civil servants) (Tolliday and Zeitlin 1991: 290–1), grew in numbers even faster than the rapidly expanding blue-collar labour force (Maurice *et al.* 1979: 5). This early adoption of bureaucracy partly reflected the 'pre-capitalist traditions of authoritarian paternalism taken over from the aristocratic *Junkers* who dominated Prussian agriculture and public administration' (Tolliday and Zeitlin 1991: 291). Labour unrest combined with the depression from 1873 to 1896 reinforced German entrepreneurs in institutionalizing discipline after army ideals (Guillén 1994: 93–4).

In our view, military socialization provided Germany with a common institutionalization of industrial behaviour by which both 'zones of indifference' and forms of authority were developed. Whereas in England, the mutuality of recognition between property owners and servants was redefined to a market relationship, the bureaucracy and a general socialization to this through the military in Germany helped make the master–servant relationship more mutual. In a bureaucratic order it is possible to change gradually the relationships between groups holding different *Berufe* by negotiating the formal rules and regulations that specify their respective social space and interrelationship. Thus fight for social space among different groups becomes a matter of formally defining numerous technicalities and rules. In a way, this formality of procedure takes over much of the space that in Anglo-Saxon countries is occupied by the so-called 'informal organization'. To achieve the professional competence to engage in the 'structured games' of renegotiating the formal structures, German unions developed a huge administrative staff in central offices. Robert Michel's theory about bureaucratic oligarchy was, in part, based on the experience of the large German Federation of Metal Workers (Guillén 1994: 96). Together with Bismarck's social reforms, this 'logic' helped give the 'reformist orientation' of the German labour movement a very special connotation. Rights and duties were much less determined by the short-termism of business cycles than in English firms. It became the 'structure of the game' that the industrial partners could not simply exploit an immediate advantage; rather they could use such situations to initiate negotiations over reforms, reflecting aspirations that gradually had been processed in their respective bureaucracies.

One aspiration of the German workers in the 1920s was to have the training system modelled after the template of the artisanal sector 'with apprenticeships of three years and the opportunity for skilled workers to advance to the level of *Industriemeister*' (Streeck 1992: 114). Thus, positions within the large corporate bureaucracies would be occupied by experts codified along the principles of the artisan sector. With this reform, industrial bureaucracy developed very differently from France, which also had strong bureaucratic traditions (Maurice *et al.* 1986). With the later law on co-determination, it was obvious how the reformist tradition would follow a very clear path-dependent road of gradually changing the constitutional order of the firm in Germany, accepting the mode of institutionalizing within a governance system based on bureaucracy.

Even more striking is the bureaucratic way in which business associations, banks, and cartels created a very regulated system of cooperation and competition among the larger firms (Lane 1992), a pattern even sanctioned by the courts contrary to in the USA (Tolliday and Zeitlin 1991). In her chapter in this book, Lane shows how this bureaucratically regulated system shapes interfirm relations very different from those in England, which allow German firms, though highly different in terms of size, to engage in complicated transactions on a much more equal footing and formalize them in written contracts. These contracts, moreover, are also accompanied by procedures allowing customers to check supplier performance, and formal quality audits are common and systematically elaborated.

In this way, the small-firm sector is under the influence of the bureaucratic ordering in the large-firm sector. Moreover, this mode of governing the large-firm sector has also served as a template for the very mode of organizing the *Handwerk*:

Artisanal firms in Germany are represented by one of the most complex, most comprehensive and most densely legally regulated systems of interest organizations anywhere in the Western world. Among its many unique features is the way in which the system combines elements of private and public law, of social autonomy and state regulation. Private law organizations with voluntary membership coexist with statutory associations of which each artisanal firm has to be a member, and at strategic points in their multi-layered structure private and public organizations of *Handwerk* are so closely intertwined that they become in practice indistinguishable. The organizational system also includes a sophisticated mix of trade specific organizations—some of which function as employers' associations—and those that represent the entire category of *Handwerk*. Moreover, artisanal interest associations have managed, in important respects, to remain 'vertical corporations' in the sense that they do not represent just employers but also workers—much to the dismay of trade unions . . . this is related to the crucial role of *Handwerk* organizations in the artisanal training and examination system. (Streeck 1992: 115–16)

As appears from Streeck's (1992) account, the system which relates groups of workers and firms, large or small, at the very decentral social space to the central state is organized in a way that makes it totally impossible to see where the state bureaucracy ends and the bureaucracies of the private sector begin. Social groups, firms, and interfirm relations are penetrated and associated through bureaucratic regulations.

The identity of the German industrial system can be characterized as a community of technical professions and vocational career stations, which have been codified into a bureaucratic system, guided in its evolution by the traditions of Roman law (Lane 1996). Two sources of authority have merged in the natural system of governance: professional authority, legitimized through the exercise of technical competence, and authority attributed to legal rights and obligations. Combined these sources define both the identity of the strategic players and the nature of the game, and truces can easily be traced in the formal agreements by which the parties have settled disputes over the years.

Compared to the two previously contrasted cases, Denmark offers a significant variation, both in terms of industrialization process and system of governance. In many ways, Danish artisans tried to achieve something close to what artisans gained in Bismark's state. However, the liberal policy of the state was maintained consistently, not least because farmers aspired to improve their situation by exporting high-quality products. However, whereas—as we have seen—in the two preceding cases publics were created over and against the state during industrialization, groups in Denmark seemed to a much higher degree to have formed publics that engaged in self-help, turning their back on the state during two crucial decades in the late nineteenth century (Kristensen 1996a). Inspired by the tradition of the folk high schools, a typical means for creating such publics would be to set up schools to help create and reproduce the identity of particular social groups. Often the social groups, having constituted their social space and created their institutions, would aspire to state financing, which they typically would receive against state auditing.

For example, the crafts were successful in institutionalizing vocational training in technical schools initiated and financed by themselves from the beginning. In setting up local and craft-wide technical schools on private initiatives, the crafts created a system which could protect their skill formation and secure their survival during the rapid industrialization from 1885 onwards. Despite the rapid growth of the working class, skilled workers were able to maintain their proportion within the class and simultaneously take the lead in organizing unions. By codifying skills in a nation-wide system of vocations and creating a technological institute to modernize education to match the emerging new technologies following in the wake of industrialization, the artisan sector and skilled workers had created an effective institutionalization of the reproduction of the nation-wide criterion for 'good workmanship' and had institutionalized pressure on individuals to observe their craft sense of honour, thereby preserving group identities. Denmark was the first country to introduce apprentice contracts regulated by law, and gradually the state took over the economic responsibility for financing this vocational training system, which developed at the same time as its counterpart in Baden-Württemberg and long before Germany made the artisanal apprenticeship also a template for large industry. Strong unions collaborated with employers' associations against unfair competition and sweating, especially in Copenhagen.

The geopolitical situation, however, also helped form a particular way of governing industrial development in Denmark. As in London, specific craft-shops concentrated in distinct streets of Copenhagen and thus mutually policed levels of honourable pay and quality, whereas the situation in the countryside made Denmark different from England. In England enclosures led to migration, but in Denmark the property of landowners was regulated in such a way that they could not abandon a farm large enough to provide a family's living. With the development of the farmers' cooperative movement and agricultural industrialization through dairies, slaughter-houses, etc., small railway towns in the countryside became centres of gravitation for self-employed craftsmen, first serving the prosperous farmers and their cooperative firms, and later developing their own firms into manufacturing firms. As a result, most transactions were carried out within the narrow bounds of small towns in the countryside, or concentrated in the streets of Copenhagen, or within the professional bounds of a craft-community, also after industrialization. As noted by North (1990: 55) contracts tend to be self-enforcing under such conditions:

Contracts will be self-enforcing when it pays the parties to live up to them—that is, in terms of costliness of measuring and enforcing agreements, the benefits of living up to contracts will exceed the costs. The most likely and indeed empirically observable state in which contracts are self-enforcing is that in which the parties to exchange have a great deal of knowledge about each other and are involved in repeat dealings, as . . . with tribal and primitive societies and with small communities. Under these conditions, it simply pays to live up to agreements. In such a world, the measured costs of transacting are very low because of a dense social network of interaction. Cheating, shirking, opportunism, all problems of modern industrial organization, are limited or indeed absent because they do not pay. Norms of behaviour determine exchange and formal contracting does not exist.

Whereas this 'natural state' depicts the transactional situation in many parts of pre-industrial Europe, many districts of proto-industrialization lost such relations by institutionalizing markets and free competition. In many localities in Denmark, however, these self-enforcing contractual relations not only survived, but changed into a principle of 'reputational relations' (Kristensen 1996a). One way of reproducing this governance principle could have been to regulate competition by continuing guild traditions, modernized through some sort of 'cartellization'. This was not the route chosen in Denmark, rather a number of principles were combined. First, unions and employers' associations, though in conflict during periods of negotiation, agreed to cooperate on enforcing wage-levels on all employers. Second, many crafts organized annual exhibitions, institutionalizing competition on quality and product innovation among their members. Third, in relation to the Technological Institute, a number of departments concentrating on testing and standard-setting were established to make it possible to monitor contracts, even though informal contracts had to be made within a framework of increasingly more complicated and science-based technologies, where traditional craft skills were unable to test reputations. Fourth, having established this technologically oriented rather than tradition-preserving identity, craftsmen and skilled workers aspired to maintain and improve the art of their crafts by using new technologies intelligently. A good reputation not only applied to the traditional criteria of excellence within the craft but also included the ability to use new technologies in developing the craft. Finally, this orientation of the crafts was reinforced as unskilled workers started to compete on the terms of skilled workers over the jobs in modern industry.

It is characteristic of the Danish trade union movement that while skilled workers organized within craft unions, unskilled workers organized consistently within general unions, one for men and another for women. Thus having defined their own social space they started to fight for its enlargement by means imitated from other groups. During the Second World War, the unskilled male workers' union organized evening classes to achieve levels of theoretical knowledge similar to those acquired by skilled workers during their apprenticeship. In the 1960s, these attempts were further institutionalized by establishing specialized workers' schools and a permanent competition between the now 'specialized (male) workers' and the skilled workers over the right to organize new 'trades' or spaces in factories as new technologies were institutionalized. Thus, to defend their place both skilled and 'unskilled' workers had to compete to gain the technical reputation that would legitimate the right to organize work at different stations on the factory floor.

Compared to Germany, thus, the game over who has the right to a certain *Beruf* is much less settled. Skilled workers have to fight continuously over demarcation lines on two fronts: towards the managerial hierarchy and towards the specialized workers. This opportunistic dynamic has the effect of making skills and the modernization of skills a strategy in which the individual simultaneously defends his or her own career opportunity and the social space of his or her particular union against other groups and unions on the factory floor. The bureaucracy of the firm and the skill hierarchy become much less well defined than in Germany, and there tends to be a continuous renewal through the shop-floor rather than through planned intervention of technical staff functions.

As this game, which is even more pronounced today (Kristensen 1992*b*), takes place within the framework of small communities, the maintenance and continuous improvement of professional reputation govern the behaviour of the individual towards the work team, the competition between work teams, and the ambitions that regulate the evolution of the firm and its way of building interfirm relations (Kristensen 1996*a*). However, as 'spectator-communities' may differ between localities and regions in their constitution and the behaviour they praise, the evolutionary dynamic that this natural governance system may guide varies a great deal from one community to the next (Kristensen 1994*a*).

In the Danish system, 'the right to a trade' is made open to all groups by the institutionalization of training institutions at all levels, but rather than being a definitive station in life, the definition of a trade is continuously being questioned and therefore continuously being challenged and defended. Neither deep class divisions nor institutionalized rights and duties defined by the demarcations of a *Beruf* are recognized. Thus, reciprocal recognition of rights within this system is dependent on acts and strategies among groups and individual workers. This in part also reflects the fact that property—in the form of land and capital—was much more evenly distributed than was the case in both Germany and especially England during industrialization, and later the welfare state universalized rights to financial security. Social divisions are fragile and it is not difficult for any group to take on the role of others and recognize their mutual right to a social space. Consequently, there is much less social space for establishing hierarchical systems than in most other countries. Bureaucracies are only legitimized if they reflect a reputational ranking order; and since that connects to persons rather than to offices, to special combinations of skills rather than to formalized skill levels, bureaucratic ordering in Denmark tends to be very volatile. However, to become a permanent 'market' player depends on the achieved level of reputation, which gives access to both communitarian support and institutional means, while failure in achieving such reputation condemns the player to the 'spot market', where actors are tested continuously and must prove either their worth to the community or become outcasts. In this respect, there is a hierarchical ordering of the market between firms, following much the same principles as those governing a worker's position toward his team and the team toward other teams.

3. MANAGERIAL ASPIRATIONS AND NATIONAL SYSTEMS OF GOVERNANCE

We have tried to ascribe to three different countries three very different types of systems of governance. Of course, what we suggest is not that market relations existed in England without any signs of bureaucracy. Neither do we believe that the legal professional bureaucracies of Germany just tied up to other bureaucracies through negotiated rules and formally codified forms of behaviour. Here, too, some zones were weakly defined leaving room for market opportunism. Furthermore, both countries harboured regions of advanced industrial districts (Marshall 1919; Sabel and Zeitlin 1985), which no doubt owed their economic prosperity to social bonds of reputational relations. Finally, Denmark's modernization did not happen without the social construction of both markets and bureaucracies. What we suggest hypothetically is, however, that market in England, professional bureaucracy in Germany, and reputational ties in Denmark structured the games which integrated the strategic calculations of the actors involved.

At the level of *work teams*, we meet these systems of governance either as norms and conventions associated with a specific social group that has succeeded in dominating the factory floor, or as rules of negotiation in cases where several groups often have to reconcile conflicts, when the existing division of labour must be redefined due to changes in markets or technology, or both.

At the level of *managerial functions and roles*, ideally we may expect to be able to identify practices for either active interpretations of these norms and conventions and continual experiments as to how they may be translated into strategies for the entire firm, or, in the second instance, a continuous search for establishing truces between the many groups by developing growth strategies for minimizing tensions among them. This argument presupposes managers to be 'governed' by the social situation outside their own group. According to Barnard (1968) managers have two functions: (1) to define the purpose of an organization, and (2) to reconcile ethical conflicts among groups, when situations occur in which two or more groups, each following their sense of honour, develop into major conflicts. The 'informal co-operative system' in Barnard's line of thought takes care of most day-to-day interaction, whereas the formal organization and executives restrict their intervention to exceptional situations in which this informal system of governance is unable to reconcile conflicts and monitor evolution. Thus, from the previous section we would expect the expansion of the executive function to follow distinct trajectories in different countries and sectors.

However, the separation from industrial practice of socialization to managerial functions through engineering and business schools, the establishment of global networks of teaching and research, and the diffusion on a universal scale of 'models of management' (Guillén 1994) simultaneously create managerial ideologies, definitions of functions, and tools and techniques which make managers try to fight for their social space in identical ways in different countries, despite variations in the way the firm is constituted, how groups are coordinated within the firm, and the institutional context in which it operates. Guillén (1994) has in great detail studied how three waves of managerial thoughts—scientific management, human relations, and structural analysis—penetrated and diffused into managerial ideological debates in different Western countries. Unfortunately, his investigations of how these new ideologies merged with managerial practices are very limited, and until recently management research has been neglecting these issues in general. At this moment, therefore, we are only able to hypothesize about how such a practice has evolved.

The general implication of these two very diverse sources of managerial evolution has been to describe the past in terms of 'traditional' patterns, whereas the present and the future seem to be dominated by changes advocated by international management science, multinational consultancy firms, and leading transnational firms imposing on its widespread affiliates managerial and organizational structures reflecting 'best practices' according to universal agreements. As mentioned in Section 1, the present conjuncture is no exception to this rule.

In the following, we shall try to trace how traditionally constituted work systems merged with scientific management principles in the post-war period by being processed through the strategic games among groups according to the rules specified in the previous section.

Scientific management combining with national systems of governance

England 1950–1970
In England, the game over definitions of 'rights to a trade' was never settled. Dependent on market conjunctures for their specific trade, workers would try to take advantage and establish relations among themselves that reflected their combined strength and the rule of 'vested interests'. Two very diverse examples show how different the outcome may have been. The first, pursued by the Flint Glass Makers, for example, was to take control over its jurisdiction: 'it led to an absolute precise adjustment, entrance to the trade and progression from grade to grade being so regulated as instantly to fill every vacancy as it occurred, but so as to leave no man in any grade unemployed' (Webb and Webb 1919: 574). To organize this hierarchy, the Flint Glass Makers had to control the number of apprentices entering ('boys') and to define a career and seniority ladder of skills. The second strategy was pursued by the cotton spinners. 'Instead of attempting to restrict the number of boys, they insist that every spinner shall be attended by two piecers, a ratio of learners to adapts ten times as great as is needed to keep up supply. This regulation is insisted on in all negotiations with employers, expressly on the ground that only by such an arrangement can the union secure for its members the highest possible remuneration' (ibid. 575).

Consequently, in the English case we see two very opposite principles for creating work teams. In the first case, the team is regulated internally through a hierarchy of seniority and skills (regulated entry). In the second case, the team employs cheap labour monitored by a skilled person, who can benefit from higher earnings the more he is able to increase productivity. What is remarkable for both strategies is that members of teams hardly recognize union politics on the shop-floor as a continuation of the class solidarity governing union issues in national politics.

In this system, managerial functions and roles were difficult to codify as firms had delegated to crafts the control of production on the shop-floor, the distribution of tasks, the pace of work, apprenticeship programmes and wage structures. Thus it is certainly understandable why Guillén (1994) finds England to be late in adopting scientific management principles, and when she did, these were already mixed up with the Human Relations school. When scientific management principles entered the game, not only were they stripped of their great ideological promises, but also the hope of institutionalizing a system separating planning from execution had been abandoned. What was left and developed, at least up to the 1960s, was piecework incentive schemes (Tolliday and Zeitlin 1986: 3).

These schemes were introduced in a period of low unemployment (from 1952 to the 1960s) and under a social democratic welfare state, during which neither financial insecurity nor a reserve army had a disciplinary impact on workers. Consequently, these managerial techniques offered shop stewards an important role in evoking recurrent negotiations over pay, giving them the air of power which labour militants in many countries envied.

But . . . job control under shop stewards was more limited and precarious than is commonly supposed. Controls over the production process did not form part of a wider union strategy but were tied instead to sectional bargaining over piecework prices, and there was little coordination even at the level of the individual factory, perpetuating wide differentials between shops and insecurity of earnings for the workforce as a whole. (Tolliday and Zeitlin 1986: 9)

In such a system it is difficult to see how authority within the zone of indifference is sustained for the majority of workers. Rather, the ranks' feelings and group attitudes toward the firm may change into extreme opportunism, reinforcing the basic structure of the English game. The implication of this, translated into Chester Barnard's terms, may have been the very collapse of the 'informal system of cooperation', which formerly enabled craft-workers to organize the lower-paid workers.

If that were the case, a cooperative system would have to be socially constructed by direct management intervention, and managers would have to take on the responsibility for motivating workers. A recent comparative study of what middle managers in fact do in Germany and England supports this interpretation (Stewart et al. 1994).

Through the very same process, however, the unions probably lost their legitimacy as guarding class solidarity, which again restricted their power to sustain the system of 'vested interests', when Thatcherism later launched its offensive.

Germany 1950–1990

Turning to the German system, 'work teams' must be put in quotation marks. The wider system is constituted as a codified system of *Berufe* with a division of labour, and German firms have in general built on this system and tried to adapt new technologies to the existing functional division of skills (Maurice *et al.* 1986). In our view, the German manager is preoccupied with technical details (Stewart *et al.* 1994: 120ff.) in response to these horizontal divisions among *Berufe*. To allocate proper jobs to proper people becomes a highly sophisticated technical task placed with the *Meister* and others in intermediate managerial positions. What happens here is a sophisticated translation of the design for a product, first to its processing needs, and second an allocation of tasks to predetermined job domains followed, finally, by complicated negotiations, where new types of processes must be aligned to marginal changes in job domains. It is well known that planning production takes time in German firms.

Paradoxically, Germany received scientific management early and with great enthusiasm. However, it was seen as a set of managerial means and techniques, disregarding its ideological promises of making skilled workers obsolete (Guillén 1994), and these kept their social space within German factories and continued to constitute their core group. Probably Taylorist techniques simply constituted a common denominator in negotiations between 'social partners', when marginal adjustments of job domains were required. Whereas Bendix (1974) views 'scientific management' in the USA as the social construction of a new authority system, Stewart *et al.* (1994) underline that German middle managers don't want to be *in* authority, but prefer to be *an* authority, constituting the 'role model' for 'their subordinates', whom they want to relate to as 'colleagues'.

Contrary to Britain, industrial unions have negotiated industry-wide wages across different *Berufe*, even at different stages of the career ladder (from unskilled groups to the *Industriemeister*). As a result, wage differentials are comparatively smaller than in, for instance, France, but the general wage level higher than in most European countries. The division of labour within plants, being largely defined through codified skills provided by the dual system, has made it possible for managers to allocate workers to different workstations and conversely for workers to control the fairness of payments and conditions. Thus, the system's transparency has made wage differential less an issue, which is constantly the case in England (Burawoy 1985).

Furthermore, through their influence on work councils and the restrictive rules for laying off workers in response to fluctuations in demand, the German skilled workers could protect their own employment by influencing hiring, dismissals, and overtime (Tolliday and Zeitlin 1986: 10). As a result of the dominant position of workers with a *Beruf*, unskilled workers have been kept in a marginal position and their access to further training restricted (their participation in this being very low compared e.g. with Denmark (Auer 1992; Höcker 1992)). Thus the loss of vested interests for skilled workers, which the English unions unintendedly prepared for themselves, was unlikely in Germany. On the contrary, Germany was just as advantageous in developing its model of 'diversified quality' production as England in undermining its ability to compete in craft-directed, low-price customized products.

Denmark until the first oil crisis
Whereas in Germany scientific management was incorporated as a new means in a governance system of bureaucracy, this was not the case in Denmark. For that reason, the evolutionary contradictions of Danish governance and scientific management are quite different from the German, which is probably one of the reasons why Denmark neither proved so prosperous after the Second World War, nor is facing many problems currently.

Like most other Western countries, Denmark found inspiration in how US firms developed new organizational forms and managerial functions. Between the two world wars, leading Danish Social Democrats, together with architects and designers, proclaimed the emergence of a new production regime, quite similar to Germany (Guillén 1994). After the war, productivity councils were set up, technical commissions evaluated and suggested changes in the Danish education system so as to produce the professional groups to man the coming hierarchies, and US-based or inspired management consultants were directly engaged in transferring new ideas and managerial techniques.

However, when transferred these American ideas were changed: (1) as the technical schools and the unions saw the new managerial functions as a way of expanding curricula, it was primarily skilled workers who, after further training, returned to firms and factories to occupy the new managerial positions, and (2) scientific management and human relations principles were merged in institutionalizing work councils, in which shop stewards and convenors negotiated the introduction of new methods with managers, both parties acting under the guidance of their organizations, which institutionalized court-like institutions to intervene in case of local disagreements.

Typically, a medium-sized, craft-based firm would try to combine its demand for flexibility with the new managerial principles by developing into a set of functionally divided workshops, undertaking welding, drilling, etc., and managed by a *Meister*. Production planning would be based on forecasts rather than actual sale to allow for larger batch sizes, without which there was no idea in trying to impose 'productivity-increasing-wage-systems', i.e. piece-rate systems, on production.

However, rather than simply reforming the identity of skilled workers from being guided by the competition over professional reputation to one in which they were guided by a self-interested striving for a middle-class level of earnings, the introduction of such managerial methods merged with the traditional sense of honour in a distinct way. Having the skills necessary to manipulate machinery and tools in many sophisticated ways, the skilled workers engaged in complicated games with the system, and the specialists, for measuring work times. Managing to operate slower while being measured than they would normally do, they not only prepared themselves for rising wages, but gained a reputation among colleagues, which was much more valuable. Often sense of honour within the community of craft-workers prevented them from using this manipulative power to earn more than the average salary, tacitly agreed among themselves.

Translating competition for reputations into such a game destroyed the harmonious relationship which had linked the reputational striving of the individual worker with the reputational striving of the entire firm. During the 1960s and the 1970s, managerial initiatives were often, for good reasons, governed by the wish to control more tightly the individual worker, and often workers considered it disadvantageous to have former colleagues act as supervisors and middle managers, since this made it difficult to pursue secretly the degenerated game over reputation. During this period, the traditionally peaceful Danish labour market often changed into its very opposite, frustrating both camps and institutionalizing a divide between managerial and blue-collar positions. Though both sides of the divide essentially originated from the craft culture and its complex of vocational training institutions, and though both groups suffered from the feeling that none of them were observing a craft sense of honour, no institutional matrix was developed to reconcile their ethical conflicts. Contrary to Germany, skilled workers taking on managerial functions were automatically excluded from being members of blue-collar unions and forced to join with people in similar occupations. Whereas an industrial union probably would have had to reconcile such a situation to keep its constituency united, the Danish union structure did not force the parties into reflexive negotiations. Attempts were made to introduce experiments with new forms of cooperation in various selected firms, but they led to no general solutions, as such attempts to reach a class compromise were met with only half-hearted defenders and very outspoken enmity within the political climate in the late sixties. In short, there is hardly any doubt that modern managerial ideologies and Denmark's natural system of governance had engaged in a vicious circle of low trust dynamics in the beginning of the 1970s (Fox 1974).

National systems of governance and current managerial practices

Discourses on managerial objectives and practices have shifted dramatically during the last decade. As both Schienstock and Loveridge/Mueller discuss in their chapters, even German firms, for long self-assured by the prosperity of their indigenous model, have turned to some aspects of the Japanese system for inspiration. Everywhere firms have felt a growing need to integrate conceptualization with execution, to reduce through-put-time and stocks with increasing differentiation of products. This has made some of them turn to Japanese manufacturing practices and related use of trusted subcontractors, although perhaps not as widely as commonly thought, as Lane points out.

A series of studies of changed organizational forms in nine EU countries, conducted between 1990 and 1993 under the auspices of CEDEFOP, found team production to be developed in all countries and considered it to be the most important part of shop-floor reorganization among a stream of associated changes. However, these studies also revealed that so far our understanding of these emerging new managerial concepts and working practices is very crude. Though the studies revealed that in most societies these novel ways of organizing work systems created problems and internal contradictions both among different skill grades of employees and toward middle managers, none analysed the distinct functions of teams, how the different participants reconciled conflicts stemming from belonging both to a professional group and a cooperating team, how the changed career prospects affected their motivation and behaviour, and how and whether middle managers were finding a new role within the emerging organization.

Such changes are simply taken as indications of a change toward Japanese practices. By now we think it is possible to—at least—qualify this view.

As demonstrated in relation to England and Denmark, the adoption of scientific management in the previous period had already caused serious contradictions specific to these countries, and no doubt the new prerogatives should also be interpreted as initiated in response to these contradictions rather than merely as an imitation of foreign managerial ideologies. What we find here, when digging a little deeper, are processes of restructuring which indeed seem very complicated.

England seems to have been very unfortunate with her attempts to restructure industry. No doubt employers had prepared themselves to fight back against the strength of labour unions and shop stewards during the 1960s. When they did in the late 1960s and early 1970s, their initiatives were inspired by American rather than Japanese ideals:

It was only in the 1960s and 70s, as a massive wave of mergers and takeovers transformed the structure of the industry, that British engineering companies decisively abandoned their indigenous model of productive organization in favour of imported management techniques such as multi-divisionalization, work study and measured day work. Far from reviving its competitive fortunes, however, this putative Americanization of British engineering was associated instead with a rapid loss of market share both abroad and at home, resulting in a steep decline of domestic production and employment. By the 1980s, ironically, the competitive difficulties of British engineering firms, like those of the Americans themselves, were frequently attributed to their inability to match the standards of product innovation and productive flexibility set by the Germans and the Japanese in meeting the demands of increasingly diverse and international markets. (Zeitlin, forthcoming).

According to Guillén (1994: 262), this change in the structure of British industry was in many cases inspired by consulting McKinsey and accompanied by growth in 'general management' courses in management schools, thus creating the preconditions for a basic change in the system of governance in England. Rather than seeing this as a sudden shift, Guillén (ibid. 254) sees it as the outcome of an increasing bureaucratization process within manufacturing. The proportion of administrative employees grew very fast, 'from 21.3 administrative per 100 production employees in 1950 to 27.1 in 1960 and 36.4 in 1970, well ahead of the average for American firms (30.3 in 1970)' (ibid. 254). Sorge and Warner (1986: 100) show that British companies created extra jobs for specialized knowledge from the shop-floor up, expanding in particular staff functions.

Simultaneously with these changes in the managerial orientation and organizational design of British industry, the country also seems to have stopped reproducing the groups and group relations which which used to constitute its system of governance in factories:

Between 1970 and 1985 the total number of apprentices in manufacturing industry fell from 218,000 to 73,000. 'Other trainees' declined in number from 200,000 to just under 40,000. . . . But over half of this contraction took place between 1980 and 1985 as firms closed or cut back on their training facilities and commitments. (Lee 1989: 159)

Instead, firms adopted a strategy to compensate for skills by extending the division of labour and using extensively supervisors and quality control inspectors (Rubery 1994: 343). Within this type of work system, there is a growing occupation of low-paid women returning to work on a part-time basis or youth taking part-time jobs during their studies (ibid. 348).

This change toward more bureaucracy within firms has not affected their interactions with surrounding firms to become more 'German'. As Lane shows in her contribution, supplier relations are less long-term oriented and less regulated by mutual negotiations and control procedures. Other studies have shown that British firms often get the less attractive jobs, for instance from large retail chains (Rubery 1994).

Moreover, the hostile environment has been reinforced especially by a wave of hostile take-overs since the mid-1980s, during which period three out of four British companies have acquired or been acquired. In short, managers seem to be living in a world no less governed by the structured game of the market than was the case in the past.

In terms of work system, England in particular is a difficult case to assess. On the surface, it seems as if the old system of apprentice training, closed shop unions, bargaining, etc., has collapsed, and yet digging a little deeper than general statistics allow, some of the old habits and strategies attributed to the previous system of governance are still in force. Dependent on 'the composition of multi-union environments, the density of union membership within plants, the types of skills employed by the company and the unions' historical role' (Heyes 1993: 301), different firms conceal different trajectories which reflect and, in part, counteract the institutional context in which they operate. In cases of a particular strong union role, apprenticeship may have been abandoned, because a new way of training is being institutionalized to enable workers to become more flexible 'functionally'. One reason for the declining number of apprentices reported for Britain may be that the parties formally have agreed to abandon the old form of apprenticeship, but still have not been able to define clear skill grades, despite the system of National Vocational Qualifications. In other cases (as noticed by Heyes 1993), the unions influence changes primarily through informal counselling, leaving the impression that they are weak. According to Stewart *et al.* (1994: 153 ff.) grievances over job jurisdictions, shop stewards, and unions still keep middle managers busy and these conflicts, paradoxically, may be a major explanation for the fast growth of managerial positions in English firms. Often former shop stewards are recruited as managers to deal with new shop stewards.

Thus the increasing number of British managers seem to be fighting desperately on several fronts simultaneously. On the one hand, they have to construct and motivate work teams, often composed of low-skilled workers with marginal experience of industrial work, and, on the other hand, they have to negotiate with unions to keep them from destroying what they have achieved on the first front. Such managers may find both inspiration and relief from their daily activities by learning about Japanese practices, but we would be highly sceptical of any report of their successful import without modification, referring to Sharpe's study in this volume.

Between 1975 and 1990, the *German model*, with its ability to cater for technically demanding niche markets, was generally seen as one of the leading models for renovating Western economies. Guillén (1994) argues that 'structural analysis' was adopted, too, in Germany during the 1960s. But his evidence is much less clear than in the English case. It seems as if problems of centralization and decentralization (the Harzburg-system (ibid. 148)), that is improvements in the functional hierarchy (the U-form-organization)), played a much more important role than discussions on and adoption of the M-form, which was introduced slowly and much more carefully planned than in both Britain and the USA.

Consequently, it seems as if German top managers are now adopting some of the M-form managerial principles and introducing market principles into the interdepartmental relations of functionally divided enterprises. Loveridge and Mueller in this volume confirm this picture.

In a tightly knit system, such as the German, this source of instability and change could not be expected to be without effect on the larger system. As Schienstock in this volume points out, the crisis of the German work system propels into the wider system. It questions the usefulness of industry-wide agreements, as firms and their new 'profit centres' take on experiments beyond what can be comprehended by bureaucrats far from the melting pot of volatile activities. On the other hand, work councils have access to information, which enables them to act, but they are at least as confused about their emerging role and authority as are the hierarchies of the German firms. In the current situation, therefore, it is very difficult to assess what the continuation of the German system will be, especially because its identity crisis is deeply connected with Baden-Württemberg, that part of Germany which was used as a model of the future for the de-industrializing parts of Germany a few years ago.

But Schienstock's evidence in this book could also be interpreted from a different position. He demonstrates that since all the institutions in Baden-Württemberg have been affected simultaneously by the current crisis, they have all initiated a search for new roles to play. In our view such a search, conducted by multiple self-interested parties agreeing to the crisis of a system, will lead to multiple solutions. Furthermore, the systematic procedure for negotiating the rules may prove useful in modifying the system in a systematic way. However, the difficult part seems to be to change relations in production, since the efforts of skilled workers are tied to the career prosperity of becoming a *Meister*, whereas the authority of the *Meister* is based on technical expertise connected to the functional division of departments and labour, both of which are being questioned with the new managerial prerogatives. Schienstock shows how 'group work' possesses a fundamental dilemma in German restructuring.

Finally, we think it is possible to read the entire situation from a third perspective indicated earlier. Slumps in the German system cannot be directly exploited by German employers, as the formally negotiated rules still constraint their behaviour to what is explicitly allowed. It might be that German managers have just launched a campaign to have existing rules renegotiated and the current situation defined as a *Notstand*. If this is the case, it is a retreat to *Notstandsgesetze*, which specify another set of rules and proceedings for how to normalize the situation.

Turning to *Denmark*, we consider a case of organizational change which we have been able to follow through field studies for more than a decade, thus offering us the chance of much more precise observations than in the case of England and Germany. As we shall see, these organizational changes are informed by Danish managers giving up the prerogatives of scientific management rather than systematically adopting 'Japanese' practices. Three factors have helped restore industriousness and make possible a new beginning in which the evolutionary dynamic monitored by reputational relations can again express itself and make even sceptics wonder why Danish industry is exhibiting such an overall dynamic, despite the difficult situation of her closest neighbours.

First, since the importance of agriculture began to decline in the 1920s, the small craft communities in the small railway towns of Jutland have developed, over the years, into manufacturing growth poles, particularly since the seventies. They could draw on a well-developed craft-educational complex (Kristensen 1992*a*), and once again the social relations of small communities have paved their way into industrial relations and prompted entrepreneurs and workers to behave according to the rules of reputational relations. Any tendency for vicious circles will soon be discovered in a small community setting, which also offers its traditional institutions for reflexive action (family celebrations, hunting parties, sports clubs, etc.).

Second, and probably more important to the survival of industrial activity in Eastern Jutland and Fünen, was the major split in orientation between managers who had risen from the rank and file of skilled workers. On the one hand, this 'group' was composed of people who strived for a middle-class position and had used their apprenticeship and vocational training to this end. To this group, union politics and the practices of shop-level games were sources of orientation that made them eager to employ managerial control techniques against their former craft community, when they crowned their skilled worker careers with a managerial position. However, other skilled workers became managers for very different reasons, simply because they were more ambitious to develop their skills than the average skilled worker as a means to help protect the shop-floor autonomy. In their mature life they found themselves confronted with an offer they could not refuse. Their skills had reached such a magnitude that the firm feared losing them, and they were offered a managerial position. If they did not accept the job a newly appointed manager would gradually take over their functions. When such workers became managers, they had to leave the union for institutional reasons and were without the protection of shop stewards. However, rather than developing a middle-class attitude toward their former colleague, they tried to enable and motivate these to follow their own career path.

Third, as in Sweden, unions, employers' associations, and researchers were continuously searching for new ways of organizing work. This widespread interest may have made industry receptive, but it never succeeded in producing more than utopian ideas, and when a 'solution' came, it was paradoxical. A group of engineers in technical high schools had found inspiration in the neglected aspect of 'scientific management' as applied in Denmark. Instead of emphasizing the operative efficiency of the individual workstation and the single worker, they emphasized continuous flow under different circumstances, be it unit, small batch, or mass production. Their work was launched as a major breakthrough, though their discovery had been an important issue in the discussions within the Taylor Society in the USA at the turn of the century. The message was spread through the Employers' Central Federation UPS Campaign and gave rise to new curricula at engineering schools and consulting firms. Faced with functionally divided workshops, new graduates from engineering schools were socialized with a strong sense of innovative mission. Design of production was something which should be continuously reconsidered rather than just taken for granted.

Simultaneously, in the early 1980s, the Danish interest rate reached a level beyond 20 per cent, making it very expensive to produce for stocks, especially as many firms produced a large number of variants of many products. Consequently, the self-evident coalition between accountants and production managers, both focusing on operational efficiency, weakened, and the emerging visions formed alliances with managers harbouring solidary sentiments toward the craft-workers at the shop-floor. Thus, long before Danish firms, managers, and their staffs discovered that team production was part of the explanation of Japan's success, a massive reorganization of factories took place, integrating workstations to achieve continuous flow.

Our studies of a sample of Danish engineering firms demonstrated that in essence two possible strategies were adopted in changing their work organization. Those engaged in the most heterogeneous forms of production, i.e. complicated large-size machines influenced to a high degree by customer specifications, would typically continue with a basic division of labour among their workshops determined by functional criteria (milling, drilling, welding, polishing). These workshops would be complemented with additional machinery of alien functionality to allow for complementary manufacturing. Hence, a 'piece' could be completed without having to zig-zag between different departments several times. The second strategy was followed by firms able to redefine their heterogeneous production into some product families (e.g. pumps, valves, fittings, etc.). They would define teams by identifying which machines were required to do most of the tasks necessary for say, a pump. Consequently, factories were changed from a functional division of processing to groups consisting of a heterogeneous set of machines and skills.

It is obvious from the first strategy that this only presents minor problems for skilled machinists. Their former specialities are in no way threatened, but they have to recapture an understanding associated with their old apprentice knowledge of a broader range of machinery. Most skills could be achieved by simply following the standard curricula of technical schools or the schools for specialized workers. However, it is also obvious that this form of reorganization favours skilled workers, whereas unskilled workers and workers with process-specific skills may suffer.

For obvious reasons, the second strategy may entail that skilled workers will have to defend their social space on the factory floor. In the case we followed in a longitudinal study (Kristensen 1986, ch. 3; Kristensen 1994*b*), managers even proposed a rotation scheme to their skilled workers, thinking that rotation would compensate for the anticipated lack of craft challenges expected to be the consequence of the new work organization. Thus, the managers prepared for the introduction of a Japanese template into a system which hitherto had been dominated by skilled workers engaged in the competitive game over reputation.

To most engineering firms in Denmark in the early 1980s, the major issue was investment in new CNC-machines. The challenge of these new machines defined the strategy of skilled workers rather than organizational experiments. Rather than believing they had to compensate for monotonous jobs through job rotation schemes, they were eager to defend their position both against the technical staff (programming) and against the specialized workers (operating), and to gain the right to man the new machines. They engaged increasingly in the dynamic of further training and gradually elaborated each individual CNC-workstation to become highly sophisticated compared with the textbook use of such machinery. What took place was simply a cross-team competition on reputation in which CNC-machinists competed with other CNC-machinists across the entire factory on how to make innovative use of the new machines.

The outcome of this reputational game had specific consequences. By now, it typically takes at least three months of intensive training, even for a skilled machinist, to acquire the necessary qualifications for manning one of these workstations so carefully elaborated by the workers. Each workstation can be changed swiftly to match changes in production flow and take over a major share of conceptual work from managerial and staff positions. Despite the managers' original intentions gradually to limit the product range and variations, the firm has been able to increase product variability while simultaneously reducing conversion time. Furthermore, it has reduced throughput time to less than a month, and is thus able to meet customers' demands when these are most critical. Also, continuous further training has become a major way of reducing poaching and keeping the workers associated to the firm, despite their increasing bargaining power in the industrial district in which the firm is located.

Consequently, the new way of organizing jobs has more than ever allowed for a game of reputational competition. For the specialized workers, this has meant increasing pressure, and in order to keep their proportion as a union on the factory floor, their response has increasingly been to recruit skilled workers (i.e. mechanics, electricians, etc.) for the vacancies, they have the right to organize.

On the other hand, *Meister*'s find it increasingly difficult to define their new role. Formerly, they were typically assigned to managerial jobs because they had gained a reputation for being particularly skilled in either drilling, welding, or milling, etc., as in the German case. With a heterogeneous set of machines, and the change to CNC technology, the source of their authority has eroded strongly. Those who have been able to redefine most easily a new role for themselves partly act as a coach would do to a football team, partly undertake to solve the problems of interaction between the different workstations of a team *vis-à-vis* the larger organization. This again is becoming increasingly dependent on close interaction between sales, production, subcontracting, and development in order to meet customer demands for deadlines and quality levels.

Compared to Japanese practices for team organization, the lack of job rotation and the game of reputational competition imply many difficulties in transferring this form of organization to a Danish setting. One effect is that the cross-workstation communication said to be so important for continuous productivity improvements in Japan does not exist and increasingly seems difficult to obtain as each workstation becomes increasingly complex. However, the question is, whether such communication is not very much institutionalized as laconic commination, or gossip, in a system where each worker knows that his reputation is contested whenever he turns on his machine. What is fairly obvious in the Danish case is that workers build up their identity through the way in which they are able to develop the individual workstation, and will often experience a tough selection process within a team, if they do not meet the standards from comparable workstations in other teams. Thus, what is communicated horizontally and directly in the Japanese system would indeed break the rules of the game in the Danish system, as it would be impossible for the worker to prove skills and gain reputation if he was instructed directly by his mates.

Direct engagement in the development of the interrelationship of the team's different workstations, or the flow of work across and between teams, arise from typical career paths and from nothing similar to Japanese quality circles. It is primarily when a distinct workstation cannot be further developed, or when a worker has learned all its aspects, making further learning marginal, that he or she starts looking for new space, either in or outside the firm, to resume enquiry into a set of technological opportunities. Having gained such deep knowledge of a set of workstations across a factory, the skilled worker is in a position to see group dynamics and problems of interactions from many angles, and is thus prepared for a managerial job when receiving an offer that cannot be refused. Thus, the new work organization is offering an ideal setting for pursuing a 'skilled-worker-career-at-work' (cf. Sabel 1982; Stinchcombe 1990).

It is important for the relationship between managerial positions and the national system of governance that these careers only seem to favour one type of manager. Whereas formerly, managerial functions imitating American practices basically favoured those that became managers in opposition to the workers' collective, the emerging pattern seems to favour those who engage in different jobs throughout the plant in order to meet new challenges. By promoting such skilled workers to managerial positions, firms may get exactly the type of managers who are able to find compromises when ethical conflicts arise out of complex social interaction. Thus, perhaps executives capable of performing the ideal roles suggested by Barnard are being cultivated?

Whereas the change to team production thus seems to have reconciled former tensions, the emerging organizational challenges seem very difficult. With the delegation of a number of managerial functions to the individual workstation and the team, Danish firms are increasingly faced with the dilemma that these teams, in practice, are in control of output and profitability. Yet, managers are still, formally, responsible for the outcome. This provides the workers with a source of power over the individual manager's career prospects, which makes the current situation unsettled. A team of workers wanting to get rid of a manager may simply manipulate their workstations so as to come up with a poor result and then encourage owners to fire the manager. This power, of course, has been checked while Denmark's economic activity level was moderate, during the 1980s, and high unemployment rates made it possible for managers to use their formal authority to sack their opponents. A change to a low unemployment regime would thus create a pressure to invent organizational forms and define managerial roles of a type to which Japanese templates seem difficult to apply.

4. OPENING UP A NEW AVENUE OF QUESTIONING

In the previous sections we have outlined a new way of reasoning concerning managerial and organizational change. Rather than accepting that managerial action can be understood as the simple imitation and import of foreign templates for organizing, we suggest these need to be viewed against the distinct national historical process which managers seek to influence, as one social group among numerous others, by ordering attempts informed more or less by foreign templates.

The historical process they seek to influence has provided the nation in question with an already established national system of governance determined basically by how the social space of different social groups has been institutionalized, how the institutionalization of that particular space defines the groups mutually and the means provided for these different groups to employ in the continuous fight for improving or defending their social space. Whereas in England the institutionalization of such social spaces was very weakly defined, in Germany they became regulated through bureaucratic relations between *Berufe*. Consequently, in England it became legitimate for any group to exploit any changes in market terms to their fullest extent when choosing strategies, whereas in Germany individual groups would engage in a structured game of bureaucratic negotiation, only indirectly taking advantage of changes in market terms, to improve their social situation. Institutional support for all groups to improve their educational standard has reinforced a community and craft-based system in Denmark in which personal reputation is a source of group reputation. Social groups secure access to and force the state to finance these educational facilities, but then depend on individual careers to gain the reputational game by which they fight mutually over social space. In effect it creates a very open and weakly defined hierarchy among social groups of very high individual social mobility.

When managers try to influence, modify, or change how these national systems of governance penetrate the operation of work systems, the way firms are organized and interfirm relations structured, their actions will enter into the very dynamic of this prestructured game among strategizing actors to produce a number of unintended consequences. We have illustrated how scientific management changed into a means for opportunistic wage negotiation among different groups of workers in England codifying, in an unregulated way, every small group of the workplace to fight for its own interests, whereas in Germany it became a means to reconcile negotiations by which a rigid system of *Berufe* could adapt to small incremental changes in technology, whereas in Denmark it pervaded though reinforced the dynamics of reputational competition within and between social groups in such a way that the reputational dynamics of firms and workers were no longer harmonious.

Furthermore, we have argued that the current importation of Japanese managerial ideas can be anticipated not only as a universalized method to meet the current challenges of a global and volatile economy, but as a way of coming to terms with the distinct unintended consequences of the interaction between national systems of governance and managerial interventions of the previous period. Thus the current managerial attempts to change work systems and the organization of firms and of interfirm relations along Japanese ideals looks like a sick man's attempt to cure two different diseases with the same medicine, totally neglecting how his antibodies will react. In our view the interaction between the national system of governance, now adapted to scientific management interventions, will structure the game in such a way that different groups within and between firms will launch strategies that will again produce unintended consequences.

Every step in this line of argument is open to questioning. We have constructed a very tentative sketch of how national systems of governance were socially constructed in three different countries based on material which was never compiled to provide such a picture. We suggest how this attributed to different social groups a distinct institutionalized social space and a structuration of the games in which they could evoke coming strategies in their fight for social space. We have only had limited access as to how social groups did in fact strategize in different past situations and how these strategies can be anticipated within the framework of a distinctly structured national game. Within each nation lies an enormous research task to enquire into the mutuality of these social group identities without resorting to the preconceived generalizations based on a universalized capitalism and its classes. We have drawn no clear line between the structured games going on in society as such at the macro-level, and what goes on within and between firms at the micro-level. We have taken for granted that the contextual game invades the game within and between enterprises, though we have not specified under what conditions this can be taken for granted. In dealing with the three countries, we have based our observations on a very heterogeneous body of material. In the English case we have relied on a rich and general history covering also diverse themes. In Germany our material is primarily taken from business historians. And finally in Denmark we are both relying on historical studies and longitudinal field studies.

However, what we have tried to demonstrate is that one step of our line of reasoning is enlightened by the other steps. Thus we invite scholars who are doing field studies in firms that are currently restructuring their organization, work system, and monitoring system to consider what is going on currently in the light of these other steps of our argument. How do different groups react and strategize to these actions from managers? Can their strategies be explained by institutional influences from the larger social fabric? What does in fact structure the game between the various actors engaged in the current dialectic? Is it possible to anticipate a pattern between the current strategies of distinct groups and how they have formerly organized collective action? Is it possible to (re)construct these particular groups' strategizing as part of a larger pattern, here conceptualized as national systems of governance, in which their ends and means are given a historical and societal meaning?

At the other end of the scale we invite scholars of general business history to connect their enquiries with the games that are currently going on in factories and firms. We certainly lack 'thick descriptions' of what Burawoy (1985) has called 'factory regimes', but often when we receive them, we have very few tools for understanding in detail the game between the actors involved, nor for telling whether what we anticipate as change or stability is indeed so. In our view, the patterning of interaction among micro-actors is only understandable through historical research, but business historians have seldom tried to connect their enquiries into the past with what goes on in factories and firms today.

Focusing on similar games and studying workers' strategies enabled Charles Sabel (1982) to challenge traditional theories of class and the labour process by showing how politics had a say. Whereas Sabel was aiming at a new synthesis, this book is an invitation to challenge how managers have received the new lessons about post-Fordist production. Rather than providing a new synthesis, this book provides a perplexing number of dimensions, aspects, mechanisms, and issues, which may be borne in mind, when researchers try to make sense of what is taking place on factory floors and within firms, not least to access whether strategic games are structured in such a way that they may lead to experiments which offer hopes of economic prosperity.

REFERENCES

Auer, P. (1992), *Further Education and Training for the Employed (FETE): European Diversity* (WZB discussion papers: FS I 92–3).

Barnard, C. (1968), *The Functions of the Executive* (Cambridge, Mass.: Harvard University Press).

Best, M. (1990), *The New Competition: Institutions of Industrial Restructuring* (Cambridge, Mass.: Harvard University Press).

Bendix, R. (1974), *Work and Authority in Industry* (Berkeley: University of California Press).

Blumer, H. (1990), *Industrialization as an Agent of Social Change* (New York: Aldine de Gruyter).

Burawoy, M. (1985), *Politics of Production* (London: Verso).

Chandler, A. D., jnr (1990), *Scale and Scope: The Dynamics of Industrial Capitalism* (Cambridge, Mass.: Belknap Press of Harvard University Press).

Crozier, M., and Friedberg, E. (1977), *Actors and Systems: The Politics of Collective Action* (Chicago: University of Chicago Press).

Dewey, J. (1927), *The Public and Its Problems* (Denver: Alan Swallow).

Fox, A. (1974), *Beyond Contract: Work Power and Trust Relations* (London: Faber and Faber).

Granovetter, M. (1985), 'Economic Action and Social Structure: The Problem of Embeddedness', *American Journal of Sociology*, 91/3: 481–510.

Guillén, M. F. (1994), *Models of Management: Work, Authority and Organization in a Comparative Perspective* (Chicago: University of Chicago Press).

Hernes, G. (1978) (ed.), *Forhandlingsøkonomi og blandingsadministrasjon* (Bergen: Universitetsforlaget).

Herrigel, G. (1993), 'Crisis and Adjustment in Baden-Württemberg; A Research Proposal Submitted to the Center For European Studies, Harvard University', 20 Dec.

——(1994), 'Industry as a Form of Order: A Comparison of the Historical Development of the Machine Tool Industries in the United States and Germany', in J. R. Hollingsworth, P. C. Schmitter, and W. Streeck (eds.), *Governing Capitalist Economies: Performance and Control of Economic Sectors* (New York: Oxford University Press).

Heyes, J. (1993), 'Training Provision and Workplace Institutions: An Investigation', *Industrial Relations Journal*, 24/4: 296–307.

Hickson, D. J. (1993) (ed.), *Management in Western Europe* (Berlin: de Gruyter).

Hirschman, A. O. (1970), *Exit, Voice and Loyalty: Responses to Decline in Firms, Organizations and States* (Cambridge, Mass.: Harvard University Press).

Höcker, H. (1992), 'Berufliche Weiterbildung für Beschäftigung in Dänemark', WZB, discussion papers FS I 92–8.

Kocka, J. (1980), 'The Rise of Modern Industrial Enterprise in Germany', in A. Chandler and H. Daems (eds.), *Managerial Hierarchies* (Cambridge, Mass.: Harvard University Press).

Kristensen, P. H. (1986), *Teknologiske Projekter og Organisatoriske Processer* (Roskilde: Forlaget for Samfundsøkonomi og Planlægning).

——(1992a), 'Strategies against Structure: Institutions and Economic Organization in Denmark', in R. Whitley (ed.), *European Business Systems* (London: Sage).

——(1992b), 'Industrial Districts in West Jutland, Denmark', in F. Pyke and W. Sengenberger (eds.), *Industrial Districts and Local Economic Regeneration* (Geneva: IILS).

——(1994a), 'Spectator Communities and Entrepreneurial Districts', *Entrepreneurship and Regional Development*, 6/2: 177–98.

——(1994b), 'Strategics in a Volatile World', *Economy and Society*, 23/3, Aug: 305–34.

——(1996a), 'On the Constitution of Economic Actors in Denmark', in R. Whitley and P. H. Kristensen (eds.), *The Changing European Firm* (London: Routledge).

——(1996b), 'Variations in the Nature of the Firm in Europe', in R. Whitley and P. H. Kristensen (eds.), *The Changing European Firm* (London: Routledge).

Lane, C. (1992), 'European Business Systems: Britain and Germany Compared', in R. Whitley (ed.), *European Business Systems* (London: Sage).

——(1996), 'The Social Constitution of Supplier Relations in Britain and Germany: An Institutionalist Analysis', in R. Whitley and P. H. Kristensen (eds.), *The Changing European Firm* (London: Routledge).

Lazonick, W. (1991), *Business Organizations and the Myth of the Market Economy* (New York: Cambridge University Press).

Lee, D. (1989), 'The Transformation of Training and the Transformation of Work in Britain', in S. Wood (ed.), *The Transformation of Work* (London: Unwin Hyman).

March, J. G., and Olsen, J. P. (1995), *Democratic Governance* (New York: Free Press).

——and Simon, H. (1958), *Organizations* (New York: John Wiley).

Marshall, A. (1919), *Industry and Trade* (London).

Maurice, M., Sellier, F., and Silvestre, J.-J. (1979), 'The Search for a Societal Effect in the Production of Company Hierarchy: A Comparison between France and Germany'. Mimeographed translation from Revue Française de Sociologie, June 1979: La production de la hiérarchie dans l'entreprise. Recherche d'un effet sociétal.
——————(1986), *The Social Foundations of Industrial Power: A Comparison of France and Germany* (Cambridge, Mass.: MIT Press).
Mead, G. H. (1967), *Mind, Self and Society: From the Standpoint of a Social Behaviorist* (Chicago: University of Chicago Press, Phoenix Books).
Nelson, R. R., and Winter, G. S. (1982), *An Evolutionary Theory of Economic Change* (Cambridge, Mass.: Belknap Press).
North, D. C. (1990), *Institutions, Institutional Change and Economic Performance* (Cambridge: Cambridge University Press).
Piore, M. J., and Sabel, C. (1984), *The Second Industrial Divide* (New York: Basic Books).
Polanyi, K. (1957), *The Great Transformation* (Boston: Beacon Press).
Rubery, J. (1994), 'The British Production Regime: A Societal Specific System?', *Economy and Society*, 23/3 (Aug.): 333–54.
Sabel, C. F. (1982), *Work and Politics: The Division of Labour in Industry* (Cambridge: Cambridge University Press).
——and Zeitlin, J. (1985), 'Historical Alternatives to Mass Production: Politics, Markets and Technology in Nineteenth Century Industrialization', *Past and Present*, 108: 133–76.
Sorge, A. (1996), 'Societal Effects in Cross-National Organization Studies: Conceptualizing Diversity in Actors and Systems', in R. Whitley and P. H. Kristensen (eds.), *The Changing European Firm* (London: Routledge).
——and Warner, M. (1986), *Comparative Factory Organization* (Aldershot: Gower).
Stewart, R., Barsoux, J-L., Kieser, A., Ganter, H.-D., and Walgenbach, P. (1994), *Managing in Britain and Germany* (New York: St Martin's Press).
Stinchcombe, A. L. (1990), *Information and Organizations* (Berkeley: University of California Press).
Streeck, W. (1992), *Social Institutions and Economic Performance: Studies of Industrial Relations in Advanced Capitalist Economies* (London: Sage Publications).
Thompson, E. P. (1968), *The Making of the English Working Class* (Harmondsworth: Penguin Books).
Tolliday, S., and Zeitlin, J. (1986) (eds.), *The Automobile Industry and its Workers* (Cambridge: Polity Press).
——————(1991), *The Power to Manage: Employers and Industrial Relations in Comparative-Historical Perspective* (London: Routledge).
Webb, S., and Webb, B. (1919), *Industrial Democracy* (London: Longmans, Green, and Co.).
Whitley, R. (1992) (ed.), *European Business Systems* (London: Sage).
——and Kristensen, P. H. (1996) (eds.), *The Changing European Firm* (London: Routledge).
Williamson, O. E. (1975), *Markets and Hierarchies: Analysis and Antitrust Implications* (New York: Free Press).

Zeitlin, J. (1997), 'Between Flexibility and Mass Production: Strategic Ambiguity and Selective Adaptation in the British Engineering Industry, 1830–1914', in C. F. Sabel and J. Zeitlin (eds.), *Worlds of Possibility: Flexibility and Mass Production in Western Industrialization* (Cambridge: Cambridge University Press).

PART 2

The Development of Governance Systems, the Formation of Interest Groups, and the Structuring of Workplace Relations

2

The Development of National Governance Principles in the Netherlands

AD VAN ITERSON

1. INTRODUCTION

This chapter explores how the connections between governance principles, collective actors, and workplace relations have developed in the Dutch business system. In order to identify the governance principles (Kristensen, this volume) which regulate the formation and interaction of social groupings in the Netherlands, attention will first be directed to the geographical and socio-economical characteristics of late medieval 'Holland' and, next, to the early history of the Republic of the Netherlands (seventeenth century) when the rebellious Dutch provinces gained unity and identity in their combat against the Spanish overlordship and the ubiquitous water, and when merchant elites grasped the opportunities offered by expanding overseas trade and the favourable location of the maritime part of the Netherlands.

It will be argued that the development of governance principles, and the formation of collective economic and institutional actors in the Netherlands, must be understood in terms of: (*a*) the late medieval and early modern agrarian and commercial activities (cattle-farming, fishing, and trading), which were not governed by a feudal owner class or centralized kingdom, but supported by municipal bourgeois ('burghers'); (*b*) the winning of land from the sea and securing it through dikes and dams, which has seen the rise of partly voluntary associations, founded on the cooperative principles of quasi-government through peer control; and (*c*) the emergence of large trade companies, 'proto-MNCs', which were coordinated by a group of *Heeren* ('Gentlemen'): rather collegiate 'management teams' representing the interests of local and regional governments. These phenomena and processes have generated a distinctively Dutch pattern of constituting and regulating social groups which continues to dominate work organization and workplace relations in the Netherlands. The central regulatory or governance principle that has become established can be summarized as the strong preference for compromise and consensus among peers, and I shall conclude the chapter by a brief discussion of how this has continued to influence the functioning of the large complex organizations that developed in the twentieth century.

2. LATE MEDIEVAL AND EARLY MODERN DUTCH SOCIAL AND ECONOMIC DEVELOPMENT

The development of organized economic activities in the Netherlands can roughly be divided into three phases:

Phase 1: from the Middle Ages to the end of the sixteenth century. This is the period of the formation of larger and larger territorial units, which eventually were united in the Habsburgian empire of Charles V and Philip II. This period ended with the revolt against the latter and the establishment of the Republic of the United Provinces.

Phase 2: from the end of the sixteenth to the end of the nineteenth century. This is the period of (i) the Republic of the United Provinces, which ended in 1795, when the Republican regime was overthrown by the revolutionaries (*Patriotten*), backed by the French military force, (ii) the Batavian Republic (1795–1806), a vassal state of the French empire, and (iii) the early decades of the kingdom of the Netherlands which was established after Napoleon's defeat in 1813.

Phase 3: from the beginning of the 'second industrial revolution' (the introduction of electrical and chemical industries in Western countries), which commenced about 1880, up to the present.[1]

In the first phase, which ended with the 1572 Revolt or the 1579 establishment of the Republic, there was no Dutch state, society, or identity. But, as in other parts of western Europe, one witnessed in the Rhine and Maas delta, too, a process of (i) feudalization, (ii) state formation, and (iii) emergence of an absolutist monarchy. However, and this is crucial for our under-

---

[1] This classification does not correspond with the generally accepted three-phases distinction in Dutch history (e.g. Goudsblom 1988*a*), in which the third phase already starts with the Treaty of Vienna in 1815, when the present Kingdom of the Netherlands was established. Although this classification is largely political, it is claimed to correspond with 'more general phases in the social development, which, next to the Netherlands, apply also for other parts of Western Europe' (ibid. 32). For my purpose, however, this distinction is not appropriate since it neglects the so-called 'industrial retardation' of the Netherlands: large-scale application of steam technology in the factory system did not coincide with the formation of the modern state, as it did in the neighbouring countries Belgium and Germany. For this reason it makes much more sense to let the third phase of Dutch economic development commence in 1880, when this type of industrialization finally 'took off'. The period between 1813 and 1880, then, must largely be seen as a prolongation of the trade, transport, and banking era which started about 1600. It will be suggested in this contribution that this era of 'trade capitalism' or 'entrepôt economy' was characterized by its own variant of 'industrialization': evidently not through the introduction of steam technology, but via other forms of mechanization and rationalization.

standing of Dutch governance, this process took a specific course here. Especially in the maritime provinces of Holland and Zeeland, feudalization was much more limited in impact than in the eastern and southern provinces, let alone the further hinterland. This is not surprising given the fact that these low-lying zones, surrounded by water and moors and a frequent prey to tidal waves and river floods, were a difficult territory to reach. Therefore, this outpost of the (weakening) German empire was quite unsuitable for the formation of a military–agrarian society in which semi-autarkic farmers lived in dependence on a warrior class. Peasant farmers were free from feudal ties and obligations already from the twelfth century onwards. Land reclamation and colonization of new territories encouraged the nobility and the church to offer attractive terms and free status in order to entice peasant farmers to work these newly cultivated areas as well as counter the attraction of migration to the same type of land in Germany (e.g. van Houtte 1964: 48–52). Earlier than in England or France, then, land was leased to peasant farmers, free from seigneurial control, for short-term money rents. By 1500, the larger part of the Low Countries was held in fee simple: 'the tendency was to parcel the land into small spots, whether it belonged to nobles, the Church, town-dwellers, or to small farmers themselves. In the newly colonized areas of the polders, the countryside became covered with large numbers of medium-sized farmhouses, . . . on small parcels of land, of standard size, deemed sufficient to support individual families. It was a trend which minimized both seigneurial influence and the pull of village institutions' (Israel 1995: 106). Even ancient common fields were parcelled out to small farmers.

Instead of the development of an agrarian-feudal society, one witnessed already in the thirteenth and fourteenth century a remarkable rise of the cities. The absence of a warrior nobility striving for extensive ruler rights offered town-dwellers the opportunity to specialize in commercial activities. Now, the same omnipresence of water (sea and rivers) explains why economic expansion was found in fishing, carrying, and transshipment. Already in the first half of the fifteenth century, the Hollanders and the Zeelanders developed the full-rigged herring buss, which ensured their dominance over the North Sea herring grounds for three centuries, and the seagoing ships which formed the basis of the rapidly increasing bulk-carrying traffic between the Baltic (grain and timber) and western France and Portugal (salt). Herring fishery, bulk freightage, and also the extensive river traffic stimulated an array of supportive activities: shipbuilding, the production of ropes, sails, barrels, casks, sacks, as well as equipping and manning.

As the peasant farmers were included in nascent urban trading networks, opportunities increased for both groups: cattle-farmers and fishermen as well as craftsmen and merchants. Also profiting were the related small-scale manufacturing industries in the cities, notably in 'inland towns' such as

Leiden, Haarlem, Delft, and Gouda. In these shipyards, ropewalks, breweries, and other *manufacturen*, and in sugar refineries, soap works, tobacco processors, and other *trafieken*, expert knowledge of commodities and craft production was crucial.

The productive cooperation between peasantry, commerce, and industry brought about strong population growth which again contributed to the continuing process of urbanization. At the beginning of the sixteenth century, nearly half of the population of Holland lived in cities—a situation only paralleled by Flanders and the Venice region (de Vries and van der Woude 1995: 86)—and these cities were usually not governed by the nobility.

The relatively weak position of feudal lords in the Dutch maritime zone contributes to the explanation why the Netherlands did not develop into an absolutist monarchy in the following centuries. The attempts of the Burgundian dukes (particularly Charles the Bold) and, later, of the Spanish Habsburg kings Charles V and Philip II, both centred in Brussels, to bring the 'Dutch' provinces under strong imperial rule, which finally seemed to succeed in 1543, met strong resistance, however, and failed in the end: the Dutch Revolt resulting in the Eighty Years' War. The result of this revolt and war was the establishment, in 1648, of a sovereign republic of seven sovereign provinces (Holland, Zeeland, Utrecht, Friesland, Groningen, Overijssel, and Gelderland). Only after that event were national institutions developed, and, among the elites, a national identity (Goudsblom 1988*a*: 36).

This is not to say that the Netherlands evolved into a strongly centralized nation. On the contrary. It has often been remarked that the political structure of the young republic was an 'anachronism': it still preserved local and provincial autonomy and privileges, whereas the emerging absolutist states had abolished these practices. Yet, at the same time the Dutch republic is as often labelled as strikingly 'modern' (e.g. de Vries 1973), since the state, the provinces, and the cities were governed by urban elites where the nobility was outnumbered by the *burghers*. The 'States General' (the Dutch legislative body) was dominated by non-aristocratic patricians from the cities, of which there was not one enjoying absolute power, despite Amsterdam's leading position. An important feature of the States General was its decision-making: the most important issues required unanimity of the voting provinces. This, again, demanded time-consuming persuasion and mutual adjustment. The same applied to the provincial legislative bodies: the seven Provincial States. As to the executive, the 'Stadtholder' (a position held by the successive princes of Orange) had to share considerable power with the Grand Pensionary, Holland's highest civil servant. The very position of the stadtholder, officially the 'servant of the States General', was questioned by the municipal elites, above all Amsterdam, leading to an—

albeit short-lived—'eternal edict' (1667) by which the stadtholdership was abolished.

Compared with the model example of state formation—feudal France into absolutist France (see Elias 1969)—the Netherlands, too, had its *Sondergang* and an early one to boot: non-feudal 'Holland' into non-absolutist Republic. The seeming paradox between the anachronistic and modern political system accounts to some extent for the simultaneous existence of traditional forms of small-scale cooperation on the basis of peer control and large-scale trade organizations such as those active in the Baltic grain and wood trade as well as the Verenigde Oostindische Compagnie (the Dutch East India Company; 1602–1798) and the Verenigde Westindische Compagnie (the Dutch West India Company; 1621–48), the first one being the world's first limited liability company and the largest multinational trading firm in the seventeenth and eighteenth centuries (Gaastra 1989, 1991). Also profiting from the open spirit of bourgeois enterprise were the (mainly Amsterdam) merchant-banking houses, which operated largely on the international market as well.

3. THE COLLECTIVE EFFORT OF DRAINAGE AND LAND RECLAMATION

The thirteenth century 'not only witnessed the start of this vast drama [of drainage and land reclamation], one of the most impressive of all examples of man's cumulative impact on his physical environment,[2] but was the period in which evolved the institutional and juridical apparatus needed to sustain it' (Israel 1995: 10). To fund, build, and maintain dikes, dams, and drainage channels, local drainage and polder boards developed. These *heemraadschappen* were committees on which villages, towns, and local nobles had their representatives, providing a mechanism for cooperation between them. As stated in the introduction, these *heemraadschappen* were not family- nor state-initiated, but 'local and spontaneous in origin' (ibid.): partly self-organized groups of experienced water tamers, so to say, and therefore often labelled as 'original democracies'. Already by the early thirteenth century, however, the count of Holland, and neighbouring princes, exerted a growing influence on this already vital framework of dike, drainage, and waterway control, especially by setting up regional jurisdictions to oversee the work of the drainage and polder boards: the *hoogheemraadschappen* (*hoog* = high). These were also committees of representatives of towns, rural localities, and the nobility. But their

[2] Note that between the 13th and 15th centuries more land was reclaimed from the sea, river estuaries, and lakes than in the early modern times.

procedures were fixed by the count and presided over by a *dijkgraaf*, a 'dike count', which, in Zeeland and Holland, was often one of the count's district officials, who combined his role in flood control and dike maintenance with policing and fiscal and judicial responsibilities. Nonetheless these regional boards were limited in reach, and, because of their character of pro-portionality, not contradictory to the associations on which they were superimposed.

In the seventeenth century, the States General took over the supervising of the water defences, the drainage boards, and land reclamation projects. The sea dikes, river embankments, and polders continued to be maintained mainly by the regional boards, but in the case of new drainage projects, where there were often rival interests, the role of the States was funda-mental. In the draining of the Schermer lake, near the city of Alkmaar, in 1631, 'prolonged negotiations took place with the States mediating between Alkmaar, a group of investors in Amsterdam, and the local drainage boards' (Israel 1995: 284). This example already indicates that supervising in the Netherlands often takes the shape of mediating.

Plessner (1974) has argued that the Dutch, in the winning of peat bogs, in the putting up of dams and dikes, and in the regulation of water via drainage channels, learned to do teamwork in a systematic way. We have seen that these teamwork activities, unlike later efforts in other estuary areas (e.g. the Ganges delta), were not initiated nor coordinated by any central government. Instead, the making of the Dutch landscape (see Lambert 1985) was mobilized by volunteering farmers and citizens, with some local government help. Upon these initiatives, governed through peer control, one has seen the rise of the above-sketched regional organizations. These formal agencies, too, were 'founded on the traditional Germanic cooperative principles of quasi-government through peer control' (Sorge and van Iterson 1995: 191). Therefore, both these local and regional water district boards are regarded here as one of the cradles of the (maritime) Dutch governance principle of consensus building via peer control of rep-resentatives of local interests. Another cradle of natural governance in the maritime provinces can be found in the large-scale trade companies which were active in the Far (South) East, in South and West Africa, in Brazil, and in the Caribbean.

4. LARGE-SCALE TRADE AND COLONIAL ENTERPRISES: THE PROTO-MULTINATIONALS

The East and West India Companies might very well have served as a blue-print for the Dutch MNCs of late eras. It is, for instance, suggested that the East India Company (the VOC) offered a bureaucratic model for integrat-ing commercial and colonial interests, which was adopted by nineteenth-century trade organizations such as the *Nederlandsche Handelsmaat-schappij*. One could argue that the VOC also provided an exemplary means of combining the need for adhering to the consensus and coalition model of the 'home country' (Holland) and the opportunity to utilize the natural and human resources of the 'host country' (particularly Indonesia).

The highest managerial functions of the VOC were in the hands of the *Heeren XVII* ('Gentlemen XVII'), who were assisted by advisory committees on issues such as accounting and auctions. These seventeen functionaries represented local boards of directors: the six *kamers* ('chambers'). The *kamer* Amsterdam supplied eight representatives; *kamer* Zeeland four; and Delft, Rotterdam, Hoorn, and Enkhuizen each one. The seventeenth *Heer* was alternating a representative of one of the five smaller chambers, so that Amsterdam could never overrule the others (Gaastra 1989).

The *kamers* set the agenda of the *Heeren XVII*: the representatives were given order to bring certain topics forward for discussion and decision and how to vote. Especially the Amsterdam and Zeeland chambers, with 12 or 13 of the 17 votes at the highest level, were quite powerful. In return, these two chambers were commissioned by the *Heeren XVII* with three-quarters of the controlling tasks (Amsterdam $\frac{1}{2}$; Zeeland $\frac{1}{4}$), such as bookkeeping and supervision of storage and shipbuilding, and of the operational tasks. Despite the dominant position of particularly Amsterdam, the VOC's higher managerial levels were strikingly horizontally decentralized, parallel to the social and political structure of the Republic. Another strikingly 'modern' feature is that managerial discretion from owners was high. Shares were remarkably widely dispersed (van Dillen 1958). And although these shareholders were represented by nine 'participants' to the meetings of the *Heeren XVII*, they had only an advisory role. Their complaints about the entanglement of commercial and political interests were not taken to heart.

This influential example indicates that early modern Dutch 'top management' operated as teams of equals, promoting the interests of stakeholding local parties rather than exclusively those of owners. For sure, this idiosyncratic pattern fits well with the contemporary situation in Dutch business, where both the executive and the supervisory board[3] are supposed to consider the interests of all stakeholders—suppliers of capital, management, workforce, and the general public alike (Schreuder 1981). Therefore, the Dutch firm could be labelled as a 'nexus of stakeholders' (van Iterson and Olie 1992) where none of the collective actors involved dominates.

[3] As in Germany, Dutch public companies have a two-tier board system. Dutch supervisories, however, are not appointed by the shareholders or by the workforce, as in Germany, but by co-option.

5. INDUSTRIALIZATION AND THE FORMATION OF COLLECTIVE ACTORS

The rise of the Republic of the United Provinces to world leadership in overseas trade and in agricultural productivity was nothing less than an alternative path to industrialization. Dutch industrialization can only be qualified as 'retarded' if one compares it with the English 'Industrialization Revolution' (de Vries and van der Woude 1995), which comprised large-scale application of steam-driven technology in the so-called factory system (e.g. Landes 1969; see also Kristensen, in this volume). What contributed to the Republic's early prosperity were technological innovations of a different nature to the flying shuttle, the blast-furnace, and the steam-engine. These innovations are to be found in precisely the sectors discussed above. Drainage, farming, and manufacturing profited greatly from the advanced windmill technology; fishing and bulk freightage from the introduction of the fast 'fluit' ship, which enabled the Dutch to sail to the Baltic twice a year instead of once. In addition, one can refer to fodder crops, methods of soil replenishment, improved sluices, harbour cranes, timber-saws, and textile looms (e.g. Davids 1993). These examples already indicate that these innovations were above all improvements in traditional devices.[4]

An essential element in the trade-oriented 'industrialization' was the unparalleled knowledge of commodities of the Dutch (Wennekes 1996), but also knowledge of classifying, testing, storing, transporting, processing, and marketing these commodities. These skills have become an enduring strength of a large number of Dutch firms in the industrial processing of drinks and foodstuffs (e.g. Unilever) and in the field of transport by road (e.g. Frans Maas) and air (e.g. KLM). The continuity between the early modern and the present era accounts for the seeming paradox that the Dutch economy has 'come to be focused on activities which are elementary and yet highly modernised and capital intensive, simultaneously pre- and postindustrial due to a high service sector share in total employment: about 72 per cent at present (including government)' (Sorge and van Iterson 1995: 191) and to 'the prevalence of very productive large enterprises in process industries' (ibid. 192). Now, because of this very continuity between the pre- and post-industrial Dutch business systems, it can be expected that the governance principles which developed in the thirteenth to seventeenth centuries are still viable in the work systems of present enterprises, both small and large scale. Before considering this, however, the formation of collective actors, competing over social and economic space in modern Dutch organizations, has to be discussed. The resulting constitution of an industrial order in the Netherlands was largely determined by the strong verti-

---

[4] Sophistication was also achieved in finance and accounting as well as warfare and punishment, but also in these fields one noticed rationalization of existing techniques rather than revolutionary breakthroughs.

cal ideological segmentation between these collective actors, known as the 'pillarization' or *Verzuiling* (Lijphart 1968), a nationally distinct socio-institutional phenomenon which has lost much of its central role in Dutch society only in recent decades.

Soon after its establishment as the state religion of the young Republic, Dutch Protestantism proliferated in a plethora of doctrines, denominations, and sects, which fragmented loyalties dramatically. Being a small, vulnerable nation, caught in an enduring fight with England which led to four sea wars, this fragmentation, however, needed to be overcome, at least among the elites involved, through coalitions. This led to a pattern of 'segregation at the bottom, coalitions at the top'. In the nineteenth century, when the (for centuries second-rate citizens) Roman Catholics, as well as the non-confessional newcomers (radical and revisionist socialists) 'emancipated' and joined the public arena, this pattern found strong enforcement through formal institutionalization. Political parties, schools, mutual health and social insurance, trade unions, professional organizations and other secondary associations, were established along these confessional and political lines. This resulted in a strongly corporatist system, which one probably would not expect in such an 'open', trade-oriented nation as the Netherlands.

Pillarization has reinforced the Dutch preference for compromise and consensus. Since neither of these different religious and ideological groups has gained absolute power in any domain, coalition building involving compromise seeking was the only way to come to decisions and to find steady governance. On first thought pillarization seems to contradict consensus and compromise. But, as already indicated, pillarization did not occur along class divisions, but ran counter to these, so that owners, managers, and workers could 'find each other' in the institutionalized defence of, for example, Roman Catholic interests. In other words, pillarization has reinforced the consensual spirit within the pillars.

These pillars, standing firmly separated from each other, carried the same roof: 'The Netherlands Ltd.', as Dutch society is often ironically called. Pillarization, in the words of van Dijk and Punch, is 'a structure of vertical divisions ... which parcelled out institutions along religious/ideological lines in a way which minimized conflicts between the "pillars". At the top, a relatively small elite bargained for the division of the spoils among the contending pillars and developed a model based on consensus, negotiation, paternalism from the top, and of "non-aggression treaties" to avoid disruptive conflict among, and open embarrassment of, elite members' (van Dijk and Punch 1993: 172).

This corporatist framework, with the accepted role of 'pillarized' associations at 'mid-field' level, and the power balance between them, has also strongly affected the governance of work systems in firms, particularly in joint-stock companies. Both in the operative co-determination system, with the accepted role of the trade unions and the works councils,[5] and in the predominating concept of the firm as a nexus of stakeholders where none of the parties dominates, coalition building and consensus seeking are mandatory to achieve business goals. Despite their large managerial discretion, as a result of dispersed share ownership,[6] but also of a failing market for corporate control and arm's length relations with governmental and financial institutions,[7] executive boards in the concentrated sectors and industries pursue the 'public' interest of the company as a whole and not the partial interests of owners, management itself, workers, or any other collective actors. This commitment to the firm's collective interest is even expected from the works council, which is, of course, officially the representative body of the workforce.

6. GOVERNANCE PRINCIPLES IN MODERN LARGE-SCALE BUSINESS UNITS

The Dutch pattern of corporatist industrial organization largely gave way to a more 'liberal' order in the 1970s and early 1980s. This must be understood in relation to the fact that contemporary Dutch business is marked by an 'hour-glass' structure: a huge number of small firms (about half a million registered companies have less than ten employees), on the one hand, and some twenty very big multinationals with world-wide operations, on the other hand, with only precious little in between (van Iterson and Olie 1992: 98). In a number of industries, the concentration degree is indeed remarkably high. First of all, there is a highly concentrated sector of large enterprises which further process natural inputs, largely in the food and drinks industry (e.g. Unilever). In addition, there is a large, concentrated

---

[5] Trade unions exert influence mainly at national and industry level, although company collective agreements are becoming more and more important in the Netherlands (e.g. Visser 1992). The unions are also active at firm level, mainly via the works councils, where union membership ratios are high: about 75 per cent. Dutch works councils are not constituted to have a top management member or to be a pure consultation and information committee, as in France and Belgium (Koene and Slomp 1991; summarized in English in Slomp 1995). Dutch works councils are independent consultation and bargaining agents, elected by the entire workforce. They enjoy co-determination rights roughly similar to those in Germany. Furthermore, they also have the right to object to a new supervisory board member. 'All considered, they have a comparatively strong position in the manufacturing of consensus in the enterprise, Dutch style' (Sorge and van Iterson 1995: 206).

[6] Except for a small number of family-owned firms, such as Heineken, Vendex International, and SHV Holdings, all modern Dutch multinationals are public limited liability companies, quoted on the Amsterdam Stock Exchange, where shares are usually widely dispersed.

[7] Unlike in France, for example, the Dutch state has never really acted as a strong coordinator of economic activities, both with respect to trade and industry. This is not surprising given the long trading tradition, the large export sector and the dominant role of large multinationals with major operations abroad. As to financial institutions, the Dutch banks never engaged in large-scale participation in national industry. Being much more commercial than investment banks, they specialized in short-term credit provisions and trade finance.

chemical industry, which is similar to the previous industry in production process type (e.g. Shell, DSM, and AKZO). Finally, one also has to count the Dutch electronics and electrical engineering among the concentrated multinational industries (Philips). These capital-intensive multinationals prefer to operate as independently as possible, or have only loose subcontracting relations with firms 'below the waist', which are both quite different from the cooperative and corporatist principle.[8] These preferences of powerful economic actors, in combination with the secularization process of 'de-pillarization' in the wider society, finally finished corporatism off. This is not to say, of course, that the same lot fell to the Dutch regulatory principles of compromise and consensus between peers.

The very size of operations of these large enterprises and the technical system used—mass and process production—could be seen to encourage Taylorist work systems. No doubt, job fragmentation and managerial coordination of complementary processes (see Whitley, this volume) are reasonably high in the largest MNC's production units. But the separation of managers from workers is much lower than in comparable units in the Anglo-Saxon world or in France and Belgium. There are numerous accounts of the low power distance between managers and workers in Dutch enterprises. The management ethos is one of aversion against overt display of power or hierarchical differences (Lawrence 1991: 128–35). According to van Dijk and Punch, '[t]he Dutch context . . . is more conducive to styles that allow for *participation* than to more authoritarian styles' (1993: 182). And many Dutch managers 'continually anticipate the expected acceptability of their proposals by subordinates' (ibid. 183). Neither is formal, task-oriented leadership, as one encounters in Germany, the main basis for authority in the Netherlands. Persuasion power is most important, followed closely by expertise. The Dutch manager has to be a problem solver, but not without consulting peers and lower hierarchical levels. Above all, he or she is expected to nurture group relations (Lawrence 1991). Consequently, one is inclined to argue, worker discretion must be higher than one would expect in large, mass or process production units, also because of the accepted role and prominent role of the unions and the works council. Dutch work systems are more similar to 'negotiated' than Taylorist ones in Whitley's terminology then, although d'Iribarne (1989) has suggested that such negotiations may be more ceremonial than real.

He argues that while the spirit of compromise ('l'esprit de compromis') and the quest for consensus ('la recherche de consensus') still regulate modern work organizations in the Netherlands, 'real' peer control in (semi-)autonomous work teams is exceptional. For sure, Dutch managers, be it in small-sized firms or in the large multinationals, show 'a willingness to listen, to talk, to consult, to explain, to restrain from verbal violence and

---

[8] Only in the agro-related sector (dairies, marketing of food) is the cooperative and corporatist principle still strong.

directives on authority' (ibid. 243). Furthermore, they 'evade to impose a measure without allowing the people concerned the time to understand and accept it' (ibid.). But it is exactly here that for d'Iribarne the other side of the coin becomes visible. Dutch consensus modern-style means that management duly informs, consults, and, if necessary, soothes the employees before decisions are taken. But the final decisions are taken in the boardrooms rather than on the work-floor. 'Le consensus néerlandais', then, is a means to manage tensions in work systems.

Overall, then, there remains the question of the extent to which large Dutch enterprises succeeded in reconciling the prevailing governance principles outlined above with the demands of coordinating bureaucratic units producing for the world market. Maybe there is little to reconcile. Maybe the Dutch have learned to live with yet another paradox or seemingly conflicting demands. Maybe the Dutch can cope well—or at least reasonably well—with the problem of conflicting regulatory principles. It would not be the first time that their ability to capitalize on ambivalence is tested and proven. These intriguing questions need to be explored further.

REFERENCES

Brunstein, I. (1995) (ed.), *Human Resource Management in Western Europe* (Berlin: de Gruyter).

Davids, C. A. (1993), 'Technological Change and the Economic Expansion of the Dutch Republic, 1580–1680', in Davids and Noordegraaf 1993: 79–104.

Davids, K., and Noordegraaf, L. (1993) (eds.), *The Dutch Economy in the Golden Age: Nine Studies* (Amsterdam: NEHA).

Dijk, N. van, and Punch, M. (1993), 'Open Borders, Closed Circles: Management and Organization in the Netherlands', in Hickson 1993: 167–90.

Dillen, J. G. van (1958), *Het oudste aandeelhoudersregister van de Kamer Amsterdam der Oost-Indische Compagnie* (The Hague: Nijhoff).

d'Iribarne, P. (1989), *La Logique de l'honneur: Gestion des entreprises et traditions nationales* (Paris: Éditions du Seuil).

Elias, N. (1969), *Über den Prozess der Zivilisation* (Frankfurt am Main: Suhrkamp).

Ferner, A., and Hyman, R. (1992) (eds.), *Industrial Relations in the New Europe* (Oxford: Basil Blackwell).

Gaastra, F. S. (1989), *Bewind en beleid bij de V.O.C. 1672–1702* (Zutphen: Walburg Pers).

——(1991), *De geschiedenis van de V.O.C.* (Zutphen: Walburg Pers).

Goudsblom, J. (1988a), 'De Nederlandse samenleving in ontwikkelingsperspectief', in Goudsblom 1988b: 30–68.

——(1988b), *Taal en sociale werkelijkheid: Sociologische stukken* (Amsterdam: Meulenhoff).

Harzing, A. -W., and Ruysseveldt, J. van (1995) (eds.), *International Human Resource Management* (London: Sage).

Hickson, D. J. (1993) (ed.), *Management in Western Europe: Society, Culture and Organization in Twelve Nations* (Berlin: de Gruyler).

Houtte, J. A. van (1964), *Economische en sociale geschiedenis van de Lage Landen* (Zeist: De Haan).

Israel, J. (1995), *The Dutch Republic: Its Rise, Greatness, and Fall 1477–1806* (Oxford: Clarendon Press).

Iterson, A. van, and Olie, R. (1992), 'European Business Systems: The Dutch Case', in Whitley 1992: 98–116.

Koene, A. M., and Slomp, H. (1991), *Medezeggenschap van werknemers op ondernemingsniveau: een onderzoek naar de regels en hun toepassing in zes Europese landen* (The Hague: VUGA).

Lambert, A. (1985), *The Making of the Dutch Landscape* (London: Academic Press).

Landes, D. S. (1969), *The Unbound Prometheus* (Cambridge: Cambridge University Press).

Lawrence, P. (1991), *Management in the Netherlands* (Oxford: Clarendon Press).

Lijphart, A. (1968), *The Politics of Accommodation: Pluralism and Democracy in the Netherlands* (Berkeley: University of California Press).

Plessner, H. (1974), *Diesseits der Utopie* (Frankfurt am Main: Suhrkamp).

Schreuder, H. (1981), *Maatschappelijke verantwoordelijkheid en maatschappelijke berichtgeving van ondernemingen* (Leiden: Stenfert Kroese).

Slomp, H. (1995), 'National Variations in Worker Participation', in Harzing and van Ruysseveldt 1995: 291–317.

Sorge, A., and Iterson, A. van (1995), 'Human Resource Management in the Netherlands', in Brunstein 1995: 191–209.

Visser, J. (1992), 'The Netherlands: The End of an Era and the End of a System', in Ferner and Hyman 1992: 323–56.

Vries, J. de (1973), 'On the Modernity of the Dutch Republic', *Journal of Economic History*, 23: 191–202.

——and Woude, A. van der (1995), *Nederland 1500–1815: De eerste ronde van moderne economische groei* (Amsterdam: Balans).

Wennekes, W. (1996), *Gouden handel: De eerste Nederlanders overzee, en wat zij daar haalden* (Amsterdam: Atlas).

Whitley, R. (1992) (ed.), *European Business Systems: Firms and Markets in their National Contexts* (London: Sage).

3

The Governance of Interfirm Relations in Britain and Germany
Societal or Dominance Effects?

CHRISTEL LANE

1. INTRODUCTION

Increased intensity of international competition and rapid technological change have rendered new types of supplier relations, based on the blue-print of Japanese obligational contracting, a panacea for beleaguered European businesses. An analysis of supplier relations in two traditional industries in Britain and Germany, based on recent empirical work, will show that a concentration on such new, supposedly universal business structures and techniques leads to a very superficial understanding of interfirm relations. To achieve a more adequate understanding of the governance of supplier relations in different national contexts one has to start from a consideration of societal effects and, only in a second step, consider to what extent and how global economic pressures and dominance effects interact with societal effects (Smith and Meiksins 1995).

In particular, the starting-point of research into supplier relations must be an understanding of national systems of governance and of the complex processes by which they have been socially constructed. These systems are seen here as institutionalized patterns of interaction between social groups, grown out of processes of conflict and cooperation in the procurement of valued resources (Kristensen 1996). Such groups, and their interaction within and between firms, have usually acquired distinctive identities and roles during the process of industrialization and subsequent formative processes in the formation of firms and markets. Although reproduction over time occurs in a non-identical manner (Sorge 1996) the continuity of societal effects is nevertheless sufficiently striking to enable the social analyst to trace governance structures from their historical roots to their current form and to distinguish them analytically from dominance effects.

Other regulatory conventions which affect economic relations are more universal sets of practices and rules, adopted by managers and policy-makers as recipes for action. They have been recommended by business schools, management textbooks, international consultancy firms, or in processes of organizational learning in interaction with foreign multinational firms. The apparently universal character and the global diffusion of such 'second-order' governance structures, however, should not disguise the fact that they also originate in distinct historical national contexts. They usually have been generated within the context of the nation, currently perceived as the economically most successful which, by virtue of its economic supremacy, is perceived as exerting dominance effects (Smith and Meiksens 1995). They are often adopted at a time of economic crisis when confidence in the national system of governance is shaken. Although Japanese economic dominance is confined to only a small number of (albeit important) industries this dominance is often generalized as a more encompassing economic hegemony, both in management textbooks (e.g. Womack *et al.* 1990) and in some social science writing. Although Japanization contains elements not solely related to Japan but which constitute, in part, a common response by all advanced economies to greatly intensified global competition, such a distinction will have to be ignored for reasons of space.

This chapter will focus on only one set of dominance effects, referred to by the short-hand term Japanization, and particularly on those of its canons which are applicable to supplier relations. The Japanese model of supplier relations envisages a high degree of integration between firms, linked to each other by obligational trust and the maintenance of highly diffuse and informally structured relations (Sako 1992). The buyer firm guarantees sales over a longer period, in exchange for the timely delivery of high-quality goods and the achievement of continual incremental improvement in both quality and price (Kaizen), as well as the provision of innovative design (Best 1990: 161 f.). Kaizen obliges suppliers to open their books to their buyer. Interdependence is achieved by such practices as single-sourcing, JIT (just-in-time) production, usually entailing computer-integration of all production-related activities or complete supply chain integration, as well as by the loaning of staff, machinery, and tools (Dore 1987). More generally, Japanese supply chains are characterized by relations of dependency between relatively powerless SMEs (small and medium-sized enterprises) and large powerful corporations with considerable bargaining leverage (Best 1990: 163; Sayer and Walker 1992: 217). Additionally, supplier firms are often horizontally linked in cooperation groups (*kyoryokukai*), orchestrated by the buyer firm, where exchange of information and learning from 'best practice' is taking place (Sako 1992; Sayer and Walker 1992). The model of Japanese supplier relations is treated as an ideal type.

Receptivity to Japanization, I suggest, depends on both industry and national context. In particular dominance effects will be less noticeable in industries less exposed to global competition. Acceptance of the Japanese model depends, first, on the degree of managers' exposure to Japanese techniques and, secondly and more importantly, on the depth of social embeddedness of national firms and markets, i.e. the degree of consistency and interconnectedness of institutional rules which impact on management behaviour and interaction between groups.

The chapter is structured as follows. Section 2 provides an analysis of the historical evolution of national governance systems, focusing on group formation and on patterns of interaction between groups within and between firms and resulting processes of identity formation, risk handling, and social divisions of economic roles (Kristensen, this volume). Processes of the structuration of groups and group interaction, in turn, have to be interpreted in the context of the national institutional framework in the way outlined by Whitley (1992 and this volume). Typification of resulting nationally distinctive interfirm relations will be made by reference to the manner in which such relations are ordered or regulated, paying regard to the varying degrees of density and interconnectedness of national systems of business norms and rules.

Section 3 is devoted to an examination of the impact of dominance effects. This entails a systematic investigation of whether and to what degree the main components of the Japanese model of supplier relations have been adopted. Finally, in section 4, typifications of interfirm relations—a British, a German, and a Japanese model—will be contrasted with patterns emerging from a recent empirical cross-national study of interfirm relations in two industries and countries,[1] and judgements can be made as to the extent and the manner in which dominance effects have interacted with societal effects in shaping supplier relations.

2. SOCIAL GROUPS, FIRMS, AND VERTICAL INTERFIRM RELATIONS: THE PROCESS OF THEIR HISTORICAL CONSTRUCTION

To understand the structure and quality of vertical interfirm relations we need to grasp how firms have been historically constituted by processes of competition and cooperation between constituent groups. A focus on owners, top managers, and boundary-spanning middle managers—the social division of economic labour between them, the shaping of their social identity, their role understandings and career paths—will throw light on what technical and organizational capabilities different types of firms can draw on, what time horizons they develop, and what product strategies evolve from the latter two. These, in turn, shape the types of supplier relations built up over time and the mechanisms by which they are governed: their length and degree of technological cooperation achieved, the extent

[1] The support of the ESRC is gratefully acknowledged. This chapter has grown out of the Contracts and Competition Research Programme and was funded by award number L 114251016. I am also indebted to all my colleagues in the Cambridge research team, but particularly to Simon Deakin for his helpful comments on this chapter.

and nature of social regulation of this relationship, and the degree of mutual dependence established. A high degree of continuity in these patterns points to the importance of societal effects whereas discontinuity may be due to changes in the institutional framework and/or to the impact of dominance effects.

Although Britain industrialized long before Germany, large, vertically integrated managerial enterprises emerged much earlier and more quickly in Germany than Britain (Kocka 1975; Kocka and Siegrist 1979; Chandler 1990; Pohl 1992). This pattern of large and even giant joint-stock companies in some sectors coexisted with the preservation of SMEs in others, due to state protection for the *Handwerk* sector (Streeck 1992, ch. 4). The pattern of ownership in the large-firm sector, shaped by the bank-based system of finance, was marked by a high degree of ownership concentration and complex patterns of cross-holdings of shares, designed to spread risk (see also Whitley, this volume). This strong presence of owners/ majority shareholders in top management positions (Pohl 1992: 471) coincided in an apparently paradoxical manner with a relatively early professionalization of both top and middle managers. In German large corporations, professional middle managers were widely accepted by the first decade of the twentieth century, and at top management level this change largely had been accomplished by the end of the second decade (Siegrist 1980).

In Britain, in contrast, large managerial firms emerged much later than in Germany, and prolonged family dominance of even large firms went hand in hand with a low level of professionalization among both top and middle managers (Pollard 1965: 23; Hannah 1976: 12; Chandler 1990: 242). When the establishment of large, managerial firms was finally completed in a whole cross-section of industries in the 1960s (Chandler 1990; Gourvish 1992) both the pattern of ownership and the underlying social relations of ownership and control differed substantially from the pattern identified in Germany. A high degree of capital concentration and a decimation of owner-managed *Mittelstand* firms of the German type coexisted with a high degree of dispersion of ownership and control. Whereas the German pattern of ownership has remained relatively persistent, despite major disruptions through defeat in two world wars, the British pattern experienced a major transformation, culminating in the early 1960s.

Contrasting national patterns of ownership and conceptions of management were accompanied by divergent forms of interfirm organization. In Germany, mechanisms, such as cartels, communities of interest (for profit pooling), and interlocking ownership in *Konzern* structures created an exceptionally high degree of interconnectedness between firms, encompassing also medium-sized firms (Chandler 1990: 507, 589; Pohl 1992: 459). The shared belief in the benefits of industrial cooperation, expressed in the formation of cartels, manifested itself equally in the founding of highly

organized and effective trade associations in the last quarter of the nineteenth century (Rampelt 1979; Chandler 1990; Abromeit 1993). This type
of interfirm coordination has persisted to this day. It has encouraged con-
formity to common business norms and technical standards and, by curbing
the opportunism of powerful buyer firms, has provided SME suppliers with
a measure of protection and support (Weber 1987). Trade associations also
have provided highly valued fora for the exchange of information and the
development of business contacts. (For further details on trade associations,
see Lane and Bachmann 1995.)

   In contrast to the German pattern of interfirm coordination, British firms
remained highly atomized economic actors. In Britain, the handling of risk
was accomplished by highly dispersed shareholding rather than by pooling
risk through cross-shareholding and by collective agreements between producers. Attempts to create horizontal links in cartels and trade associations
proved either ineffectual or short-lived (Chandler 1990: 287; Turner 1988).
The ineffectual character of trade associations in the regulation of interfirm
relations has remained a feature up to the present day (Heseltine 1993; May
et al. 1994). Their capacity for collective problem solving and normative and
technical regulation of their member firms is still considered low (Willis and
Grant 1987; Grant 1993), as is their ability to prevent destructive competition and to protect SME suppliers from the market power of large firms
(Lane 1996; Lane and Bachmann 1995).

   Contrasting national patterns of ownership of industrial firms are
expressed in and reinforced by very different social identities and role
understandings of both owners and managers. German owners are much
more locked into and identify with a given firm. They develop an ownership psychology which, amongst other consequences, results in the development of long-term time horizons and an emphasis on stable growth,
rather than quick maximum returns on investment. The resulting stability
in ownership (few hostile take-overs), together with aspects of employment
and promotion policies, has reproduced this same ownership psychology
also among professional managers.

   Various aspects of the stock market-shaped British concentration
process, from the 1930s onwards, removed owner-managers much more
comprehensively from both large and medium-sized firms than in Germany.
The highly dispersed share ownership means that shares in a given firm are
regarded as a financial asset to be moved according to stock market dictates, and owners do not generally develop a strong identification with a
given company (Hutton 1995; Lane 1995; Whitley, this volume). This has
resulted in shorter time horizons, affecting not only investment and product
strategy, but also employment policy. As in Germany, these propensities
among owners have been absorbed also by managers. Although British
government policy towards SMEs has greatly changed during the last two
decades and the creation of entrepreneurial firms is now strongly champi-

oned (Storey 1994) this has not, for various reasons, led to the emergence of a strong group of medium-sized firms on the *Mittelstand* pattern.

Apart from patterns of ownership, a number of other historically founded circumstances have shaped the professional and social formation of higher and middle managers in the two countries. Management formation, in both countries, was shaped by the examples of organizational forms for coordinating economic activity and the models of production organization and associated skill creation available in each society at the formative stages of industrialization. In Germany, two pre-industrial traditions influenced the evolution of managers and corresponding patterns of enterprise coordination and professionalization processes in apparently contradictory ways. Due to the deep entrenchment of rational-legal bureaucratic patterns of administration in both (local) state and military organizations, the first, highly influential model, ideally suited to the management of large-scale economic units, was bureaucratic coordination (Kocka 1970).[2] Hierarchical coordination, functional specialization, a high level of education, a slow progression up the career ladder and, above all, a system of impersonal rules to coordinate activities were characteristics of this model, widely embraced by German managers during the founding years of the large joint-stock company (see also Kristensen, this volume). A high level of juridification of intra- and interfirm relations became one expression of this tradition, leading to a strong representation and powerful position among early German managers of legal specialists (Hartmann 1989).

The second highly influential model was that of craft organization. The very much later transition in Germany than Britain from the guild to the industrial stage and the protection of the craft sector by the state had kept the craft traditions vital in Germany (Doran 1984; Lane 1991; Streeck 1992) and provided a model, counterbalancing the bureaucratic one (Dornseifer and Kocka 1993: 235). One aspect of this tradition—a focus on technical skill, vocational training, and pride in the product—came to influence approaches to management formation. Another element—flexible and non-hierachical forms of coordinating production within firms and close association with other producers in product-based formal associations to regulate competition—became another powerful influence on both intra- and interfirm organization (Lane 1991). Although the craft model was initially most prevalent in the *Handwerk* sector and in firms of the *Mittelstand* by 1914 it had spread also to larger firms (Doran 1984: 74), while some principles of bureaucratic coordination diffused downward to SMEs. During the post-Second World War period, the ideology of the Social Market Economy has continued to champion *Mittelstand* firms and the commercial legal code

---

[2] Dornseifer (1993), in a historical analysis with continued contemporary relevance, also points out that preferences for bureaucratic styles of interaction in German firms should not lead us to overlook the fact that many aspects of organizational structure deviate strongly from the bureaucratic type.

echoes some of the values of a *Mittelstandspolitik*, such as notions of fairness and mutual responsibility in arrangements between trading firms and the protection of weaker from stronger firms.

In Britain, neither the bureaucratic nor the craft model were influential in the formation of management. The British legal and political traditions, with their disdain for codification and universally applicable rules, also came to affect management style where legal regulation and binding rules have found only half-hearted acceptance and voluntarism is very influential. The weakness of the craft model was due to a number of related factors: the much earlier destruction of the guild system (Lane 1991) and the pervasiveness of economic individualism; the influence of the highly developed merchant tradition (Landes 1969; Fox 1985); and the widespread adoption of a system of internal subcontracting of production tasks to work groups, coordinated by senior craft-workers. The resultant distancing of owners/managers from the production process and the emphasis on experience-based knowledge are emphasized in Lazonick's (1994) model of market-coordinated, proprietary capitalism. Formal management education was given low emphasis and was much delayed, and the concept of management education which eventually evolved put more stress on the process of managing and appropriate leadership skills than on the acquisition of product-related skills. (For further details, see Kristensen, this volume.) This model of hands-off management was embraced particularly by higher management whereas the craft model retained some significance among middle managers, promoted upwards from the shop-floor (Chandler 1990). All these influences converged to mould divergent managerial roles, identities, and forms of management interaction in the two societies. Although contextual changes over time have recast these roles in some respects—more so in Britain than in Germany, in both societies changes to management roles and relations between different sets of managers have occurred, by and large, within the general mould set during the early stages of industrialization (Landes 1969; Lazonick 1994: 46).

The German emphasis on specialized knowledge/expertise has resulted, from the very beginning, in a higher proportion of either vocationally trained or highly educated managers whereas the British preference for practitioners and generalists has led to recruitment criteria, placing experience, leadership quality, and social skill above academic qualification (Locke 1984). German top managers traditionally have been, in descending order of esteem, engineers/scientists, lawyers, and commercially trained specialists (*Kaufleute*), and the top management team (*Vorstand*) has always contained at least the technical and the commercial specialism (Dornseifer 1993). The technical function has traditionally been dominant not only in production but also in R&D, marketing, and strategic management (Dornseifer and Kocka 1993). The dominance of technical staff, together with the tendency to develop binding rules and norms, has become manifested also in the elaborate German system of technical standards and their wide diffusion throughout industry. (For greater detail on technical standards, see Lane 1997.)

The majority of British top managers, in contrast, have either had non-specific tertiary education or no academic education at all. Since the firm establishment of managerial enterprises from the 1960s, a general management education has become a more widely held qualification. This is widely attributed to the dominance effects of the then hegemonic American model (Dunning 1993). But specialist qualifications are not totally absent among British higher managers. The growing importance of the stock market has placed a high value on an accountancy qualification and has propelled accountants into pivotal positions within corporations (Earl 1983). Both their practices and general ideology have ensured their dominance over those, committed to R&D/technical criteria or manufacturing concerns (ibid.). Engineers are a significant minority in management positions of the largest manufacturing firms (Wood 1991). But, in contrast to the German situation, in many firms the clear distinction between line and staff positions forces managers with an engineering background to give up their technical activities and interests (Lee and Smith 1992: 3). This low profile of engineers, together with weakly developed associational ties and a disdain for binding standards, finds expression also in the only patchily developed and unevenly diffused system of technical standards.

In more recent decades, a number of external influences have led to some shifts in management practices and preferred qualifications. In both countries, there has been an increasing demand for graduate and postgraduate academic qualifications, but the prior head start in this respect by German managers has been retained (NEDO 1987: 3; Eberwein and Tholen 1990; Stewart *et al.* 1994; Wood 1991), as has been the specialist versus generalist management concept.

In Germany, the craft tradition and the credentialism of the bureaucratic ethos in management formation appear to have merged in recent decades. Academic qualifications have not totally replaced vocational qualifications but are often acquired in addition to them. Thus, around 50 per cent of managers had both qualifications in recent studies (*Manager Magazin*, II (1986); Eberwein and Tholen 1990). Within the top and second level management functions, engineers appear to have lost ground to managers with a background in Business Economics (*Betriebswirtschaft*) (Eberwein und Tholen 1990)[3], and in some large MNCs financial specialists have acquired influential positions (Porter 1990). Engineers and scientists (in the chemical industry) are thus less dominant than in the past in defining the image and preferred operating principles of firms. But they still

---

[3] German *Betriebswirtschaft* differs from Anglo-Saxon management in that it has more to do with techniques and the various business functions than with the process and principles of management (Stewart *et al.* 1994: 49).

outnumber the managers with a non-technical education by a small margin (Eberwein and Tholen 1990: 36) and 'pride in the product' has not disappeared among technical *Vorstand* members (ibid. 129). In manufacturing industry, the once influential lawyers have lost in numerical weight and have been increasingly sidelined into specialist legal staff departments (Hartmann 1989: 445). Their number is nevertheless said to be two-and-a-half times as high as in Britain (*Management Today*, June 1992: 50–3).

In Britain, the increase in university-educated managers has not led to a greater stress on specialist qualifications at any level of management. Even in the 1990s, about half of all positions were open to graduates of *any* discipline (*The Independent*, 3 December 1992, p. 18). The two exceptions to this rule are the heavy weight of accountants at all higher levels and the greater importance of specialists in marketing. (In 1992, accountants formed 20 per cent of the graduate intake (ibid.), and many more qualify through post-entry part-time study.) In addition to university qualifications, those awarded by professional bodies also carry weight, e.g. from the Institute of Accounting or the Institute of Marketing (Stewart *et al.* 1994: 50).

These different national processes of professional socialization have both grown out of and reinforced the different role conceptions moulded by ownership relations and the historical evolution of management roles. The German specialist with a hands-on orientation who also manages may be contrasted with the British generalist, hands-off manager whose authority is derived from his management role. These differing role conceptions of British and German managers receive further impetus from different national managerial career paths. The specialist bent of German managers, together with the greater weight accorded employee loyalty and pride in a given firm, mean that they progress slowly within one or two enterprises within the same industry and rarely change functions (Eberwein and Tholen 1990: 33 f.). However, this has been increasingly less applicable to the recruitment of top managers (ibid. 66). Credentials invariably form the basis for promotion (Stewart *et al.* 1994: 55). The career progression of British managers, in contrast, is much less determined by considerations of preserving specialist experience and loyalty. It therefore occurs through more or less pronounced 'job-hopping' between functions, firms, and industries and at a much faster pace (Warner and Campbell 1993; Stewart *et al.* 1994: 60f.).

These differing qualification profiles, social identities, and role understandings strongly shape the capabilities, product strategies, and operating procedures of their employing firms, including processes of interaction in vertical interfirm relations. German firms are less prone to define work roles through written rules, but there pertains a higher *de facto* degree of institutionalization of organizational structures and procedures, and rule-following is more ingrained (Eberwein and Tholen 1990: 190; Stewart *et al.* 1994: 67–8). A number of studies show that highly formalized modes of communication provide a secure framework for informal organizational practices and, indeed, render the latter more manageable (Dornseifer and Kocka 1993; Lane and Bachmann 1996). Middle managers nevertheless find bureaucratic office procedures constraining, particularly if they want to innovate or introduce change (Stewart *et al.* 1994: 81).

In British firms, the looser role definitions have called forth a greater formalization of their task content. But the more pronounced British inclination to renegotiate roles and the lesser tendency to adhere to bureaucratic rules makes for more flexible structures and procedures, as well as generating more opportunities for organizational innovation (Stewart *et al.* 1994: 84). However, the high degree of uncertainty also generates a much greater volume of managerial coordination activities (ibid. 75). But despite the greater German tendency towards a bureaucratic style, both vertical and horizontal linkages between technical operations have been better developed in Germany than Britain (Maurice *et al.* 1980; Dornseifer 1993: 74). Management control appears to be more centralized in Germany than Britain (Stewart *et al.* 1994), and at middle management levels quite different modes of control are prevalent. These different kinds and degrees of formalization and organizational integration within firms are bound to reproduce themselves in enhanced form in vertical interfirm relations.

Managerial technical competences and organizational capabilities, institutionalized in structural arrangements and operating procedures, have shaped and become reinforced by national market strategies. German firms in most industries, from the end of the nineteenth century, have put prime emphasis on low-volume/high value-added segments and niches and customer service, as well as on quality and technological sophistication (Dornseifer 1993: 71 f.; Warner and Campbell 1993). The dominance of engineers and the complexity of technical organization have led to a low emphasis being placed on cost control in German firms, and this has caused conflict between technical and commercial specialists throughout this century (Dornseifer 1993: 88). Mass production methods did not bypass German firms during the post-Second World War period. But they have been less dominant than in British firms, which have been more concerned with manufacturing low-cost, standardized goods than high-quality, technologically sophisticated niche products (Chandler 1990). During the last decade or so, however, cost considerations have been added to the other priorities in Germany, and this may lead to a further weakening of technically oriented managers *vis-à-vis* the bureaucratic big head (*Wasserkopf*). British firms now place a greater emphasis on quality, but this new preoccupation does not appear to be reflected in a strengthening of technical functions, and control through accountancy remains strongly entrenched.

The interrelated intrafirm features and managerial profiles and strategies outlined above have, in turn, influenced the construction of supplier relations. German supplier relations are moulded by the following influences: a market strategy concentrating on 'diversified quality products' and customer service; the dominance of technical criteria and functional specialization in both managerial orientation and firm structures. This product strategy, together with the high degree of both organizational stability and continuity of managerial staff, positioned at the intersection between firms, has fostered the development of long-term supplier relations, oriented towards cooperation. Long-term relations need careful social regulation, and the mechanisms adopted are influenced by the bureaucratic-legal tradition, the collaborative, technical problem-solving style, and the ability to externalize some of the monitoring costs to various types of producer and technical associations. Control procedures are shaped by managers' specialist training and hands-on attitudes, as well as by their rule-bound behaviour. The bureaucratic-legal mode of regulation is partially moderated by the abilty to rely on long-standing interpersonal connections, based on relatively high continuity of boundary-spanning staff. Bureaucratic modes of interaction are also moderated by personal contacts with managers of other firms and awareness of their firms' reputation, developed in the various associational fora. All these influences combine to orient managers to forge long-term, cooperative relations, based on close technical integration and regulated by a mixture of personal reputation-based trust and a whole network of market, technical, and legal rules, conducive to system trust (Lane and Bachmann 1995 and 1996; Lane 1997).

The availability of a large pool of *Mittelstand* firms of the 'technological problem-solver' type further influences the nature of supplier relations in decisive ways: it fosters 'competence' trust (Sako 1992) and reduces risk. An abundance of associational, technical, and legal rules about competition and contracts reduces power asymmetries between large firms and SMEs. This, in turn, safeguards the autonomy of collaborating firms and stresses interdependence, rather than hierarchical forms of dependence. More recently, global competitive pressures have forced a stronger attention towards product costs and the ability to combine technological ingenuity and quality with competitive price. Inevitably, these new pressures have come to exercise a strain on the cooperative nature of supplier relations which has borne most heavily on SMEs.

British supplier relations have been moulded by the following factors: a market strategy which, in many industries, puts low cost above technological excellence, complexity, and customer service; the low saliency of technical qualifications and experience in specialist roles; a preference for constant renegotiation of rules and procedures, due to the weak development of a bureaucratic-legal tradition; a growing instability of firms and a much greater flux among managers, creating discontinuity at the vital intersection between firms; a voluntaristic and flexible approach to intergroup and -firm relations, with a more short-term and situational orientation to cooperation; a greater shortage of technically advanced medium-sized supplier companies, and a strong tradition of enterprise autonomy and, with the more recent increase of hostile take-overs, even adversarialism, obviating both external regulation of interfirm relations and the sharing of risk. These influences predispose managers to seek to establish supplier relations which demand low mutual integration, can be constantly renegotiated and which, because only minimally prestructured by standard rules and operating procedures, depend on individual management initiative and personal contact. They are usually more short-term and more flexible, but they also involve less mutual commitment and are more open to adversarial tactics (Lane and Bachmann 1996). The latter have been encouraged also by more asymmetric power relations between large and smaller firms (A. T. Kearney 1994). Due to the absence of social supports for more relational forms of contracting, recent attempts to move away from pure market relations have been realized in only a patchy and partial manner.

3. INFLUENCES ON THE FORMATION OF GROUPS, FIRMS, AND INTERFIRM RELATIONS

The historical analysis of managerial groups, firms, and interfirm relations in section 2 has made evident the relatively high degree of continuity in national governance systems and the strength of societal effects. Some indication has been given of the role of social institutions in reproducing governance structures, and a more systematic analysis of societal institutions with an impact on firms and markets can be found in the author's previous publications (Lane 1992, 1995, 1996, and 1997; Lane and Bachmann 1995). Section 3 will therefore concentrate on dominance effects and explore to what extent and how dominance effects have moderated reproduction processes. Here the focus will be on the impact of the model of Japanese supplier relations.

Dominance effects

The empirical identification of dominance effects will take two forms. It will examine the quantitative and qualitative aspects of Japanese inward investment into Britain and Germany and the broader economic context in which it has occurred. It will then explore how far elements of the Japanese model of supplier relations, detailed in section 1, are perceived to have impacted on national governance systems.

Britain has consistently attracted a significantly higher proportion of foreign direct investment (FDI) and has been penetrated to a much greater extent by foreign MNCs than Germany. According to statistics, provided by Julius (1990: 51), at the end of the 1980s, Britain had attracted 38 per cent of all Japanese European investment and Germany a mere 8 per cent. This meant that 30 per cent of all European employment in Japanese firms was

located in Britain and 15 per cent in Germany. Furthermore, in Germany
no industry is entirely dominated by Japanese MNCs as are several British
industries where supplier firms are more strongly compelled to orient themselves to foreign ways of managing. Although Japanese investment is only
a relatively small proportion of total foreign investment in both countries
its rapid increase during the second half of the 1980s, together with Japan's
phenomenal increase in competitiveness in a number of core industries, has
rendered its impact disproportionally strong in most advanced societies.

Given this investment pattern, Germans are less likely than British
people to be employed by, managing, or supplying to Japanese firms and
hence less likely to have direct experience of foreign ways of organizing
economic activity. But it would be simplistic to derive the degree of expected Japanization simply from degree of direct exposure to the Japanese
model in the course of inward FDI. Additional factors, such as degree of
superior performance by foreign firms, of cultural similarity, of vulnerability to Japanese competition and the degree of perceived industrial crisis by
the host country are all of importance. It is deemed, however, that the most
important influence on the degree of receptivity to the Japanese model is
the degree of social embeddedness of host country firms and, more particularly, the degree and consistency of social regulation through national
governance structures.

Dominance effects from Japanese models of intra- and interfirm organization have given rise to a whole field of mainly Anglo-Saxon literature,
and I shall concentrate here only on those aspects of Japanization directly
connected with outsourcing. The Japanese model of supplier relations has
already been outlined in section 1. It is notable that the initial impact of the
Japanese model has been far greater in Britain than in Germany. The indirect impact on British management processes through reorganized supplier relations is assumed to have been considerable although this applies
more to the copying of isolated techniques rather than of the integrated
Japanese model (Oliver and Wilkinson 1988; Trevor and Christie 1988;
Morris and Imrie 1992; Sako 1992; Oliver 1993; A. T. Kearney 1994; Elger
and Smith 1994). This has manifested itself in more pronounced increases
in productivity among those British firms supplying to Japanese companies
than in a control group not connected to Japanese firms (Andersen
Consulting 1992: 35). An overview article of recent studies of supplier relations by Imrie and Morris (1992) emphasizes the following qualitative features of the adoption process: changes have occurred only in a few industrial
sectors and, within them, in a few 'leading edge' firms; adoption of the
model has been patchy, even in cases where only individual elements have
been adopted. More particularly, Imrie and Morris (1992) note the incom-
pleteness of most JIT systems, the continued priority of price over quality
in supplier selection, and the inability of many suppliers to reach required
quality standards and to meet time limits. Other researchers, such as

Rainnie (1991) and A. T. Kearney (1994), also stress the continuing asymmetry in power between large customer firms and their smaller supplier firms and the imposition of demanding terms on them. Supplier firms continue to guard their autonomy and are loath to divulge too much financial information to their large customers, for fear of weakening their bargaining power (Sako 1992). There is little evidence that demands for higher standards in quality, design capacity, and efficient logistics systems have led to new patterns of training and role understanding among managers, or that design capacity of supplier firms has markedly increased (Sako 1992). The incidence of close, collaborative relationships is much rarer than the hype about them suggests (Imrie and Morris 1992), and obligational contracting is impossible to develop in the absence of a shared sense of fairness concerning the conduct of the stronger partner against the weaker (Sako 1992).

In Germany, the Japanization theme initially had low salience. Since the publication of the comparative study of the car industry by Womack *et al.* (1990), however, the concept of 'lean production' (LP) has been taken up very widely by German managers, trade unions, and academics, and it has been claimed that German interest in the book has surpassed by far that in other countries (Cooke 1993). LP is a holistic concept embracing the whole value-creation process, and a new approach to supplier relations is only one of its many constituent elements, particularly the techniques of JIT production and supply chain integration. Insight into the wider consequences for organizational structures and managerial processes is gained from a study of Baden-Württemberg engineering firms, supplying to the car, electronics, and machine-building industries (Cooke 1993; see also Schienstock, this volume).

Cooke sees elements of LP being widely accepted by these German firms. He emphasizes above all management effort to achieve cost saving on all inputs to and stages of the production process, without lowering quality, and the increase in outsourcing to *Mittelstand* firms. One notable effect of this has been a struggle between engineers and purchasing managers over the 'make or buy' decision, a further intensification of the pressure on engineers to become more cost-conscious and a consequent partial loss of status and power to purchasing managers (Cooke 1993: 82, 88). He also perceives a much increased pressure on *Mittelstand* firms resulting from the combination of demand for lower costs and the threat to undertake more foreign sourcing. They have responded in a variety of ways: the strong world-class firms avoid the demanding car industry buyer firms—'independent, excellent and conscious of their status, many will simply not play the LP game' (ibid. 81); the less well-placed have either combined into cooperative associations with competitor firms to withstand the pressure and/or have introduced LP themselves; or they have sunk into a lower tier of the subcontracting hierarchy, been acquired, or ceased trading (Cooke 1993: 17,

92). The traditional pride among SMEs in independence is also being undermined by new demands for 'open-book accounting', but this is still being fiercely resisted (ibid. 83).

More generally, it appears as if LP has been adopted as a set of techniques which, as it still demands technological ingenuity, skill, and high quality, has not *fundamentally* altered the German production paradigm. The engineering specialism has come under further pressure to show more awareness of cost and to avoid the traditional German 'overengineering'. But engineers will by no means be marginalized. Technological excellence now has to be combined with adhering to cost targets. LP's demand for greater organizational flexibility may effect a further shift away from the bureaucratic German tradition in favour of its craft tradition. The close relations between buyer and supplier firms entailed by LP are not new in Germany (Porter 1990: 374; Bannock and Albach 1991: 19), even if the character of collaboration is different. However, LP is putting the traditionally supportive relation of large buyer firms towards their *Mittelstand* suppliers under severe strain, particularly in the car and electronics industries. As the relationship is often an interdependent one there are, however, limits to how far large buyer firms can 'push their luck'. Lastly, the increased demands on smaller supplier firms for cost-efficient quality and design capacity is sometimes overtaxing them and may compel them to accept merger which will reduce the pool of flexible *Mittelstand* firms.

4. SUPPLIER RELATIONS IN COMPARATIVE PERSPECTIVE: SOME RESEARCH FINDINGS

This section will answer the questions posed at the beginning of the chapter. To what extent have firms and interfirm relations in two more traditional industries been influenced by societal and dominance effects? Have dominance effects, in the form of Japanization, been less insistent than in the more globalized industries? What, if any, are the differences in these respects between the British and the German firms and how can they be explained? Before addressing these questions, brief descriptions of the research project and the industries are in order.

Supplier relations have been studied in two German and British industries—mining machinery and kitchen furniture—during 1993 and 1994. A case-study approach involved the administering of semi-structured interviews to managers in forty-two buyer and supplier firms, supplemented by additional interviews with officials in trade associations and standard-setting institutions. The mining machinery (MM) industry makes technologically complex, small-batch/customized producer goods, requiring massive investment in process technology, materials, and skilled employees. Customer demands for quality, technological ingenuity, safety, and after sales service are extremely high in this industry, but cost has become an increasingly important factor. The industry has been greatly affected by political considerations in both countries. (For a fuller description of both industries, see Lane and Bachmann 1995.)

The German MM industry is world market leader in terms of quality and technological sophistication and has a significantly higher share of export markets than its British counterpart (Korfmann 1992; calculations from *British Industry Monitor*). In Germany, the industry is geographically highly concentrated in the Ruhr area, whereas in Britain firms are more geographically dispersed. The German industry has a high proportion of *Mittelstand* firms, whereas in Britain many firms are part of a large group.

The kitchen furniture (KF) industry makes complex, but technologically less advanced consumer goods. In Germany, the industry caters for middle and top market segments, selling modular and customized kitchens all over Europe, whereas in Britain the industry is dominated by firms oriented to the lower market segment which sell mainly in home markets. The German industry is much larger and more competitive than its British counterpart. This difference is reflected in the firms populating both industries. Whereas in Germany, medium-sized *Mittelstand* firms predominate, in Britain the majority of firms are very small and often unstable. German high geographical concentration can be counterposed to British complete dispersion.

In contrast to supplier relations in highly competitive world market industries, interfirm relations in these two industries are little affected by Japanization or Lean Production. Supplier firms in both industries and both countries are in no way dependent on their buyers.[4] Although the latter practised single-sourcing for a few individual components this was by no means the rule, and in neither country did suppliers depend on only a few buyers. The wish for independence was strongly affirmed by both sides and was also expressed in structural terms. Although delivery had to comply with some time schedules in about 50 per cent of firms, fully-fledged JIT production was not found. Only a minority of firms put security of delivery as the highest concern. (It would, in any case, be inappropriate for the small batch/customized MM industry). Close synchronization between buyer and supplier firms was therefore rare, and computerized links, which were usually only partial, existed in less than half of all British and German firms. Some German supplier firms which sell both to the car and the furniture industry spontaneously affirmed the marked differences in degree of synchronization between the two industries. Open-book accounting by supplier firms was completely absent in both German industries and in the British KF firms, and was practised by only a minority of British MM firms. Other

---

[4] MM manufacturers of end-products, however, are (have been), very dependent on quasi-monopsonist buyers, the two national coal boards. (Our interviewing preceded British privatization.)

means to bind suppliers closely to their larger buyer firms, such as common training of staff and the loaning of tools and machinery were practised by only a minority of mainly German firms.

Although managers in both countries and industries aspired to close and longer-term relations there was little evidence of diffuse social relations or of the cultivation of obligational trust, as defined by Sako (1992). Trust relations were not absent, but trust was built on bases different from those common in the Japanese paradigm (Lane and Bachmann 1995 and 1996). The combination of legal regulation with interfirm trust, common in Germany, would not be found in Japanese firms (Sako 1992). Although supplier associations existed in the German furniture industry these were not buyer-coordinated, and, instead of competing with one another, their main purpose was to increase their collective strength so as to improve their bargaining position *vis-à-vis* buyer firms.

Thus, in neither country was there a notable dominance effect. British firms showed themselves to be more familiar with some of the concepts entailed in the Japanese model, such as the notion of partnership dealing and JIT production, but adaptations to the new model were as inconspicuous as among German firms. The only marked change in both countries and industries was a stronger preoccupation with the main perceived sources of competitiveness—quality and price—in response to sharply increased competition. The concern with cost was particularly marked among German firms and echoes the situation outlined by Cooke (1993). Whereas anxiety about costs may not have been a new and therefore salient development for British firms it was a new circumstance for German enterprises. This is evident from the fact that prices are an important factor in supplier rating systems in the majority of German firms and much less frequently in British firms. In Germany, buyers had increased their control over prices during the preceding five years significantly more often than in British firms, and more British suppliers, particularly in the KF industry, claimed that they determined price levels themselves. German firms were, however, not abandoning their concern with quality but were now striving for cost-effective quality.

To conclude this section, both British and German firms had not been much affected by dominance effects. This finding is in contrast to previous writing on the impact of Japanization and Lean Production on British and German firms. This must be due to the fact that most previous studies have focused on the leading-edge world market industries whereas our study has centred on more traditional industries. The more pronounced impact of global economic pressures on German than British firms, particularly in the KF industry, can be explained in two ways. First, in the latter industry, only German firms are inserted into foreign markets and hence more strongly exposed to their pressures. Second, German firms in both sectors traditionally have been concerned with quality rather than low cost and are now compelled to accomplish both simultaneously. British firms, in contrast, competing traditionally on low cost, showed few signs of moving up into higher market segments.

Despite the similarity between supplier relations in Britain and Germany in their low exposure to dominance effects, we found many marked differences between them which appear to be due to different societal effects. These amplify and echo the observations made in section 2. There was a striking difference in the length of supplier relations between the two countries. Whereas among the German firms there were only two instances of relations with the main suppliers/customers of less than eleven years' duration in Britain the corresponding figure was nine. At the other end of the scale, one British firm with more than forty years' business connection with a supplier/customer can be contrasted with seven such German firms. Of these seven German firms, some of the MM firms had ties going back to the last century, and in both sectors many firms had been in family possession for at least two generations. Greater German stability in interfirm relations was accompanied also by a significantly greater use of long-term contracts and, in contrast to the British firms, a strong disdain for short-term contracts. Thus, although managers in both British and German firms expressed themselves in favour of long-term relations in Britain the distance between hope and reality was significantly greater than in Germany.

This more marked long-termism in Germany than in Britain can be ascribed to the different financial systems into which the two national groups of firms are inserted, as well as to the more pronounced technical collaboration between German customer and supplier firms and the greater commitment of their owners and managers to their firm and industry. Our case-study data show a higher degree of ownership instability in Britain, and industry data also show a much higher incidence of bankruptcy in the British than the German KF industry.

Another notable difference was that, although managers in both countries expressed a commitment to quality, in Germany alone was this consistently accompanied by procedures to check supplier performance on quality. Only in Germany were formal quality audits common. 71 per cent of firms had them or were affected by them, contrasted with 35 per cent of British firms. Similar results were obtained for the use of/submission to supplier rating systems where 78 per cent of German firms but only 33 per cent of British firms were affected. This difference is likely to be connected both with the different skills of owner managers/middle managers in sales departments, as well as by the different attitudes to control (see section 2). The German penchant for rule-bound systematic behaviour, derived from the bureaucratic tradition, together with managers' more pronounced cultivation of specialist skills, inclines them to these more systematic control procedures than are commonly applied by their British counterparts.

Control is, however, rarely allied to punitive measures, as the long trading records bear out.

The German craft tradition and the emphasis on technical excellence, lacking in Britain, is also clearly expressed in our comparison of supplier relations. This is evident from the more frequent association by the German firms of mutual visiting with the express purpose of technological collaboration. German supplier firms also were seen more frequently to be investing special knowledge into the subcontracting relationship. The greater German value put on technical matters is additionally expressed in the wider use of technical standards. The difference was particularly marked in the KF industry.

The contrast between British voluntarism and German preference for legal regulation, referred to in section 2, is also clearly expressed in the governance of supplier relations in the two industries. Not only was the use of formal contracts more common in German firms but they also were more often long-term and played a more important role in the ordering of business relationships. But this greater use of legal regulation was not connected with a greater recourse to litigation. The higher degree of regulation of business conditions by trade associations and the greater use of unambiguous technical standards, together with the stronger formal and informal pressure to adhere to conditions, mean that court action is both less prevalent and more rarely contemplated by German than British firms. Contracts remained mostly in the background of supplier relations, and in long-term relations were rarely activated. They were entered into to plan the details of the nexus and to provide mutual reassurance. Although the reassurance function was also found in British firms, there were more cases in Britain where contracts were used in an adversarial manner, and significantly fewer British than German managers saw contracts as a device to build trust in business relations.

The greater juridification of German interfirm relations is thus both a reflection and a reinforcement of the long-termism noted above, and the reverse applies in the British case. This greater formality in German than British supplier relations does not, however, preclude the development of more informal personal ties. These were no less prevalent than in British firms. As was indicated in section 2 for intrafirm relations, flexible forms of organization can often flourish within the safety of a high-regulation framework.

5. CONCLUSIONS

This study of the social construction of actors, firms, and interfirm relations in Britain and Germany has tried to determine the relative importance in this process of societal and dominance effects. Empirically, these effects cannot be easily distinguished one from the other, as well as being constantly reshaped by key groups of organizational actors. Hence it is impossible to draw firm conclusions on causation, but some cautious generalizations can nevertheless be made.

First, the recurrence of particular social patterns of business relations over long historical periods, such as general value orientations, expressed in role understandings, role division, and structural arrangements, together with their replication in different aspects of business organization and different industries, suggests that societal effects have been far more influential in both countries than dominance effects. Governance structures, regulating supplier relations in the two countries, show a surprising degree of continuity over time, and any change which has occurred tends to be an adaptation within the dominant mould. Thus, although British management education and practices changed substantially from the 1960s onwards, partially under the influence of American dominance, a generalist approach has been preserved and technical skill is still underemphasized.

It is too early to formulate firm conclusions about the 'Japanization' factor. Structural factors, such as the degree of interpenetration of the British economy by Japanese firms and their greater dominance over certain industries, would suggest a more marked vulnerability of British firms also to this dominance effect. It would also appear that structural and cultural features of German firms and interfirm relations make them more resistant to the 'Japan' factor. Here I refer to the highly integrated nature of the German industrial economy, where associational networking is constantly being reinforced by a common set of values and norms, derived from a curious amalgam of the craft and the legal-bureaucratic traditions, overlaid with an emphasis on mutualism derived from the philosophy of the Social Market Economy. The much lesser degree of institutional embeddedness of British firms and the greater autonomy of individual firms and actors within them, coupled with the greater weakness of the industrial economy, would seem to make British managers more receptive to foreign 'best practice'.

But this tendency should not be overstated. The analysis of interfirm relations in two more traditional British and German industries has clearly shown that Japanization hype has consistently overlooked the 'industry' effect and has unduly generalized from a few important but not necessarily typical industries. Even in the more globalized industries, however, the pronounced British individualism in business relations must act as a strong brake to the slavish copying of 'foreign ways'. Adoption of some Japanese techniques can coincide with the continuation of traditional British ways of doing business. Most importantly, the very pronounced differences between Japanese and British governance systems make it highly unlikely that many British firms would ever adopt the integrated Japanese model of supplier relations.

REFERENCES

Abromeit, H. (1993), 'Unternehmerverbände', in U. Andersen and W. Woyke (eds.), *Handwörterbuch des politischen Systems der Bundesrepublik Deutschland* (Opladen: Leske & Budrich), 548–51.

Andersen Consulting (1992), *Worldwide Manufacturing Competitiveness Study* (London: Andersen Consulting).

Bannock, G., and Albach, H. (1991), *Small Business Policy in Europe*. Report for the Anglo-German Foundation (London: AGF).

Best, M. (1990), *The New Competition* (Cambridge: Polity Press).

Chandler, A. P. (1990), *Scale and Scope* (Cambridge, Mass.: Belknap Press of Harvard University Press).

Cooke, P. (1993), 'The Experiences of German Engineering Firms in Applying Lean Production Methods', IILS (ed.), *Lean Production and Beyond: Labour Aspects of a New Production Concept* (Geneva: International Institute for Labour Studies).

Doran, A. (1984), *Craft Enterprises in Britain and Germany*. Study for the Anglo-German Foundation by the Economists' Advisory Group (London: AGF).

Dore, R. (1987), *Taking Japan Seriously* (London: Athlone Press).

Dornseifer, B. (1993), 'Zur Bürokratisierung deutscher Unternehmen im späten 19. und frühen 20. Jahrhundert', *Jahrbuch für Wirtschaftsgeschichte*, 1: 69–94.

——and Kocka, J. (1993), 'The Impact of the Preindustrial Heritage: Reconsiderations on the German Pattern of Corporate Development in the Late 19th and Early 20th Centuries', *Industrial and Corporate Change*, 2/2: 233–48.

Dunning, J. H. (1993), *The Globalization of Business* (London: Routledge).

Earl, M. J. (1983), 'Accounting and Management', in M. J. Earl (ed.), *Perspectives on Management* (Oxford: Oxford University Press).

Eberwein, W., and Tholen, J. (1990), *Managermentalität: Industrielle Unternehmensleitung als Beruf und Politik* (Frankfurt am Main: Frankfurter Allgemeine Zeitung).

Elger, T., and Smith, C. (1994) (eds.), *Global Japanization?* (London: Routledge).

Fox, A. (1985), *History and Heritage: The Social Origins of the British Industrial Relations System* (London: George Allen and Unwin).

Gourvish, T. R. (1992), 'British Business and the Transition to a Corporate Economy: Entrepreneurship and Management Structures', in B. Supple (ed.), *The Rise of Big Business* (Aldershot: Edward Elgar).

Grant, W. (1993), *Business and Politics in Britain*, 2nd edn. (London: Macmillan).

Hannah, L. (1976), *The Rise of the Corporate Economy* (London: Methuen).

Hartmann, M. (1989), 'Zwischen Stabilität und Abstieg: Juristen als akademische Elite in der Wirschaft', *Soziale Welt*, 40/3: 437–53.

Heseltine, M. (1993), 'Speech on Trade Associations at the CBI' (June). Unpublished typescript.

Hutton, W. (1995), *The State we're in* (London: Jonathan Cape).

Imrie, R., and Morris, J. (1992), 'A Review of Recent Changes in Buyer-Supplier Relations', *Omega: International Journal of Management Science*, 20, 5/6: 641–52.

Julius, D. (1990), *Global Companies and Public Policy* (London: Pinter).

Kearney, A. T. (1994), *Partnership or Power Play?* (London: A. T. Kearney).

Kocka, J. (1970), 'Vorindustrielle Faktoren in der deutschen Industrialisierung', in M. Stürmer (ed.), *Das kaiserliche Deutschland: Politik und Gesellschaft 1870–1918* (Düsseldorf: Droste Verlag).

—— (1975), 'Expansion—Integration—Diversifikation: Wachstumsstrategien industrieller Grossunternehmen in Deutschland vor 1914', in H. Winkel (ed.), *Vom Kleingewerbe zum Grossbetrieb* (Berlin: Duncker and Humblot).

—— and Siegrist, H. (1979), 'Die hundert grössten deutschen Industrieunternehmen im späten 19. und frühen 20. Jahrhundert', in N. Horn and J. Kocka (eds.), *Law and the Formation of the Big Enterprise in the 19th and early 20th Century* (Göttingen: Vandenhoek and Ruprecht).

Korfmann, H.-D. (1992), 'Die deutsche Bergbaumaschinen-Industrie vor neuen Herausforderungen.' *Glückauf*, 128/5: 348–58.

Kristensen, P. H. (1996), 'Variations in the Nature of the Firm in Europe', in R. Whitley and P. H. Kristensen (eds.), *The Changing European Firm: Limits to Convergence* (London: Routledge).

Landes, D. (1969), *The Unbound Prometheus: Technological Change and Industrial Development* (Cambridge: Cambridge University Press).

Lane, C. (1991), 'Industrial Reorganisation in Europe: Patterns of Convergence and Divergence in Germany, France and Britain', *Work, Employment and Society*, 5/4: 515–39.

—— (1992), 'European Business Systems: Britain and Germany Compared', in R. Whitley (ed.), *European Business Systems: Firms and Markets in their National Contexts* (London: Sage).

—— (1995), *Industry and Society in Europe: Stability and Change in Britain, Germany and France* (Aldershot: Edward Elgar).

—— (1996), 'The Social Constitution of Supplier Relations in Britain and Germany: An Institutionalist Analysis', in R. Whitley and P. H. Kristensen (eds.), *The Changing European Firm: Limits to Convergence* (London: Routledge).

—— (1997), 'The Social Regulation of Inter-firm Relations in Britain and Germany: the role of technical standards', *Cambridge Journal of Economics*, 21, 2 forthcoming.

—— and Bachmann, R. (1995), 'Cooperation in Supplier Relations: The Role of Trade Associations and Legal Regulation'. Working Paper of the ESRC Centre for Business Research, University of Cambridge, CBR.

———— (1996), 'The Social Constitution of Trust', *Organization Studies*, 17/3: 365–95.

Lazonick, W. (1994), *Business Organization and the Myth of the Market Economy* (Cambridge: Cambridge University Press).

Lee, G., and Smith, C. (1992), 'British Engineers in Context', in G. Lee and C. Smith (eds.), *Engineers and Management: International Comparisons* (London: Routledge).

Locke, R. R. (1984), *The End of Practical Man: Entrepreneurship and Higher Education in Germany, France and Great Britain 1880–1940* (Greenwich, Conn.: JAI Press).

Maurice, M., Sorge, A., and Warner, M. (1980), 'Societal Difference in Organising Manufacturing Units', *Organization Studies*, 1: 63–91.

May, T. C., McHugh, J., and Taylor, T. W. (1994), 'Trade Associations: Preliminary Analysis of Results'. Unpublished research paper. Department of Politics and Philosophy, Manchester Metropolitan University.

Morris, J., and Imrie, R. (1992), *Transformations in the Buyer-Supplier Relationship* (London: Macmillan).

National Audit Office (1990), *Promotion of Quality and Standards* (London: HMSO).

NEDO (1987), *The Making of Managers.* Report on behalf of the MSC, NEDC, and BIM (London: NEDO).

Oliver, N. (1993), 'Making it in Britain'. Working Paper. Judge Institute of Management, University of Cambridge.

——and Wilkinson, B. (1988), *The Japanization of British Industry* (Oxford: Basil Blackwell).

Pohl, H. (1992), 'On the History of Organisation and Management in Large German Enterprises since the 19th Century', in B. Supple (ed.), *The Rise of Big Business* (Aldershot: Edward Elgar).

Pollard, S. (1965), *The Genesis of Modern Management* (London: Edward Arnold).

Porter, M. (1990), *The Competitive Advantage of Nations* (London: Macmillan).

Rainnie, A. (1991), 'Subcontracting and the Small Firm', *Work, Employment and Society*, 5/3: 353–76.

Rampelt, J. (1979), 'Zur Organisations- und Entscheidungsstruktur in west-deutschen Unternehmerverbänden: Ein Literaturbericht'. Discussion paper. International Institute of Management, Wissenschaftszentrum Berlin.

Sako, M. (1992), *Prices, Quality and Trust: Inter-firm Relations in Britain and Japan* (Cambridge: Cambridge University Press).

Sayer, A., and Walker, R. (1992), *The New Social Economy* (Oxford: Basil Blackwell).

Siegrist, H. (1980), 'Deutsche Grossunternehmen vom späten 19: Jahrhundert bis zur Weimarer Republik', *Geschichte und Gesellschaft*, 6/1: 60–102.

Smith, C., and Meiksins, P. (1995), 'System, Society and Dominance Effects in Cross-national Organisational Analysis', *Work, Employment and Society*, 9/2: 241–68.

Sorge, A. (1996), 'Societal Effects in Cross-national Organization Studies: Conceptualizing Diversity In Actors and Systems', in R. Whitley and P. H. Kristensen (eds.), *The Changing European Firm: Limits to Convergence* (London: Routledge).

Stewart, R., Barsoux, J.-L., Kieser, A., Ganter, D., and Walgenbach, P. (1994), *Managing in Britain and Germany* (New York: St Martin's Press).

Storey, D. J. (1994), *Understanding the Small Business Sector* (London: Routledge).

Streeck, W. (1992), 'The Logics of Associative Action and the Territorial Organization of Interests: The Case of German *Handwerk*', in W. Streeck, *Social Institutions and Economic Performance* (London: Sage).

Trevor, M., and Christie, I. (1988), *Manufacturers and Suppliers in Britain and Japan* (London: Policy Studies Institute).

Turner, J. (1988), 'Servants of Two Masters: British Trade Associations in the First Half of the Twentieth Century', in H. Yamazaki and M. Miyahoto (eds.), *Trade Associations in Business History* (Tokyo: University of Tokyo Press).

Warner, M., and Campbell, A. (1993), 'German Management', in D. J. Hickson (ed.), *Management in Western Europe* (Berlin: De Gruyter).

Weber, H. (1987), *Unternehmerverbände zwischen Markt, Staat und Gewerkschaften: Zur intermediären Organisation von Wirtschaftsverbänden* (Frankfurt: Campus).

Whitley, R. (1992), 'Societies, Firms and Markets: The Social Structuring of Business Systems', in R. Whitley (ed.), *European Business Systems* (London: Sage).

Willis, D., and Grant, W. (1987), 'The United Kingdom: Still a Company State?', in M. P. van Schendelen and R. J. Jackson (eds.), *The Politicisation of Business in Western Europe* (London: Croom Helm).

Womack, J., *et al.* (1990), *The Machine that Changed the World* (New York: Rawson Associates).

Wood, W. J. (1991), 'The Influence of Directors' "Qualifications" on Profitability in U.K. Manufacturing Companies', in D. Bennett and C. Lewis (eds.), *Achieving Competitive Edge* (Berlin: Springer Verlag), 439–44.

4

The Social Regulation of Technical Expertise
The Corps and Profession in France and Great Britain

ELISABETH CAMPAGNAC

GRAHAM WINCH

1. INTRODUCTION

This chapter forms part of a larger programme of work comparing the national business systems of France and Great Britain, and the development of contemporary capitalism in the two countries which revolves around the essentially *étatique* nature of the regulation of the French system compared to the market regulation of the British (Boyer 1996). While this contention is not original at the general level, exactly how these differences manifest themselves in the governance of particular work systems has rarely been systematically explored in a comparative mode. In order to provide greater precision in the analysis we have decided to focus upon one particular type of work system which, as we will show, has historically had an especially profound influence on the development of national business systems—transport infrastructure engineering—and to explore the problem of how technical expertise is developed and deployed in modern capitalist societies. This relatively narrow focus does not imply wider irrelevance. As will be demonstrated, it was in the construction sector that this problem was first tackled, and the distinctive ways in which those two countries now deploy technical expertise are deeply embedded in the ways in which the construction sector developed during the early phases of industrialization.

Our argument will be that in those nations, such as Great Britain and France, where the state existed in a strong form prior to industrialization, the state plays a fundamental role in the formation of economically important social groups and their related modes of governance. Choices by the state regarding the way in which transport infrastructure[1] was to be pro-

---

[1] Dobbin (1994) has already demonstrated how valuable an exploration of policy towards the railways is for understanding the formation of national industrial policy.

vided formed the social and economic context for the development of the social groups required to engineer it. Where infrastructure construction was at the instigation of the state, as in France, the *corps* was formed by the state to ensure the provision of technical expertise. Where infrastructure construction was at the instigation of the private sector, a self-regulating group—the *profession*—emerged to provide the technical expertise required. These two solutions—both clearly established by the 1820s—then went on to shape the entire development of the organization of technical expertise in the two countries and are still profoundly influential throughout their contemporary business systems. The argument will therefore concentrate upon the role of what Torstendahl (1990) has called 'knowledge-based groups' in industrialization as a complement to the craft-based groups discussed by Kristensen. This argument forms an essential preliminary to the investigation of the division of labour within the enterprise which is the focus of current research.

The chapter will start with a conceptual orientation, identifying the relationship of the argument to the central propositions regarding the governance of social groups that run through this volume. It will then analyse the national industrial policies with regard to the provision of transport infrastructure, and in particular, policy towards that great nineteenth-century phenomenon—the railway. Next, the principal institutions for the formation and mobilization of technical expertise for the construction of transport infrastructure—the Corps et École des Ponts et Chaussées, and the Institution of Civil Engineers—will be described, analysed, and located in the context discussed in the previous section. The chapter will end with some concluding thoughts.

2. TECHNICAL EXPERTISE AND THE GOVERNANCE OF WORK SYSTEMS

In the introduction to this volume, Kristensen develops further the role of social groups in the governance of work systems, focusing particularly upon the emergence of nationally distinctive social groups amongst skilled factory operatives during initial industrialization. The argument here will both broaden this perspective, and also provide greater focus. It will broaden the perspective by moving beyond manufacturing. The creation of a manual workforce accustomed to the rigours of factory discipline is only one of the many problems that an industrializing economy faces. Similarly, when manufacturing typically accounts for less than a quarter of GDP in advanced economies, no comprehensive analysis of the character of contemporary business systems can rely upon evidence from the manufacturing sector alone. This chapter will explore the ways in which the governance of work systems through social groups has been applied to another problem that any industrializing economy must solve—that of providing a transport infrastructure so that raw materials can be brought to the factory and finished goods distributed. The sector which produces this infrastructure—construction—is also one of the largest single sectors in any economy. Construction expenditure typically accounts for up to 12 per cent of GDP in west European countries, and up to 20 per cent in rapidly growing economies such as Japan in the 1980s. The chapter will also provide focus, because it will concentrate upon a particular sector, for as Winch (1996a) argued in the previous volume in this series, it is the sector which gives the activities of the firm meaning.

Our problem immediately leads us to the literature on the sociology of the professions. Originally rooted in sociology of social structure, rather than economic sociology, the sociology of the professions has increasingly turned its attention to the economic implications of professional organization (Larson 1977; Abbott 1988). Professions are here defined not in the loose sense of the emergence of a 'professional' middle class encompassing civil servants, the liberal professions, and the managerial layers of the corporation developed by neo-Weberians such as Perkin (1969, 1989), but in the more restricted sense of the members of specific social institutions whose task is to form and legitimize expertise—what Millerson (1964) has called the 'qualifying associations'. In this sense, we part from Weber and side with Parsons in defining professionalism as an *alternative* to bureaucracy, not as its most sophisticated expression.[2] However, our work will also show the limitations of the concept of *profession*, and how it needs to be complemented by that of the *corps* as two distinctive types of knowledge-based social groups in contemporary capitalism.

Larson (1977) argues that professionalization is a process which brings together two distinctive elements—a body of relatively abstract knowledge and a potential market for services derived from that knowledge. It is the standardization and codification of professional knowledge which can be made distinct and recognizable to a potential client which is central to realizing this market and coalescing the profession into an effective group. Until this process of codification is complete then competing groups can lay claim to the monopoly of expertise in a market. Abbott (1988) investigates in his analysis the division of expert labour between the competing professional groups in the social construction of the system of professions. Both go on to explore historically the development of the major professions, mainly in the United States, but also in Britain and France.

It is from the work of Abbott that our chapter takes its central problematic. In a later article, he poses the question how expertise in society is socially structured, where expertise is defined as the 'ability to accomplish complex tasks' (1991: 19). He contends that this approach inverts the traditional functionalist approach which identifies an institution and then

[2] See Parson's introduction to Weber (1947).

searches for the function that it fulfils, by identifying a social function, then looking for how it is met. He also contends that the definition of expertise is action-oriented, including within its scope the ability to mobilize the knowledge of others through social interaction, rather than as a property solely of individual's knowledge. We pose this question more precisely by focusing on technical expertise, and asking how societies ensure that their requirements for public works—essentially transport infrastructure—are met efficiently, effectively, and without danger to their users. Thus we do not start with the concept of profession and then range internationally trying to find examples of its existence as a social phenomenon, but with a social problem and ask how it is solved in specific national contexts. Our answer will be that it is through the development of nationally embedded types of social group—the corps and the profession.

3. THE INSTITUTIONAL CONTEXT OF THE PRODUCTION OF TECHNICAL EXPERTISE

The organization of the technical expertise in construction offers both similarities and strong disparities between France and Great Britain. In order to understand these, it is necessary to examine the place, the role, and the status of the expertise that has been produced, historically and socially, in each of the two countries. We will explore in this section the historical context of the production and deployment of technical expertise in public works in the context of highly contrasting institutional relations.

The case of France

The case of public works and the organization of its technical expertise is, without doubt, the most convincing example of the difficulty of isolating the institutional modernity of post-revolutionary France from its fount in the *ancien régime*. Here we follow the argument of Legendre (1992), who has identified the ways in which the administration of the French state has its source in the institutions of the *ancien régime*, and forms a homogeneous entity which is strongly differentiated from the British model. In this respect, the organization of public works which was implemented in France represents a particular conception of the relationship between state and market which is expressed first in the mercantilism advocated by the crown and subsequently in the interventionism of the liberal state of the nineteenth century.

During the *ancien régime*, the crown invested in order to lift the barriers which feudal society placed against the free circulation of goods, as well in the development of commerce and industry. This investment took different forms—state participation in banking institutions, taking direct charge of what traditionally had been collective goods as well as the provision and maintenance of the road system by the Administration des Ponts et Chaussées. This role in the provision of infrastructure proved vital in the unification and control of the national territory as well as aiding the development of commerce and industry.

The French state responded to the challenge of the industrial revolution in various ways. On the one hand it modernized the Colbertian institutions established under Louis XIV, for the post-revolutionary state in France had neither negated the fiscal monopolies, the methods of the formation of technical expertise, nor the methods of support through taxation established by the *ancien régime*. On the other hand it took inspiration from the policy of royal privileges and concessions (Bezançon 1995) to give France new infrastructure through the method of the concession for public works such as railways and urban transport systems, or the concession for public service such as water, gas, and electricity. The concession took the place of the public monopoly, and put in place, beside the civil code, a specific public code—the administrative code—which extended the competence of the state.

This tradition of royal concession stood the French state in good stead when it came to building the infrastructure for industrialization. It was assumed that the state should take the lead in developing the transport infrastructure, yet capital shortages meant that private sector involvement was required—the formula of the *concession* solved this dilemma. The solution was that the state, through the Corps, would define the rail routes required, finance land acquisition and the grading of the route, and the construction of tunnels and bridges, while the concessionaire would finance track, installations, and rolling stock, and operate the route. Fares were set through the *cahier des charges*. The Corps not only controlled where the lines should run, but how they should be built. The Corps' overriding aim was to link secondary centres with Paris by fast lines with gentle grades and curves, bypassing other towns which would have doubled traffic, built to a very high specification. In 1832 a commission was set up to plan the rail network, and by 1835 the plan was complete. The Corps then granted concessions to dozens of private companies after its enactment in 1842, which were reorganized in 1852 into six regional concessions (Dobbin 1994, ch. 3; Smith 1990).

These concession contracts were given a regulatory framework at the level of the state in 1836, and of local authorities in 1837. Whilst the concession contracts let by local authorities evolved in the context of a fluid legal framework, occasionally subject to the review of the state, the state itself adopted at the national level a series of laws relating to each new form of infrastructure concession, imposing new controls during their negotiations with the enterprises, thereby assuring the homogeneity of the rules, without exercising the function of entrepreneur. A general model of concession contract was established at the beginning of the twentieth century.

The development of the concession was by no means restricted to France, but its implementation in France had a number of peculiarities which are worthy of note:

1. First, it was not restricted to the provision of public works and commerce, but extended to industrial sectors. The state intervened in a number of industries, reconciling the provision of the requirements of industrialization with the spirit of proprietor. Thus the *loi Minière* of 1810 extended the system to mines, and led to the creation of the Corps Impérial des Mines in the same year.

2. It is difficult to oppose the absolute state (symbolized by Louis XIV) and the modern liberal state, for the French institutional model is realized through a combination of the two. Moreover, it is when Legendre (1992) defines interventionism in France as the product of this synthesis, and emphasizes that it is here that the contradiction between 'liberty' and 'equality' is concealed, that foreign observers fail to understand France.

3. The French concession is characterized by a sharing of risks between the private and the public sectors. Thus the *loi Minière* organized a regime of concessions by means of the payment of allowances by the state to the proprietor, and the payment of rents in return. In turn this led the state to control prices. It was this same idea of action for economic progress which justified the complex formulas for concession utilized during the nineteenth century. Such a conception cannot but deform the rules of competitive markets, and it underlines the role which the French state played in the struggle against risk. This was distinctive of 'l'ésprit du capitalisme français', which led enterprises to claim protection against risks from the state, and for the state to accord it, all justified in the name of effectiveness.

4. Thus a fourth characteristic of the French concession system is that it largely favoured the industrial power of the enterprise. Developing from a strong economic nationalism, the policy of the concession of privileges has as its objective the stimulation of the development of new firms as well as the existing large corporations.

5. Finally, the French legal system is characterized by a centralism embodied in the existence of a *bloc massif* of administrative codes relating to public contracts (*codes des marchés publics*) and concessions which marks France very clearly off from England with its common law system. The appearance of the administrative codes is closely linked to institutional developments after the revolution based on enlightenment notions of the rationality of the law.

The system of concessions was a considerable success, despite the opposition of the socialists, but in the period before the First World War, a struggle was waged against the monopolistic capitalism which it allegedly generated. During the first half of the twentieth century, the growing role of the state was fulfilled through the development of *la régie*—implying the direct execution of its functions by the state—not *la concession*. During the 1970s, and even more during the 1980s, there was a return to the concession due to the combination of a number of different factors, particularly the national political context, the rise of neo-liberalism, and the new policies of competition at the European level.

The case of Great Britain

To this tradition Great Britain presents a strong contrast. The Glorious Revolution of 1688 led to the foundation of what developed into a constitutional monarchy in which the power of the sovereign was negotiated with the other sources of power in the land—both the aristocracy, and increasingly, parliament as representative of the people. At the same time, London was taking over from Amsterdam the role of Europe's financial centre and embarking upon the rise to global economic and political dominance that peaked during the mid-nineteenth century when Britain became not only the workshop of the world, but railway builder to the world (Linder 1994).

While France represented the first political nation state, Britain represented the first economic nation state (Braudel 1979). The earlier economic powers had been city states. In their day, they were dominant financial and manufacturing centres, appropriating the flows of merchandise around the Mediterranean, and the flows of gold and silver from the Americas by exporting financial services and high-quality manufactured goods. What Britain achieved was the extension of the market to the national level, thereby benefiting from economies of scale as the extent of the market expanded. On the basis of the wealth derived from increasing dominance of world trade, the improvements in agricultural productivity which allowed the rise of a purely urban population, and the development of (for its day) a relatively good infrastructure, and ready access to raw materials, British entrepreneurs embarked upon the industrial revolution.

As this revolution gained momentum, the mercantilism inherent in the granting of charters to the great trading companies came under attack. Slowly, the advocates of free trade won the day, their most symbolic victory being the reform of the corn laws in 1846. What distinguished Great Britain from France and all other industrializing nations save the United States was the absence of the state from economic initiative. The state saw its role as ensuring the rule of law, and granting rights to the exploitation by private capital of common goods in areas as varied as the enclosure of common land (thereby allowing the rise of agricultural productivity), international trade (thereby facilitating the accumulation of capital), and the construction of turnpikes, canals, and railways (thereby enabling the provision of infrastructure).

Meanwhile, the provision of infrastructure developed on a very different basis from that of France. The first turnpike in England was started in 1654, and built steadily to an effective network of main roads. The state was only interested in the strategic routes to Scotland and Ireland—the rest of the network was built by private entrepreneurs at their own initiative. Canals began to be financed and built in the same way from 1755, and the development of the railways followed in due course. From the Liverpool and Manchester railway of 1825, the pattern of entrepreneurs presenting bills to parliament, justified on the basis of the public interest, in order to enable the expropriation of private property so that the lines could be built remained the same throughout the railway building boom of the mid-nineteenth century. By 1848, a network of lines linked the principal industrial centres to London, and the railway entrepreneurs began to turn their attention to the rest of the world.

This approach to the provision of transport infrastructure may be called the *charter*, to distinguish it from the *concession* of France.[3] It is sometimes forgotten what a central role private capital and initiative played in the construction of the British transport infrastructure during the nineteenth century. The canals and railways, with the exception of a few in Ireland, were built entirely at private initiative and expense without any guarantees from the state. The process was subject to detailed parliamentary scrutiny because the construction of a railway or canal inevitably involved the expropriation of private property lying along the route. But the role of the state was largely to protect private property interests, not to ensure the construction of transport infrastructure. Once the benefits of rail transport had been clearly established by 1840, Parliament readily granted charters to rail promoters on the basis of detailed technical submissions. Parliament otherwise mainly limited its intervention in the operation of the railways to the safety of the travelling public (Dobbin 1994, ch. 4).

Discussion

The differing experiences of France and Great Britain in solving the problem of providing a transport infrastructure show a remarkable contrast, which is summarized in Table 4.1. The role of the state was profoundly different in the two countries. The principal objective of the French state was to ensure that a transport infrastructure was built, and private sector participation was only acceptable under the close control of the Corps—it therefore chose the *concession* as the legal form for the railway company. The British state's objective was to protect the private property and safety of its citizens affected by the activities of the railway promoters—it therefore chose the *charter* as the legal form for the railway company. These two

---

[3] This distinction is developed further in Winch (1996*b*).

policies were developed in the context of detailed knowledge of the other. The Corps recoiled from the anarchy and cheapness of the British rail system, while the British engineers were appalled at the extravagance of the French. Both policies were contentious within their own countries. Many French engineers and industrialists outside the Corps were heavily critical of its approach, arguing that the very high level of specification demanded held back the development of the system and uselessly absorbed capital. One argued in 1883 that the Corps had 'made the country poorer while trying to make it richer' (cited Smith 1990: 683). In Britain, the speculative adventures of the railway promoters became known as 'railway mania' in the 1840s, while many in Britain railed against the waste inherent in promoting competing lines, which was another way of uselessly absorbing capital. No less a figure than the duke of Wellington called for planning of the system in 1838. However, as Dobbin shows (1994), it was the policies most in line with the predominant business system which were the ones adopted.

TABLE 4.1. French and British Railway Policy Compared

France	Great Britain
Planning	
All routes planned by the Corps	No centralized route planning
National rather than local needs favoured	Promoters choose routes to maximize immediate returns
Finance	
Pervasive system of grants and profit guarantees	No state involvement
Broader socio-economic returns emphasized, even at the cost of immediate primary returns	Primary returns from routes emphasized
Capital shortages forced concession approach	Capital abundance encouraged speculative fever
Technical coordination	
Technical expertise lay with the Corps	Technical expertise lay with the promoting company and their engineers
Efficiency of use major criterion	Cost of construction major criterion
State determined all aspects of technology	State only interested in safety
Concessions specified detailed technical choices	Charter bills specified detailed technical choices
Competition	
Cahiers des Charges set by the state	Virtually no regulation of rates

These contrasts in the institutional context of construction in France and Great Britain illustrate clearly the impact of the societal on the sectoral. The state-led economic development of France encouraged the state to solve the problem of the provision of public works by sharing risks with the private sector, while the market-led economic development of the British economy left the risks entirely with the private sector. The state restricted itself to providing a regulatory context for that activity. These differences in the role of the state led to profound differences in the formation and mobilization of technical expertise, and it is to that question we now turn.

4. THE ORGANIZATION OF TECHNICAL EXPERTISE

The construction of a rail network required the mobilization of considerable levels of novel technical expertise, both for the construction of the tracks, particularly bridges and tunnels, and also the provision of the rolling stock. Both countries were able to draw upon their experience of building canals and roads, but unprecedented challenges remained. The ways in which this technical expertise was mobilized were strongly influenced, if not determined, by the very different ways in which the construction process was organized, which has been discussed in the previous section.

The case of France

The production of technical expertise in French public works can be studied through the example of the Corps des Ingénieurs des Ponts et Chaussées. Even if they do not represent all the technical expertise in French construction, they occupy the positions of power in the body of the public administration and the construction corporations (Thoenig 1987). The Corps is the best known in France and as de Tocqueville (1952) noted, it is 'le grand agent du gouvernement central en matière de travaux publics', and the archetype of French centralism. The case of the ENPC is, therefore, a very good example of the manner in which the formation of technical expertise, essentially on behalf of the state, simultaneously serves to create a social elite. The engineers of the Corps des Ponts et Chaussées belong to the *noblesse d'état* analysed by Bourdieu (1989). Without doubt, this relationship between the *grandes écoles*, the culture of the engineer, and the *grands corps de l'État* defines the specificities of the French system.

Founded in 1747, the École Nationale des Ponts et Chaussées is the oldest of the French engineering schools, and one of the leading schools in the world. It was established at a period when engineers remained rare in both France and Great Britain. It is very much a product of the mercantilism *à la française* analysed above, and its functions cannot be understood without reference to the interventionist role of the state. Previously, infrastructure had been the responsibility of local agencies—*seigneurs*, communities, associations of merchants, and religious orders. Although Henri IV had created the office of *grand voyer* at the instigation of Sully in order to solve the problems posed by the circulation of goods and people, this ambition remained a dead letter due to the absence of local technical competence. In 1669, Colbert had reminded all his staff of the importance of transport routes for the grandeur and wealth of the kingdom, and exhorted them to surround themselves with competent technicians. Bringing together architects and engineers, he formed the kernel of the Corps des Ponts et Chaussées. Charged with the construction and the maintenance of the communication routes in their areas, the engineers of the Corps initially had considerable autonomy due to a lack of overall coordination.

The creation of the ENPC by Perronet and Trudaine was intended to rectify this problem through the homogenization of the formation of technical competence. In this spirit, Trudaine began in 1744 by creating a central organization charged with preparing maps of all the existing and planned roads, but he still wished to raise the level of recruitment and to establish a distinctive training. By a decree of 14 February 1747, considered to be the founding act of the ENPC, he asked Perronet to instruct the draughtsmen and geographers in map making, but also in the techniques necessary for fulfilling the functions of the various parts of the Corps such as trigonometry, geometry, architecture, and surveying. From the start an important place was accorded to individual incentives, and a competitive spirit dominated each class. Here were the essential traits of the ENPC.

With the creation of the ENPC, the management of infrastructure provision was assured through the provision of a technically competent corps. It was at the school that the professional identity of the Corps was established. After the creation of the École Polytechnique in 1794, the decision was taken to select from amongst its graduates, the entrants to the ENPC. During this period, the theoretical capacity of the engineers increased considerably as a consequence of an increasing reliance upon mathematics in the syllabus. Thus this period saw the emergence of a new actor 'l'ingénieur moderne' in distinction to the 'l'ingénieur artiste' of before (Picon 1992). This new figure of the modern engineer came to incarnate the values of progress which legitimized its growing role in technical processes.

These developments did not take place without problems or debates. One of these related to the very conception of *l'ingénieur*. Should the engineer be a pragmatic technician mobilizing expertise on the project, or should the engineer be more knowledgeable on the model of the École Polytechnique? How should the technical competence be formed—around the mathematical formulation of techniques, or around the economic issues relating to technical choices? During the eighteenth century, the engineer had a relatively feeble understanding at the scientific level, but was more competent in economic questions. Training became much more scientific during the nineteenth century, but also less open to the economic issues.

The increasing role of mathematics in technical competence contributed to the transformation of the idea of public works. However, the engineer was also led to think in terms of processes, and thus to be interested in the division of labour, and the control of work. Public policy debates regarding roads also served as an apprenticeship in social conflict. Having recourse to a distinctive competence, and possessing the opportunity to implement the results of their analyses of the division of labour, the engineers adhered to a rationality distinct from that of the foreman or worker they instructed. This rationality of the engineers of the Corps led to a desire to bring to the process of production the scientific knowledge of the physical world. Thus it was through the figure of the *ingénieur des ponts* that technical competence led very early to a capacity for rationalization in France.

In the case of those engineers acting on behalf of administrative functions of the state, it very soon appeared to be difficult to reconcile the requirements of public service with the maintenance of privileges granted to corporations. This reconciliation was effected at the ideological level through the mediation of the *ésprit de corps*. In this respect, the extension of the role of the ENPC through membership of the Corps was critical. It was also fundamental to the formation of the technocracy, which is one of the specificities of the French model.

The case of Britain

Two sorts of technical expertise were organized during the early years of the industrial revolution in Great Britain—that deriving from the crafts, and that deriving from those educated in natural philosophy.[4] When the duke of Bridgewater promoted the construction of the Bridgewater Canal to carry his coal to market he retained James Brindley, an apprenticed wheelwright, to engineer the project in 1759. This was the world's first arterial canal, independent of existing rivers. At the same time, John Smeaton, a lawyer with strong links to the Royal Society and a passion for machines was retained to rebuild the Eddystone Lighthouse. It was Smeaton who first used the term 'civil engineer' in 1768, and saw himself as the social equal of a lawyer or physician. The principal difference between Brindley and similar engineers, and Smeaton and others such as John Rennie, a graduate of Edinburgh University, was that the latter were more educated and could therefore read French and Latin, enabling them to follow developments in continental Europe, and especially at the École des Ponts.

---

[4] Much of what follows is based upon Buchanan (1989) and Watson (1988).

It was civil engineers of the latter type who came together in 1818 to form the Institution of Civil Engineers (ICE), with the objective of 'facilitating the acquirement of knowledge necessary in [the] profession and for promoting mechanical philosophy'. The Institution elected Thomas Telford, the leading engineer of the day, as president in 1820, and was granted its royal charter in 1828. At this time, the term 'civil' was used to distinguish the membership from military engineers, and for the next century, the ICE claimed to represent all engineers. That it did not do this very successfully is indicated by the formation from amongst its membership of the Institution of Mechanical Engineers (IME) to meet the needs of those concerned with engines in 1847, and the forerunner of the Institution of Electrical Engineers (IEE) in 1871. However, the ICE petitioned against, and managed to prevent, those two institutions gaining royal charters until the 1920s.

These developments were in conscious and knowledgeable contrast to the French approach. As Thomas Telford, the president of the ICE, put it in his inaugural address in 1820, 'in foreign countries similar establishments were instituted by government, and their members and proceedings are under its control; but here, a different course is being adopted' (cited Buchanan 1989: 63). Many British engineers admired the theoretical elegance of French engineering and Telford allegedly learned French in order to read about its works, but the French approach was not seen as an appropriate way to deliver the infrastructure of the world's first industrial nation. I. K. Brunel, whose father was French, and who had been educated in France, was scathing about the relevance of French engineering texts for practice, and advocated instead visiting blacksmith's shops.[5] Advances were made in Britain through the empirical testing of models, not abstract theory. The rationality of British engineering was, therefore, very close to that of the workers it directed.

Although some of the very early railway engineers—notably the Stephensons and Brunel—were themselves promoters of railway companies, most engineers either worked on behalf of contractor-promoters such as Brassey or the railway companies themselves. Typically, this was not as an employee, but as an independent adviser to a number of different promoters. Thus the role of the consulting engineer evolved, and the distinctive organization of the professional engineer in independent practice emerged. The activities of these practices were then regulated by the professional institution in order to assure purchasers of the quality of the intangible service rendered.

The rise of the professional institutions in Great Britain is very much a nineteenth-century phenomenon (Reader 1966) in response to what Perkin

---

[5] The fact the Corps had little idea how to build railways and was obliged to rely almost entirely on British entrepreneurs such as Brassey for the actual construction of the first generation of lines during the 1840s (Middlemas 1963) provides support for his case.

(1969) has called the entrepreneurial society which had ushered in the industrial revolution.[6] The ICE is a distinctively modern organization, which provided the original model of the professional institution which has become such a distinctive feature of the British business system (Millerson 1964). With its links to the Royal Society, and its foundation principle of the acquisition and dissemination of technical knowledge, the ICE was very much a response to the challenges posed by the industrial revolution that could not be solved through the market. In this sense the professional institution evolved as an essential complement to the market, where market transaction governance was inadequate due to imperfect information.

As the century unfolded, the task of the engineer became more and more complex, and increasing demands were made upon them, but although chairs in civil engineering were established at University College London and Glasgow University in the 1840s, there were no formal links between the universities and the Institution until 1867, when a student class of membership was established. The usual route to membership, and hence the highest status of engineer, was by serving a pupillage and having five years' subsequent employment in the profession, but a formal education was not yet seen as necessary, or even desirable, for the training of an engineer. Only in 1897 was an educational qualification for entry to the associate member class, and hence the ladder to full membership, implemented, while practical training and experience remained part of the membership requirements. It was not until after the general reform of engineering education in the UK during the 1960s that it became obligatory in 1974 to have a university degree in order to obtain membership.

The crucial point about the 1897 reform from a comparative perspective is that the examinations were set by the ICE itself, not by the universities. Universities sought to have graduates of their degree programmes *exempted* from the Institution's educational requirements, and this remains the situation today. The central importance of self-regulation as opposed to state regulation to the ICE in particular and the British engineering institutions in general was well demonstrated by the reaction against the recommendations of the Finniston Report in 1980, which advocated a statutory Engineering Authority for the registration of engineers. The government backed down from implementing this proposal and the charter-based Engineering Council was founded instead (Jordan 1992).

The ICE provided a model for the formation and deployment of technical expertise for the other nascent engineering professions in Britain such as the IME and IEE which took it as a model. Equally importantly for the argument here, it also provided the model for the development of the

---

[6] Millerson (1964) has shown that, despite some formal organizational similarities, only two of the professional institutions of the nineteenth century can trace their roots back to the pre-industrial guilds—the pharmacists and the surgeons—both meeting timeless needs.

engineering profession in the United States. It is contended here that, just as the Corps and École des Ponts formed the model for the invention of the modern engineer and organization of technical expertise in France, the ICE formed the model for the organization of technical expertise in Britain, the United States, and throughout the Anglo-Saxon world.

Discussion

We have, therefore, identified two very different types of knowledge-based social group with two distinctive types of governance system for the organization of technical expertise in public works—the corps and the profession. The first is deeply embedded in a national system where the mode of regulation is *étatique*, while the latter is similarly embedded in a national system where the mode of regulation is through the market. As Thompson (1968: 149) argued, 'short of state-controlled academies and institutions . . . the voluntary professional association was the only way which could be devised of fitting professional activities into the workings of a free economy'. On the basis of the evidence from the construction sector in

TABLE 4.2. The Corps and the Profession Compared

Corps	Profession
Governance system	
Founded at state initiative	Founded at private initiative
Regulated by the state	Self-regulated by charter from the state
Mainly employment by the state or large corporation	Mainly employment in independent practice
Knowledge base	
Formal education in schools dependent upon the appropriate state ministry[a]	Pupillage and/or formal education in general purpose universities regulated by the professional institution
Bias towards theoretically acquired knowledge	Bias towards empirically acquired knowledge
State/enterprise relations	
Relations between the state and the enterprise closely coordinated through the corps	Relations between the state and the enterprise clearly separated and mediated by independent professionals

[a] The *grandes écoles techniques* are distinctive within the French higher education system because they are financed by the ministries which they serve, unlike the *universités* which are financed by the ministry of education. All British higher education is funded by the ministry of education.

these two countries we can propose the principal differences between the corps and the profession to be as summarized in Table 4.2.

5. SOME CONCLUDING THOUGHTS

It has been our contention in this chapter that the organization of technical expertise in France and Great Britain is profoundly influenced by the institutional context in which it takes place. This context is the result of the social construction of institutions leading to historically distinctive paths of development which facilitate distinctive kinds of social networks. We propose that the Corps and the Profession are distinctive social formations for the mobilization of technical expertise in advanced industrial nations, which cannot be reduced one to the other. Just as the Corps des Ponts et Chaussées could not exist in Great Britain, the Institution of Civil Engineers could not exist in France. To take the title of Antoine Picon's book—both the ICE and ENPC indeed invented the modern engineer, but it was a very different type of engineer that was invented in each case.

Thus our work presents two challenges to the current approach to the analysis of knowledge-based groups through the sociology of the professions. By taking the perspective of the national business system rather than the national social structure, and asking the question of how technical expertise is organized in advanced capitalist societies, we have identified two distinctive types of knowledge-based groups. This is in contrast to the prevailing argument in the sociology of the professions that national differences are simply variations on a theme, a position argued most recently by Burrage (1990), who is dismissive of the contention of Jamous and Peloille (1970) that the Corps is a more appropriate concept for analysing French doctors than the Profession. Secondly, by a focus on the demand for knowledge-based services and how it is fulfilled, rather than their supply, we have shifted the analytic emphasis away from the self-creation of professions through social closure to their economic role in providing vital elements of the industrialization process. It thus represents an advance on the work of those such as Larson (1977: 12) who have attempted to relate supply and demand for professional services, but without a clear elaboration of the nature of the demand.

If we are to take the concept of national business systems seriously, then we should expect common problems to be solved in different ways, and our methodological approach should not start by importing concepts developed in the analysis of one type of business system to the analysis of another, but through the analysis of the problems that each business system is trying to solve nationally and at the level of the sector. This approach has established that the Corps and the Profession are the dominant governance modes for the organization of technical expertise in France and Great Britain respectively, and that they need to be understood in the context in which they each developed—the provision of transport infrastructure in the world's first two nation states. In the former the state was the primary actor, and so a state-regulated corps was established; in the latter the entrepreneur-promotor was the primary actor through the market, and the self-regulating profession established itself to meet its needs. These two models have gone on to pervade the national business systems of the two countries, and have been influential throughout the world. Their distinctive strengths and weaknesses,[7] the implications of these governance modes for the division of labour within firms and on projects, and their implications for national competitive advantage are currently the subject of further work.

REFERENCES

Abbott, A. (1988), *The System of Professions* (Chicago: University of Chicago Press).
——(1991), 'The Future of Professions', *Research in the Sociology of Organizations*, 8.
Bezançon, X. (1995), *Les Services publics en France* (Paris: Presses Ponts et Chaussées).
Bourdieu, P. (1989), *La Noblesse d'état: Grandes écoles et esprit du corps* (Paris: Minuit).
Boyer, R. (1996), 'Le Capitalisme étatique à la française à la croisée des chemins', in C. Crouch and W. Streeck (eds.), *Les Capitalismes en Europe* (Paris: Éditions la Découverte).
Braudel, F. (1979), *Le Temps du monde* (Paris: Armand Collin). Translated as (1984) *The Perspective of the World* (London: Harper Collins).
Buchanan, R. A. (1989), *The Engineers: A History of the Engineering Profession in Britain 1750–1914* (London: Jessica Kingsley Publishers).
Burrage, M. (1990), 'Introduction: Professions in Sociology and History', in M. Burrage and R. Torstendahl (eds.), *Professions in Theory and History* (London: Sage).
de Tocqueville, A. (1952), *L'Ancien Régime et la Révolution* (Paris: Gallimard).
Dobbin, F. (1994), *Forging Industrial Policy: The United States, Britain, and France in the Railway Age* (Cambridge: Cambridge University Press).
Jamous, H., and Peloille, B. (1970), 'Professions or Self-Perpetuating Systems: Changes in the French University-Hospital System', in J. A. Jackson (ed.), *Professions and Professionalization* (London: Cambridge University Press).
Jordan, G. (1992), *Engineers and Professional Self-Regulation* (Oxford: Clarendon Press).
Larson, M. S. (1977), *The Rise of Professionalism* (Berkeley: University of California Press).

---

[7] Both systems had difficulties in coping with the emerging technologies of chemical and electrical engineering in the late 19th century (Shaw 1995).

Lasserre, H. (1989), *Le Pouvoir de l'ingénieur* (Paris: L'Harmattan).

Legrende, P. (1992), *Le Trésor historique de l'état en France* (Paris: Fayard).

Linder, M. (1994), *Projecting Capitalism* (Westport, Conn.: Greenwood Press).

Middlemas, R. K. (1963), *The Master Builders* (London: Hutchinson).

Millerson, G. (1964), *The Qualifying Associations* (London: Routledge and Kegan Paul).

Perkin, H. (1969), *The Origins of Modern English Society, 1780–1880* (London: Routledge and Kegan Paul).

——(1989), *The Rise of Professional Society: England since 1880* (London: Routledge).

Picon, A. (1992), *L'Invention de l'ingénieur moderne: L'École des Ponts et Chaussées 1747–1851* (Paris: Presses Pont et Chaussées).

Reader, W. J. (1966), *Professional Men* (London: Weidenfeld and Nicolson).

Shaw, C. (1995), 'Engineers in the Boardroom: Britain and France Compared', in Y. Cassis, F. Crouzet, and T. Gourvish (eds.), *Management and Business in Britain and France* (Oxford: Oxford University Press).

Smith, C. O. (1990), 'The Longest Run: Public Engineers and Planning in France', *American Historical Review*, 95.

Thoenig, J.-C. (1987), *L'Ère des technocrates: le cas des Ponts et Chaussées*, 2nd edn. (Paris: L'Harmattan).

Thompson, F. M. L. (1968), *Chartered Surveyors: The Growth of a Profession* (Routledge and Kegan Paul).

Torstendahl, R. (1990), 'Introduction: Promotion and Strategies of Knowledge-Based Groups', in R. Torstendahl and M. Burrage (eds.), *The Formation of Professions* (London: Sage).

Watson, J. G. (1988), *The Civils: The Story of the Institution of Civil Engineers* (London: Thomas Telford).

Weber, M. (1947), *The Theory of Social and Economic Organisation* (New York: Free Press).

Winch, G. M. (1996a), 'Contracting Systems in the European Construction Industry: A Sectoral Approach to the Dynamics of Business Systems', in R. Whitley and P. H. Kristensen (eds.), *The Changing European Firm* (London: Routledge).

——(1996b), *The Contracting System in British Construction: The Rigidities of Flexibility* (London: Le Groupe Bagnolet Working Paper 6).

5

Financial Security, Welfare Regimes, and the Governance of Work Systems

GLENN MORGAN

1. INTRODUCTION

European societies are currently undergoing profound transformations as they attempt to adapt to the challenges arising from international competition. Central to this process of adaption is the creation of forms of work system which are competitive against those arising in other parts of the world. As other chapters in this collection reveal, this process of transformation is structured by underlying forms of institutions and social relations. The direction and outcome of change processes within national systems under pressure from international competition is dependent on these underlying institutions and the capacities and capabilities of these institutions and key actors to produce new ways of working.

In order to understand these processes, it is therefore necessary to identify the key features of this underlying set of institutions and actors and how these influence the capability of firms to develop new forms of work systems. This collection demonstrates that there are a variety of approaches to this issue. Two complementary approaches can be distinguished. The first approach begins with the work system and identifies how changes at this level are shaped by the institutional context. Thus the main object of attention is the problem of creating new systems of work governance which can enhance competitiveness. In this approach, research tends to be focused at the organizational level and the methodology treats the categories of actors and structures as given observing how new rules are being developed.

The second approach begins from the institutional context and examines how categories of social actors and structures are themselves historically constituted. In methodological and research terms, this approach tends to be more historical, examining how institutions and actors are shaped in particular national contexts. Within this approach, it is possible to distinguish between levels of institutional analysis. One level of analysis deals with what may be termed proximate institutions which have a direct and obvious impact on the governance of work systems through structuring the nature of the inputs, e.g. occupational categories, training, and skills. The second level of analysis is concerned less with particular institutions and more with the way in which they interact to shape particular rules of action in society as a whole and organizations in particular.

This chapter is based within this second type of institutionalist approach. It focuses on the broad area of the wage labour nexus as the arena in which a number of institutions come together to pattern the constitution of and relations between social actors. This nexus is conceived not as a simple 'spot' contract between an individual employee and an employer but as a specific social relationship constituted through an array of organizations including the state, the firm, workers' organizations, and financial institutions. Within this context, the specific point under consideration relates to the dual purpose of the wage. Under conditions of capitalist production, one part of the wage is utilized directly by the worker for immediate consumption purposes within the domestic arena; the other part is either compulsorily or voluntarily saved to manage periods outside the labour force (either for reasons of illness, unemployment, or age). This second element of the wage may be understood as the attempt by wage labourers to create a form of financial security or welfare regime against the vicissitudes of the labour market and in this way to reduce their dependency on employers. All capitalist societies develop their own particular sets of institutions to manage this element of the wage relation. The concern of this chapter is to explore the implications of these institutional arrangements for the governance of work systems in different societies.

2. FINANCIAL SECURITY, WAGES, AND WORK SYSTEMS

As an economic system, capitalism is dependent on the existence of landless labourers with nothing to sell but their labour power. Thus capitalist societies are structured around the wage nexus and the effort bargain between managers and employees. Crouch summarizes what he terms the 'problem central to relations between employers and employees under any economic system that separates those who perform work from those who control its performance' as follows:

On the one hand the employers need pure contract in their relations with labour, so that effort and its reward can be bound closely together; but they also want workers to co-operate like willing partners. For their part, workers do not want to give any more than they are being paid for, but also want to be treated like reasonable human beings. (Crouch 1993: 28)

From this perspective, employers and managers wish to link rewards to the specific labour input contributed by workers. However, a 'spot' contract between employees and the employer does not necessarily provide the worker with anything other than immediate needs. The individual worker

who lacks any other form of subsistence will seek to raise wages and benefits to a level which can sustain him or her (and his or her family unit,
allowing that some others within this unit will also be employed, whilst
others will not) even in times of unemployment, whether from sickness, old
age, or unemployment. In societies where subsistence is primarily through
wage labour, either the wages must be sufficient to enable this to occur
or some other means to achieve this goal must be institutionalized. The
institutions which arise beyond the wage relation to secure this financial
security can be referred to as a welfare regime.

At a conceptual level, there are essentially four ways in which welfare
regimes can be constructed. These may be termed individualized self-help,
collective self-help, employer-organized help, and state-organized help.
Although each of these is likely to be present in one degree or another in
any particular society, it is also likely that at particular periods of history,
one of these will constitute the dominant set of principles and institutions
for the organization of financial security. Each of these welfare regimes has
different implications for the relationship between the worker and the
employer.

In historical terms, individualized self-help is the earliest form of
response to the requirement for financial security. Individualized self-help
in this context refers to families which seek to manage the reproduction of
their members and generations over time solely through the waged and
unwaged activities of the individuals who compose the kinship unit. In this
context, there is no pooling of the risk other than that which can be sustained within the family. This type of individual self-help welfare regime is
characteristic of the early stages of industrialization and urbanization in
most countries where subsistence agriculture and forms of obligation
between landowners and peasants break down, pushing large numbers of
landless labourers and their families into towns and wage labour. The des-
perate search for work and subsistence in such circumstances led to what
contemporary commentators such as Engels in Manchester (Engels 1969)
and Mayhew in London (Thompson and Yeo 1973) perceived to be a break-
down in social reproduction. The wages which were being paid in some circumstances were barely sufficient or stable enough to sustain immediate
consumption needs for the individual wage-earner, never mind enable the
reproduction of the family unit over time (see also Seccombe 1993).

Such a system is unstable as the destruction of the working-class family
leads not only to social disorder, crime, and rebellion in the cities and the
countryside but also to instability within factories and other types of work
setting. How this instability is resolved is a complex question relating to the
specific characteristics of particular societies. In the current period, the com-
plexities of international trade exports from developing countries and the
response of the industrialized countries to the conditions of work in these
societies (through the enforcement of World Trade Organization agree-

ments as well as human rights conventions) leads to a variety of pressures from outside on the resolution of these instabilities. Internal political systems may resist these external pressures and manage the process through coercion, rather than democratization if international institutions lack any means of enforcement of other standards. During the industrialization of Europe in the nineteenth century it was characteristic of the process that coalitions of benevolent capitalists, radical intellectuals, and small artisans and the most prosperous of the working class (normally male skilled workers) emerged to create systems of regulation and control that reduce the worst excesses of this system (e.g. through Factory Acts which restrict female and child labour, Public Health Acts which improve sanitary conditions, and trade union legislation to legalize workers' collective action) and establish institutions for the moral and educational welfare of the working class (e.g. religious and state education). In other parts of Europe, such as Germany, the state stepped in to create some of these conditions.

In types of welfare regime based on individualized self-help, employers are able to enforce spot contracts with individual employees, reducing the wage to the minimum that can sustain current consumption. Unable to save or to gain any sort of independence from the labour market, the employee is subjected to the dictatorial power of the employer over the work process.

Societies move out of this initial stage of individualized self-help in three different ways. First, workers themselves join together to provide mutual support. The traditional identification of mutual support with trade unionism and industrial relations conflicts has led to a neglect of the more common phenomenon of mutual support through the creation of savings and provident funds (see Hopkins 1995 for a detailed consideration of the British case). The timing, extent, nature, and significance of these funds varies across Europe, but in general terms they are based on the capability of workers to put aside part of their income towards saving. These small savings are then pooled into membership schemes; constitutions set up the principles under which members can call on the pool of funds as a whole as opposed to simply retrieving their own limited share. Membership is usually confined to a defined population which shares a similar social background. Some are based on insurance principles—against death, illness, disability, old age. Some are based on banking principles where credit is supplied either for emergencies or for the purchase of small items or, most common of all, for housing. The central problem for such funds tends to be that the needs and demands of members for help far outweigh the capability of the group to save, since this remains dependent on the wage relation. This problem is exacerbated where the risk pool which is the basis of the fund lacks diversity, e.g. where it is based on a single location, industry, or occupation. A threat to this base affects all equally and there is therefore little capacity to redistribute from an unaffected to an affected group. The most successful forms of mutual association have generally been those which gradually broadened the pool of contributors and turned over their management to a specialized group of professionals working on established actuarial or banking principles to manage contributions, outgoings, and investment.

Self-help funds involve a definite, if often only marginal, increase in the power of the workforce as they provide a small source of funds separate from the wage relation. Worker and trade union power to resist employers' demands is increased if they have sources of funds enabling them to survive periods of unemployment caused by strikes, lockouts, or unemployment. If periods of illness, injury, and old age can be similarly covered by such schemes, a degree of independence is attained by the workforce from the domination of the employers. However, as these funds become 'professionalized', managed by professional bankers and actuaries, they simultaneously become more secure and yet less effective as a form of collective self-help amongst workers. They are no longer available to be utilized directly for political or industrial relations purposes as their terms and conditions become increasingly subjected to a bureaucratized form of rationality.

The second response is where employers themselves explicitly take on responsibility for financial security and the reproduction of the labour force. There may be a range of motivations, stretching from outright paternalism in which 'cradle to grave' welfare is provided by the employer to undermine any radical politics through to more calculated forms of provision, where employers devise welfare schemes in order to secure the labour of their most important employees.

The third form of financial security is that which is organized through the state. Here again, it is important to recognize the mixture of motivations which can exist. In Bismarck's Germany, the establishment of welfare benefits was part of a deliberate strategy to undermine the radical politics of the emerging Socialist Party. In other countries, the expansion of welfare benefits through the state arose as a result of various political and social coalitions determined to improve their standard of living by using the state as an instrument of redistribution.

The intervention of the state in welfare invariably builds on and adapts existing self-help institutions rather than creating an entirely novel structure. In this way, earlier institutions become embedded in new structures of relationships. Thus, it is impossible to judge unequivocally the role of the state *per se*; rather the crucial issue is the way in which the state organizes the reconstruction of the existing systems and the role which is allocated to individual, collective, or employer dominated forms of welfare as opposed to state provision *per se*.

To summarize the argument thus far, I have suggested that there are four broad ways in which financial security is generated. At this theoretical level,

TABLE 5.1.   Forms of Financial Security and Impact on
Power of Employers and Employees in the Workplace

Form of financial security	Impact on power of	
	Employers	Employees
Individual	+	−
Collective self-help	−	+
Employer sponsored	+	−
State	?	?

it is possible to hypothesize how these different forms of security impact
on the power of employees and employers.

3. FINANCIAL SECURITY AND WELFARE REGIMES: THE IMPACT OF THE STATE ON RELATIONS BETWEEN EMPLOYERS AND EMPLOYEES

During the process of industrialization in European societies, forms of
financial security were engendered by the political and social conflicts
between groups in particular societies. In this process, particular institutions
and sets of relationships were established that were taken up and adapted
by the state from the start of the twentieth century. Over the first half of
the twentieth century, most western European societies developed systems
in which the state took the main role in organizing and underwriting the
welfare regime. As Boyer and Drache state, 'Each national welfare state is
the outcome of deeply embedded compromises and . . . these compromises were the result of past struggles that shaped social stratification,
politics and economic specialization' (Boyer and Drache 1996: 5).

By the 1950s, therefore, there were a range of welfare regimes organized
through the state in western Europe. However, it is helpful to follow the
French-based Regulation School further and note that these regimes shared
a certain role in the structuring of the post-war social and economic order
(see Aglietta 1979; Boyer 1990). From the point of view of this discussion,
this role can be described in terms of the creation of an integral relationship between a Fordist system of production and a Keynesian Welfare
regime. This is not to assume that a single model of production or welfare
became common across Europe but rather that a particular form of the relationship between the two was established that took on different characteristics depending on the structure of social relationships and institutions in

each country. The essential unifying element of this system of regulation was that the welfare system was organized through the state to maintain a level of consumption that could sustain full employment (in Keynesian terms) and therefore guarantee both social order and profits for the main productive enterprises within the society. Within national systems, the work organization of the enterprises could be different—based on mass production in France and the UK, diversified quality production in Germany and Denmark etc. Similarly, the welfare system could be differently organized, based on occupational funds in France and Germany, the state in Scandinavia, and a mixture of forms in the United Kingdom. Nevertheless, the same relationship was maintained with the state managing levels of consumption through the system to ensure full employment and profits (a system which Lash and Urry 1987, amongst others refer to as 'Organized Capitalism').

Three broad types of welfare system developed in this period when the system of Organized Capitalism dominated (Esping-Andersen 1990, 1994). They reflected the particular historical constitution of financial security in different societies and the way in which the state incorporated these to create a Fordist welfare regime, i.e. a system that guaranteed consumption and thereby the conditions for full employment and production.

4. THE SOCIAL DEMOCRATIC WELFARE STATE

The social democratic welfare state is based on a universalistic solidarity between groups which attempts to undo traditional or market-induced inequalities by the use of the state. The level of benefit which is offered is based on providing the citizen with an adequate level of income in old age and unemployment. Baldwin has argued that a crucial determinant in this process was the role of the middle class. Contrary to other interpretations which see the triumph of social democratic welfarism as the result of working-class struggle, Baldwin shows that 'Neither the working class nor the left was here (in Scandinavia) the motor of reform. The unique features of the Nordic welfare state were determined by the interests of the politically emergent agrarian middle classes neither to be excluded from the benefits of social policy, nor to bear more of the costs than could be displaced to their urban opponents' (Baldwin 1990: 290).

It was this coalition between the middle class and the working class that was crucial to the form which the welfare system took. Both classes looked to the state, in Baldwin's terms, for 'statutory generosity' and in return they were willing to forgo their traditional modes of organizing security. Thus working class and trade unions transferred the responsibility for welfare from their own self-help organizations to the state. Similarly, the middle class was willing to give up individualized control over its own savings surpluses. State provision directly replaced private provision and access to benefits was defined on the basis of the rights of citizenship and 'tied not to past contributions and past wages/salaries but, primarily, to the current growth of living standards'. This system developed very specifically from the way in which Scandinavian societies had managed the transition to industrialization and the creation of a class compromise. It reflected at all levels the power of the social democratic ideal which was dominant in these societies.

The social democratic model as instituted in the Nordic states provided levels of benefit to the population as a whole which reduced the dependence of particular workers on the employer. It became a right of citizenship rather than a deferred benefit dependent on and derived from one's occupational position. It was therefore an element in a fundamental shift in power between employers and employees. This particular element was part of the broader extension of the power of labour across these societies where trade union membership and social democratic parties' share of the vote in general elections has far outstripped most of the rest of Europe in the post-war period (see Crouch 1993: 224 and 276; Therborn 1995: 309). The generosity of the welfare payments and the relative lenience with which they were paid pressurized employers to adapt their own policies in ways which encouraged workers to remain in their specific employment rather than taking advantage of the system to move around. This in turn contributed to improved conditions of work, trade union recognition, and the general reinforcement of the power of labour at the expense of employers. It also reinforced a more general solidarity amongst the population, all of whom shared approximately the same level of benefits in illness, unemployment, and old age.

5. THE LIBERAL WELFARE STATE

The second of Esping-Andersen's models is that of the liberal welfare state. This system carries through elements of individual self-help but recognizes the role of the state as providing a safety net for those in need. Thus on the one hand, the system encourages private savings and provision as widely as possible. On the other hand, there is a recognition that the nature of the labour market is such that certain groups will either be excluded altogether (the disabled and the infirm) or will only be able to participate intermittently (because of family responsibilities) and/or at a low level of reward (due to poor education, low skill attainment, etc.) and therefore need to be given temporary help.

The liberal welfare state therefore tends to combine two elements which vary in their significance. The first is the provision of universal insurance benefit and the second is the provision of means-tested benefits. Rights to

the universal insurance benefits are dependent upon labour force participation and a certain level of contribution to the insurance fund. Thus the
state acts as a disciplinary agent encouraging workers to stay in jobs, as
failure to do so can affect one's rights to benefit. However, the universal
benefit itself is kept low in order to act as an incentive on individuals either
to provide for themselves (as liberal self-help ideology prefers) or to return
as quickly as possible to the labour market. In these systems, the universal
benefit is usually only offered for a limited duration (except in the case of
the old age pension) and failure to get back into the labour market thrusts
the worker into the category of those who are offered means-tested benefits. This category consists also of those with little or no record of participation in the labour force. It is characteristic of these systems that
means-tested benefits are administered in a stigmatizing and niggardly
manner to 'discourage malingering'.

The liberal welfare system represents an uneasy compromise between
the aspirations of labour as a social actor for welfare standards guaranteed
by the state and the proponents of self-help. This is clearest in the case
of the United Kingdom, where working-class institutions of self-help
declined in significance as the Labour movement pinned its hopes on the
rise of the welfare state in order to guarantee its financial security. However, unlike the Nordic countries, the adherence of the more well-off
sections of the society to the system was never secured. They continued
to maintain and develop their own private sources of security outside the
state system. Generous sickness and pension arrangements were provided for white-collar workers in the private as well as the public sector.
These groups preferred the extension of their private privileges to the
growth of public provision. The public system of welfare reflected these
differences.

In this system, the state acts as a disciplinary agent, making labour force
participation essential for the worker. Employees were discouraged from
unemployment and from reliance on the state for benefits. Whilst the state
provided a minimal level of support, this was frequently at or below what
was considered to be the poverty line and could only be supplemented by
going through means testing procedures, which were in turn designed to
discourage claimants. This system did not therefore create a welfare regime
which counter-balanced in any significant way the power of the employer
over the employee. If anything, it reinforced that power by opening up a
range of alternative management strategies. On the one hand, the employer could effectively operate 'spot contracts' with labour. Whilst this might
be limited by trade union power, the consequences of unemployment were
highly undesirable and therefore employees would have to settle for low
wages, poor work conditions, and insecurity of employment. On the other
hand, employers could operate to encourage the stability of their labour
force by offering 'perks' that supplemented the low level of state benefit.

As with paternalist employers of the nineteenth century, they effectively tied in their workforce at a relatively low cost, thus improving cooperation and management control.

This system was also highly divisive as far as the society as a whole was concerned. It divided off the poor and the unemployed, those dependent on state benefits from the rest. It became relatively easy for politicians to capitalize on this division and blame the poor for their own situation. Those in employment or with their own savings felt little solidarity with this group or wish to defend it. It divided workers between those in relatively secure jobs where benefits supplemented the state system from those in insecure, temporary work who feared that they would have to fall back on the low level of state insurance in the future. It divided workers in different firms off from each other as benefits became dependent on the prosperity of one's own firm, rather than the industry or nation as a whole. Furthermore, it reflected and reinforced the divide between a middle class in lifelong careers with increasing earnings capacity and the ability to save at various stages of the life cycle from those more precariously perched on the ladder of stable employment, whose income was rarely sufficient to allow for any-thing more than minimal saving. Thus the cross-class solidarity that is so characteristic of the Nordic countries was non-existent in these systems and therefore defence of the state system as anything more than a safety net tended to rely on trade unions and working-class parties, which in turn are much weaker in these societies than they are in Scandinavia.

6. THE CONSERVATIVE, CORPORATIST WELFARE STATE

The third model which Esping-Andersen identifies is the conservative, cor-poratist welfare state and is characteristic of most continental European societies. In these systems, there is no commitment to universalism or egali-tarianism. Rather rights to benefits reflect one's status and position in the labour market in a direct manner. The welfare state is inegalitarian, grant-ing benefits according to one's earning power on the labour market, not as a right of citizenship.

Esping-Andersen notes the historical origins of these systems which con-tinues to be reflected up to the present day:

The Continental European powers were the vanguards of modern social policy and historical circumstance came to nurture a peculiar blend of étatist and especially, corporatist approaches to social solidarity. The early timing of program institution-alization meant that it drew its logic from an economy still influenced by guilds, cor-porations and other occupational associative monopolies, such as the German Stande or the French cadres. . . . corporatism and status differentiation came to be the foundation of welfare state organization in Austria, Belgium, France, Germany and even Italy. (Esping-Andersen 1994: 718)

These systems derived from their own distinctive form of class compromise in which the inequalities of the labour market and employment status were reproduced in the welfare system, only this time, the state acted as ultimate guarantor of the right to an unequal benefit. The nature of the compromise was distinctive from both the social democratic and the liberal model. On the one hand, all groups looked to the state to guarantee its benefits; there was therefore a basic solidarity of citizenship which was engendered and enhanced. On the other hand, the benefits which the state supplied to its citizens were unequal. This compromise came about because the existing systems of collective self-help were gradually incorporated into the new state structure, yet kept their relative autonomy as representing the financial interests of the specific status group involved.

The French system of pensions reveals one form of the structure which underlay these systems. The French system was based on a number of principles. The first was that the pension should be earnings related and not a flat rate benefit. This implied that the system should not be redistributive between classes in its impact. Rather there was to be a form of redistribution between generations; those who were in retirement received their pensions directly from the contributions of those still in employment. The second principle was that groups should in the main be self-defined and self-administering in order to fund equitably the pension on an earnings-related basis.

There was no single underlying principle of how to create the groups. The system became highly complex and variegated:

The scheme was to be administered by an assortment of *caisses* among which insured persons were, in theory free to choose. By the end of the 1939 war there were 727 caisses, of which 86 were departmental or inter-departmental, 176 were set up by mutual benefit societies, 78 were Catholic 'family' caisses, 96 were employers' caisses, 52 trade union caisses and the other 239 were a miscellaneous group, mainly occupational. Some important groups of employees were excluded from the 1930 scheme, since they were already covered by schemes of their own (*regimes speciaux*). These schemes covered officials in the public sector, railwaymen, miners, seamen, tramway workers and others. The agricultural sector insisted on having its own separate scheme. (Lynes 1985: 12)

An attempt by the left after 1945 to merge these together and create a universalist, redistributive social democratic welfare system (known as the *régime general*) was defeated by groups which wanted to sustain their separate identity and privileges. Two of the most important groups in this category were the self-employed and the cadres.

The self-employed (small employers, shopkeepers, liberal professions, artisans, and farmers) were a significant group in French society. Over a third of the employed population of France still worked in agriculture as late as 1939 (the figure in Britain was 6 per cent at this time: Therborn 1995: 66). They objected to the level of contribution which they were being asked to make to the *régime general* and suspected that they would lose out from any redistribution. They also wished to maintain their status differentiation from the rest of the population. In the event, a series of self-employed pension schemes were set up to reflect their own differences from one another and to limit any form of redistribution to those within the same category.

The cadres also objected to entering the *régime general* and demanded their own supplementary scheme. The way in which this was institutionalized had a significant impact on the overall system. Benefits were based on contributions and paid out as a percentage of earnings. As a group, the cadres were the wealthiest group of employees. They wished to limit the redistributive impact of the system by keeping their contribution to the *régime general* as low as possible, whilst making their contribution to their own fund relatively generous. In this way, the benefits of their high income were confined to their own status category. The consequence was that the *régime general* was relatively poorly provided for, inducing other groups to also demand their own supplementary pension scheme:

By 1961 all wage earners were compulsorily affiliated to such schemes, blue and white collars each in their own. The ultimate effect of this flight to supplementary arrangements, in which redistribution was limited—provoked as it had been by the solidaristic intent of postwar initiatives—was therefore to prevent the reformers' ambitions for significant statutory intervention from being fully realized. (Baldwin 1990: 171)

Meanwhile, the *régime speciaux* which had been established earlier for particular groups such as civil servants, miners, railway workers, electricity, and gas employees were all maintained.

The complexity of the system, based on different funds and statuses, was reinforced by the complexity of the rules on benefits and contributions. As all the systems were 'pay-as-you-go', they depended on inter-generational solidarity, based on a sense of equity within the status category. However, the balance between contributors and beneficiaries was not static. Some occupations declined in numbers increasing the burden of contribution which would have to be sustained by their surviving employed members. Others increased in number and could afford to pay benefits which reflected their new status and importance. The decline of certain groups was particularly problematic forcing the state to intervene in the sense of both providing funds to ensure the caisses did not go bankrupt and to try and persuade the 'social partners' running the caisses to reconstruct the levels of contributions and benefits in order to put the system back on to a firm financial foundation.

As an exemplar of the conservative, corporatist welfare state, the French case has its own specificities. Nevertheless, the way in which it works indicates how this system differs from those previously analysed in terms of its impact on employer–employee relations. Most notable is that the system depends on the continuing economic and political solidarity of each status group, in distinction both to others and to employers. At one level, the system reinforces occupational differentiation, ensuring that employees see their interests as distinctively associated with their own category. In some cases, this creates or reinforces forms of solidarity that do not appear in other systems—such as the identity of the 'cadres' and of the different groups of self-employed. At another level, it creates a form of universal solidarity in the sense that all the different groups want to protect their own privileges and will therefore join together to present a united front if the principle of the special schemes appears to be under attack. The system can also operate to sustain trade unions when in every other respect they may be weakening. In France, for example, the trade union representatives on caisses wield an influence far beyond what one might expect in a society where only around 12 per cent of the labour force are members of unions.

From the point of view of the employee, participation in the labour force is the key to achieving access to the benefits of the welfare system. In this respect, the system differs substantially from the social democratic model in terms of how it enables the employee to become independent of the employer and labour market conditions. However, unlike the liberal system, where the state effectively acts as gatekeeper to welfare benefits and sets the conditions for and level of the benefits in a way that disciplines the employee and forces the employee back to work, in the corporatist system, the gatekeeper role is held by the associations which administer and control the funds. This is a crucial difference as these associations are frequently dominated by trade unions or worker representatives. These groups do not act in an overtly disciplinary way in terms of the conditions which they set for receiving benefits. Rather as might be expected, they lean in the other direction, seeking to minimize the conditions and maximizing the benefit (partly through trying to keep employer contributions to the fund as high as possible). This power is limited for two reasons. First, there are the countervailing powers of the other social partners on the committee to run the funds. Secondly, the demographics of occupational change can force the fund to seek state assistance which may only be granted on the curtailment of certain privileges and the exercise of a more disciplinary role.

As far as employers themselves are concerned, the system tends to reduce their power over the workforce. Earnings-related benefits paid at a relatively generous level and administered by worker representatives leave little room for employers to offer added incentives to their own workforce. It also makes it more difficult to threaten employees with unemployment as the schemes will act to cushion their impact for a while at least. On the other hand, the schemes do remain linked to the labour market and they do require certain levels of contributions on the part of the workforce, thus encouraging some stability and cooperation.

The different routes into the conservative, corporatist welfare system clearly affect the form this takes. Thus the example of France which has been discussed in some detail clearly differs from Germany. In Germany, the existence of strong industry-wide trade unions bargaining with organized employers' federations helps reinforce the cooperative elements of the model both by simplifying the operation of the system and by reducing the possibility that union representation on the fund associations is used to undermine labour market disciplines. Thus there are variations in how the conservative, corporatist system works and its implications for employer–employee relations.

In conclusion, Table 5.2 can be presented as a representation of the key features of the three models of welfare regime.

7. FROM FORDISM TO NEW FORMS OF WELFARE?

In the Fordist era, European societies developed their own forms of welfare with the implications which have been outlined. In this period, the welfare system contributed to sustaining the levels of consumption necessary to maintain full employment and high utilization of the factors of production. As the Fordist system began to decline, so the pressure for change in the system of financial security increased. Yet, the relations which had been institutionalized both within organizations and within the state meant that the capacity to change and the potential direction of change would differ according to the type of welfare system which existed.

The general crisis of the system relates to the ability to continue to fund welfare in the old way as conditions change. Although some of these changes in demand arise from factors partially exogenous to the economic situation (such as the fact that people are living longer), they are significantly influenced by the breakdown of Fordism and the increase in international competition. This has led to higher numbers of unemployed within most of the European societies as well as a shrinkage in the number of years people actually spend in the labour force, relying on longer years of

TABLE 5.2. Impact of Welfare State Regime on Employees and Employers

Type of regime	Impact on employees		Employers' power
	Solidarity	Power	
Social Democratic	+	+	−
Liberal	−	−	+
Conservative Corporatist	−	+	+/−

training at the start of their career and earlier retirement at the end. Payments to the unemployed, the training, and the retired are therefore increasing. However, these transfer payments need to be funded out of taxation or borrowing but, it is frequently argued, this simply exacerbates the situation in two ways (as described by O'Connor 1973 in his classic study of the fiscal crisis of Western states). If the transfers are funded out of taxation on employers and employees, it increases the costs of goods produced under those conditions relative to the costs of goods produced in low taxation systems. It thus reduces competitiveness further, causing more people to lose their jobs, causing transfer payments to rise again, etc. If the transfers are funded out of borrowing, it results in higher interest rates all round the economy, thus fuelling inflation and undermining investment, leading again to declining competitiveness.

These developments indicate that the old systems of welfare are in severe crisis. However, this is not just a fiscal crisis. It is also a broader crisis in the way in which the welfare regime affects incentives to work and accept changes at work. As has been shown, welfare regimes can be interpreted as mechanisms through which workers manage their relative independence from employers. The higher the level of relative independence which they enjoy due to their ability to draw on welfare rights beyond the firm or the labour market, the more difficult it will be for employers to enforce changes in work practice that workers wish to resist. Therefore, the attempt to shift welfare from the state into private provision is not just a fiscal measure but an attempt to rebalance power in the workplace in favour of the employers.

Jessop has characterized this as a move towards what he terms a 'Schumpeterian' workfare state (Jessop 1994). In such a system, welfare provision is essentially privatized with the responsibility falling on the individuals within the family to save for their own old age or illness. State benefits are confined to 'workfare' rather than 'welfare'; unwillingness to participate in the labour market is effectively punished by the withdrawal of all benefits. State expenditure more generally concentrates on improving the productive efficiency of the society through investment in training, education, and infrastructure. The goal of the state is no longer to utilize the welfare system to maintain consumption and full employment which is anyway an impossible task for the nation state in an open international economy with high levels of competition. Instead the state's aim becomes to create internationally competitive firms by maintaining a fiscal regime which reduces the social overhead costs of firms and a welfare system which encourages worker cooperation by getting rid of alternative safety nets to labour market participation.

It is clear that within Europe, the UK has gone furthest down this route. This was possible because the liberal welfare system which had become established there was already an unstable compromise of public and private provision and the Thatcher government gradually pushed the system further towards private provision. Thus whereas in the 1970s, there was cross-party agreement on the need to improve state pensions (through providing an earnings-related element) and to enhance company pension schemes (i.e. where benefits are dependent on participation in a single company for a long period of time), during the 1980s the Tories abandoned both; as Waine states, 'For the New Right this approach was inadequate; their opposition was to both state earnings related provision *and* occupational pensions' (Waine 1992: 135). The result has been the creation of a system of personal pensions, purchased by the individual from a financial institution. The personal pension is portable between jobs and offers an alternative to company or occupational pension schemes. Although there are many long-standing company or occupational pension schemes which still survive and offer a relatively generous level of benefit, the conditions for these are gradually being made less favourable, as is the state welfare system itself, thus inducing more people into the private system of individual self-help.

In those parts of Europe dominated by conservative, corporatist forms of welfare, change is more difficult. In late 1995, the Gaullist government of Alain Juppé brought forward its plans to reduce welfare spending by the state and to encourage forms of private provision. The reaction was a massive rejection of these plans by demonstrators on the streets of Paris. This relates very much to the existing system of welfare in which every citizen expects their own rights to be protected and upheld by the state. In spite of the fact that these rights provide unequal benefits, there is a shared dependence on the maintenance of the system and a shared unwillingness to see them scrapped. This shows the dual nature of the corporatist system. The potential for class-wide solidarity is undermined as it is status groups which are the basis of entitlements. Such differentiation has meant that French employers have generally been able to operate with less worker resistance than their counterparts in the UK (Gallie 1978). However, when it comes to resolving this broader system-level problem, there is less capability in the French context of moving towards a new model of welfare than there was in the UK because of the very strength of these status groups.

In Germany, similar issues are beginning to reach the agenda. In April 1996, Chancellor Kohl announced the need for a fundamental shake-up of the German system of welfare, involving a reduction in public spending of 2 per cent, equivalent to DM70 billion in 1997 and necessitating a fall in unemployment benefits, a reduction of sick pay and a rise in the retirement age for both men and women. *The Economist* commented that 'because generous welfare payments help give everyone a stake in the system, and hence buttress consensus, it is hard to unravel the welfare state without affecting the other parts of the consensual system too' (*The Economist*, 4 May 1996, p. 22). Unlike the French system, where work organization tends to be hierarchical and based on mass production principles, the German system depends at the level of the enterprise on high involvement by the skilled workers in the actual production process. This involvement was premissed on the expectation of continued employment or in exceptional circumstances, generous unemployment benefit, supplemented by high levels of pensions and sickness pay. If these pillars are withdrawn, can the German system of work governance be sustained?

In the Scandinavian countries, the pressures on welfare are bringing to the fore the underlying differences which exist. In Sweden, the system of work governance has, with some notable exceptions, been predominantly based on mass production. As competitive conditions for these industries have changed, a similar debate to that elsewhere has emerged with conservative parties urging a reduction in public spending. As might be expected, however, where the welfare system has been based on principles of broad social solidarity and there has been little competition from the private sector, it is proving highly difficult to create a stable right-wing majority for reform and following a short period of conservative government, the social democrats returned to power committed to maintaining the system. In Denmark, on the other hand, the work system has proved highly effective at competing under the new conditions and therefore the social solidarity binding the welfare system together has not yet been seriously threatened.

8. CONCLUSIONS

Each national system faces the same challenge of international competition and the need to adapt. However, this chapter has argued that the speed of adaptation and the ability to change clearly varies due to the institutionalized patterns which have been built up over a long period of time. Over the last decade, these welfare regimes and their consequences have been subjected to fierce criticism (see Pierson 1991 for a review of these criticisms). This raises the question of the capacity for change which exists within particular social systems and how this may be related to broad ideological currents about the future of welfare and national economic development.

It is clear that there is a dominant perspective which is based on the belief that state welfare funding needs to be reduced and replaced by private provision. This view draws its power from a specific interpretation of the economic order in which international competition necessitates a particular set of responses from European governments. New nations are emerging onto the international market that lack any semblance of a Western welfare state. These are deemed to offer a challenge to which the European countries must respond by cutting back on their own welfare systems. In some countries, workers are left almost entirely to provide for themselves on the basis of their wages, which given the plentifulness of labour in these countries are extremely low. In other countries, the state is sponsoring private forms of provision e.g. Singapore and Malaysia, thus creating high forms of compulsory savings which are diverted to support state infrastructural investment, whilst holding down state expediture and taxation as a whole. In Eastern Europe, the old systems of welfare have been thoroughly shaken up, if not smashed (Whitley *et al.* 1996; Dittrich *et al.* 1995; Gowan 1995). The World Bank and the International Monetary Fund support this approach to development as the only possible route. Not surprisingly, there is a strong tide for similar reform in Western European economies (see Biersteker 1995 for a critique of this process).

However, as has been shown in this chapter, there are strong forces of resistance to this, depending on how the welfare state was originally built and developed. These forces will guarantee that there is no single solution or convergence towards a privatized system of welfare. Boyer goes further;

This decade will probably experience a major turning point, from promarket and conservative strategies towards more solidaristic policies oriented by rejuvenated state intervention in the domains of taxation, welfare, innovation and education . . . But alternative rules of the game will have to be defined at the international level. This is a matter of political will and bargaining, not the spontaneous outcome of the homo oeconomicus's rational calculus. (Boyer 1996: 110–11)

In conclusion, this chapter has argued that work systems are influenced by the way in which financial security for employees is attained. In western Europe, there remains a high level of diversity between these systems, though they all involve the state to one degree or another. As new societies enter the world market with low wages and non-existent state welfare systems, the western European models are being challenged. Clearly, this is only part of a broader process of confrontation between different models of capitalism that is at the heart of recent debates on international competitiveness. However, this chapter has tried to show that it is a very important part of that confrontation in a number of ways. First, these systems do embody costs and benefits for firms, employers, and employees in particular societies which have a differential impact on international competitiveness. Secondly, these systems embody different capacities for change; it is clear that institutional barriers to change are stronger in some countries than others and this is not simply related to the political complexion of the government. For these reasons, it is worth studying these interrelationships both within western Europe and more widely.

REFERENCES

Aglietta, M. (1979), *A Theory of Capitalist Regulation* (London: New Left Books).
Baldwin, P. (1990), *The Politics of Social Solidarity: Class Bases of the European Welfare State 1875–1975* (Cambridge: Cambridge University Press).

Biersteker, T. J. (1995), 'The "Triumph" of Liberal Economic Ideas in the Developing World', in B. Stallings (ed.), *Global Change, Regional Response* (Cambridge: Cambridge University Press), 174–96.

Boyer, R. (1990), *Regulation Theory: A Critical Introduction* (New York: Columbia University Press).

——(1996), 'State and Market: A New Engagement for the Twenty-First Century', in Boyer and Drache 1996: 84–114.

——and Drache, D. (1996) (eds.), *States against Markets: The Limits of Globalization* (London: Routledge).

Crouch, C. (1993), *Industrial Relations and European State Traditions* (Oxford: Clarendon Press).

Dittrich, E., Schmidt, G., and Whitley, R. (1995) (eds.), *Industrial Transformation in Europe* (London: Sage).

Engels, F. (1969), *The Condition of the English Working Class* (London: Fontana).

Esping-Andersen, G. (1990), *The Three Worlds of Welfare Capitalism* (Cambridge: Polity Press).

——(1994), 'Welfare States and the Economy', in N. Smelser and R. Swedberg (eds.), *The Handbook of Economic Sociology* (Princeton: Princeton University Press), 711–32.

Gallie, D. (1978), *In Search of the New Working Class* (Cambridge: Cambridge University Press).

Gowan, P. (1995), 'Neo-Liberal Theory and Practice for Eastern Europe', *New Left Review*, 213: 3–60.

Hopkins, E. (1995), *Working Class Self-Help in Nineteenth Century England* (London: UCL Press).

Jessop, B. (1994), 'The Transition to Post-Fordism and the Schumpeterian Workfare State', in R. Burrows and B. Loader (eds.), *Towards a Post-Fordist Welfare State* (London: Routledge), 13–37.

Lynes, T. (1985), *Paying for Pensions: The French Experience* (London: Suntory-Toyota International Centre for Economics and Related Disciplines, LSE).

O'Connor, J. (1973), *The Fiscal Crisis of the State* (London: St James's Press).

Pierson, C. (1991), *Beyond the Welfare State?* (Cambridge: Polity Press).

Seccombe, W. (1993), *Weathering the Storm: Working Class Families from the Industrial Revolution to the Fertility Decline* (London: Verso).

Therborn, G. (1995), *European Modernity and Beyond* (London: Sage).

Thompson, E. P., and Yeo, E. (1973) (eds.), *The Unknown Mayhew* (London: Penguin).

Waine, B. (1992), 'The Ideology and Practice of Personal Pensions', *Economy and Society*, 21/1: 27–44.

Whitley, R., Henderson, J., Czaban, L., and Lengyel, G. (1996), 'Continuity and Change in an Emergent Market Economy', in Whitley and Kristensen 1996: 210–37.

Whitley, R., and Kristensen, P. H. (1996) (eds.), *The Changing European Firm* (London: Routledge).

6

Bargaining for the Future
The Changing Habitus of the Shop Steward System in the Pulp and Paper Mills of Finland

KARI LILJA

1. PULP AND PAPER MILLS AS FIELDS OF ACTION

A distinctively Finnish feature of community development is that it has been formed in connection with a saw mill, pulp mill, and/or a paper mill or coevolved with the establishment and growth of such mills and mill combines. Thus, for instance, Tarmo Koskinen has characterized Finland as an 'archipelago of forest industry communities' scattered in the backforests along the water ways and along the coastline (Koskinen 1987*b*). Looking from this 'Braudelian' perspective, industrial Finland was clearly invented by its geography: availability of forests, water ways, and water power. They constitute the foundation upon which the economic, social, and political institutions of the Finnish society have evolved. This foundation has remained the same for over 100 years while the economic, social, and political institutions have been transformed several times, mainly due to external political and economic pressures. Thus the economic and social field which emerges from the availability and refinement of the wooden raw material is an obvious key to the understanding of the functioning of the Finnish society. It provides a sectoral cross-cutting of the whole society (cf. Raumolin 1984; Lilja *et al.* 1992).

On the national level, the chemical forest industry is currently dominated by three large European-wide forest industry corporations. To give an idea of their importance in the Finnish society, it is sufficient to point out that the two largest of them account for 28 per cent of all exports from Finland in 1995 (Lehtinen 1995: 29). But the domination of the industry by these large corporations does not go unchallenged. The functioning of the mills is dependent on the skills and consent of the workers. Their interest representation is mediated by a powerful union, the Paper Workers' Union, and at the local level by the shop steward mechanism. Through other stakeholders this economic core is integrated to the society in its totality.

For the shop steward mechanism of interest representation the economic and social system of the mill has been the initial field of action. In this
field the bargaining rights of the workers were fought for and as an aggre-
gate result of these fights bargaining rights have been gradually codified into
the industry level collective bargaining contract. In Finland this stage was
reached rather late, especially when comparing with its Scandinavian neighbours: industry level collective bargaining became the rule only after the
Second World War (see Lilja 1992). Even after that the mill communities
were governed via a comprehensive paternalistic regime which structured
the everyday life both in the mills and in the community (Koskinen 1987*a*).
The shop steward institution became established by a general agreement in
the middle of the 1940s but it started to gain wider influence only since the
1960s. The growing significance of the shop steward mechanism could be
especially seen in the pulp and paper industry where important aspects of
wage determination were decentralized to the mills at the end of the 1960s.

In this chapter I describe and analyse how the character of the shop
steward system has changed as its fields of action have extended beyond
the immediate labour process and its regulation. One clue to this change of
character is to say that the shop steward mechanism of interest representation has turned from a mouthpiece of the workers towards a skilful societal actor. Instead of only acting as a spokesman of the feelings of the
constituency this skilful actor is able to take into account a large variety of
contingencies and turn them into a resource in bargaining as well as in more
implicit games with the management at the workplace and within the wider
corporate context.

The traditional view of the function of the shop steward system is that it
is involved in local negotiations on wages, manning levels, and other conditions of work. Empirical research has also shown that a large part of the
local negotiations are linked to the administration of the industry level collective bargaining contract, making local adjustments with a style which
looks more reactive than proactive, resembling the model of 'muddling
through'. Such a view was also prevalent among the actors interviewed
during the beginning of the fieldwork on which this chapter is based.
However, repeated visits to the mills over the years have led to a complementary interpretation of what is going on in the day-to-day interaction of
shop stewards with the various layers of management: it also constitutes a
bargaining arena for the future. This arena consists of various strategic plans
which are revised yearly and submitted to the corporate headquarters.
These consist of explicit technological trajectories of the mill combine
which have direct implications for the social trajectories of the mill community. These economic and social models compete for support at the workplace, within the wider corporate context and in the local community. They
are used as slogans for mobilizing different types of constituencies as well
as hammers for threatening and disciplining both workers and managers.

The more complex the system of participation becomes, the greater the potential for widening the area of bargaining and the more there are issues for coordinating with opponents (cf. Grieco and Lilja 1996).

Because both the management and the workers are active in several fields of action the dyadic relationship of the workers and the management is too simple to constitute the overall system of action. These two actors have multiple logics of action in each of the fields of action. To approach this multi-level system, it is suggested that the overall structure is conceptualized as a collection of interdependent games (Crozier and Friedberg 1980: 57).

With the access to new fields of action shop stewards have been forced to develop new ways of thinking and acting. Following Bourdieu (1990: 52–65) we will use the concept 'habitus' to cover the variety of practices at the disposal of the shop steward system. The purpose of the chapter is to describe how the habitus of the shop steward system has changed in relationship with the changing structural and institutional context.

2. A COMPLEX SET: THE HABITUS OF THE SHOP STEWARD MECHANISM OF INTEREST REPRESENTATION

For some decades the shop steward system in Finland has consisted of a senior shop steward and of departmental shop stewards. In addition to these positions, there are also other institutionally defined representatives, like the chairman of the local union and labour protection representatives, which contribute to the local level leadership function of the interest representation of the workers (cf. Lilja 1987: 200–3). For explicating some of the formal institutional features of this representational mechanism in the pulp and paper industry in Finland, it is of interest to point out that in mill combines where the number of workers exceeds 500, the senior shop steward is freed from work in the labour process. He acts as a full-time negotiator and local trade union organizer, with good office facilities at the mill site. Even in smaller workplaces the senior shop steward is practically freed from work in the labour process because the foremen cannot count on his presence, due to administrative duties. Thus, in fact, we are dealing with a special type of a working-class intellectual, elected by all the workers in a mill site in periodic elections.

In the paper mill context, there is no doubt that the position of a senior shop steward has a high status. The personalities which become chosen are very distinct. Earlier their oral skills were very important as well as their courage to stand up against the social, economic, and political pressure put upon them by the employer. They were representatives of a counter-culture of the working-class movement. Since the end of the 1960s, the required competencies and expectations on the role behaviour of the senior shop steward have been changing. This is due to the fact that the legitimacy of trade unionism in Finland has increased and the rights of the senior shop steward as well as other shop stewards have been secured by contracts and laws. In the pulp and paper industry, a senior shop steward is expected not only by the workers but also by the local management to be capable of mediating the conflicting pressures of the different constituencies and divisions among the workers. In his relationship with the management he is expected to be capable of articulating a strategy of interest representation which takes into account the leeway of the local management and the position of the workplace in the competitive system of the industry as a whole (cf. Batstone *et al.* 1977). Thus in the workplaces of the pulp and paper industry, the senior shop steward appears more and more like a statesman figure.

Thus it becomes of interest to ask what kind of dispositions are involved in the practices of the shop steward mechanism, constituting its habitus, and how they have changed. In structuring the description, three dimensions are used: the multiplicity of the temporal horizons, the multiplicity of conflict and cooperation in the mosaic of games and the type of the knowledge bases on which to draw information and scripts for action.

3. TEMPORAL CONTEXTS

Every workplace is a field of negotiated orders between a number of actors. The system of negotiated orders covers many temporal intervals from the day-to-day aspects of the work organization to the long-term survival of the workplace as a business operation and as a source of income. In pulp and paper mills, there are several institutional practices and contextual conditions which have shifted workers' perspective from the immediate present to the rather long-term future.

The first aspect concerns the system of employment. For a significant part of the workforce, a pulp and paper mill provides an opportunity for lifetime employment. Within this system there is also a chance for career advancement: workers in the internal labour market move from one position to another in order to learn the various jobs along the production process. To become a paper machine tender it takes typically twenty years to go through the job ladders in internal labour markets. There are also other similar occupations at the top of a career ladder. This concerns even maintenance occupations: in mill communities craft-workers have the mill or the mill combine as their first priority for employment due to their stability of employment and also high levels of payment. In towns where two corporations had mills, it was typical that an informal agreement existed between employers that recruitment of workers from the other firm was prohibited. The system of lifetime employment and career orientation of the workers put increasing emphasis in the interest representation system to the long term in comparison to immediate rewards.

Secondly, there is a parallel system of 'careers' in the local union and in the shop steward system. Before being elected as the senior shop steward, a person has served in various functions in the local union and as a departmental shop steward. He has received an extensive training from the courses of the national union and those of the federal union. Typically it takes about twenty years before a person is elected to the position of the senior shop steward. Thus the period during which he is under the evaluation of his work mates is very long. During this period the person really earns the literal name of the trusted person which is the Finnish (and Scandinavian) term for the shop steward. The layer of skilled workers and those aspiring to get into such a position is large enough to dominate the administration and policy-making of the local trade union. Typically, the senior shop steward is elected among these workers. From the point of view of a candidate, a good timing for the candidacy is after he has built his own house. It is a symbol of good housekeeping and commitment to the local community.

The political groups of the labour parties, social democrats, left-wing socialists, and communists have had a special interest in the position of the senior shop steward. Such a resource is unquestionably of high relevance for local political activities. Until recently, party political linkages have been important in the electoral process. However, strong personalities have always been able to overcome party political sympathies of the electorate, despite the fact that they represent other parties than those supported by the majority of the electorate. Though the political competition has caused various splits in the trade union movement, it has also maintained a tradition of rank-and-filism in the Finnish trade union movement.

To complicate further the scene for elections, it must be added that the management also has a keen interest in the person to be elected. One way to influence the electoral process from the managerial side is to give concessions in bargaining to a departmental shop steward or the senior shop steward whose personality best fits the task from the managerial point of view. Such preparations for the electoral contest take years and become linked with micropolitics in the social system of the mill and the mill community.

The employment model and the elitist system of workers' representation stretch the relevant time span from the present to the future. But there is a further aspect in the field which is derived from the dynamics of the industry: the time span for which a pulp mill or a paper machine is technologically and business-wise viable is about twenty to thirty years. Thus the industry logic sets a time bomb to tick after the technological features of the mill design have been decided. It takes, however, ten to fifteen years since the start-up before the time bomb is recognized in the social system.

This lag is due to the optimism which a successful start-up creates. The cost efficiency of a new production line and newly defined manning levels are good shelters for job security. However, in the long run there is a need for a large expansion project to signal the commitment of the corporation to the locality (Lilja 1989; Laurila 1995).

For the workers, new machine and mill investments create new top positions and open up jobs for the next generation. For the engineers and management, the advancement of professional competencies is a major concern and it can be accomplished best by being involved in the development of new generation mill designs. This contains the possibility of being exposed to presentations of the suppliers and being able to scan recent advances of competitors, also by getting access to the premises of competitors via the suppliers who want to present their technology-in-use as show-cases for the most modern solutions. New operations provide also new openings for career advancement, which is the main way of rewarding experience and loyal service (cf. Lilja and Tainio 1996: 163–4).

For all of the personnel of the mill site, the expansion of the critical mass of inhabitants in the local community has beneficial effects for personal finances, e.g. as to the value of their real estate. In small towns, which are dominated by one large employer or not more than a few, small changes in the employment levels have wide repercussions in the local housing markets. The expansion of personnel and local inhabitants facilitates a 'second career' in the housing market, for moving into better houses, building one's own house without the risk that the present house is not being sold, or at least avoiding the downward spiral of real estate investments due to shrinking employment levels. New migrants help to influence also the regional authorities to allocate better education—secondary schools, high schools, vocational schools and colleges—for children, closer to their parents.

The above description elaborates contexts for substantive games at the workplace and in the local community. The long term has a concrete meaning in everyday life, especially through the values which define the sense of honour of each of the actors. In a closely knit community such mentality leaves little space for opportunism. This is reflected in the elections of senior shop stewards in that candidates who have shown that they understand and share a concern for the long term have better chances of being elected. This makes it possible that in the day-to-day interaction with the management the long-term interests of the workers are turned into action in a consistent way.

4. THE DUALITY OF CONFLICT AND COOPERATION

The postulate of an underlying conflict of interest between the capitalist and the workers is based on an abstraction which separates the labour process from other contexts of everyday life. In contrast to this abstraction, fieldwork-based studies have conceptualized the relationship between the employer and the employees as a complex mixture of both conflict and cooperation. For instance, they have showed that the social climate of the workplace periodically shifts from a cooperative climate to a conflictual bargaining climate depending on the stage of the negotiation for a workplace level collective bargaining contract (Daniel 1973). Similarly, the code for social relations can also switch suddenly during negotiations, allowing off-the-record talks when a so-called strong bargaining relationship has been established through years of integrity in the actions of the opponents (Batstone *et al.* 1977). Such switching of codes is common between the context of the labour process and that of the bargaining table or that of the workplace and the neighbourhood (cf. Chua and Clegg 1989).

Additionally, there are other structural contexts and fields of action to which the shop steward system is connected. One concerns the lateral scope of the activities of the working-class movement. In Finland there is a wide scope that allows the extending of the bargaining issues from the work-related issues to other spheres of life in the local community and the wider regional context. Another Finnish feature is the centralized organization of the working-class movement extending to trade union movement, political parties, and the national polity. For instance, in the career paths of senior shop stewards one of the ultimate top positions is in the headquarters of the unions or even to become a member of the parliament. These structural contexts and social connections are relatively unexplored dimensions in the study of workplace industrial relations (cf. Edwards *et al.* 1995: 296). However, through them important resources are channelled to localities and to the workplaces. These linkages add to the totality of potential games played in the field of a workplace. Workers have very cost-efficient ways of influencing managerial decision-making by signalling a threat or a potential reward which is slumbering in one of these 'latent' fields of action. Small acts can have strong consequences if reference is made to the above-mentioned 'latent' structures or fields of action beyond the workplace which are critical to the managerial agenda. This explains also why there is space for cooperation between the employer and the employees even during conflicts.

Three kinds of latent sources of influence which workers' representatives can draw upon in bargaining with managers and which encourage longer-term collaboration can be readily identified. These concern their collective skills, the common interests of specific mill sites in competition for new investment, and their links with local political and administrative agencies. Considering first the role of workers' skills in structuring workplace relations, it is important to note that employment models which rely on internal labour markets and lifelong employment systems delegate a considerable amount of managerial and supervisory work to the workers themselves. Workers are the main agents of informal socialization of new entrants to the teams where also collective skills are reproduced and expanded. This creates at the same time rigidities in the use of labour power. An extreme example of the way in which the seniority principle in career advancement could be guarded by the workers is the following: skilled workers gave intentionally wrong advice to a worker who was speeded up in the career ladder by management against the implicit seniority rules. The wrong advice caused huge damages in the production runs and the worker had to quit. Vague advice or non-responsiveness can lead to similar outcomes without any trace of intentionality.

The establishment of new mills in old mill communities has the danger that work cultures from old mills diffuse to the new mills through the transfer of workers. This may hinder the development of new organizational structures and patterns of responsibility which are made possible with new generations of process technologies. On the other hand, when greenfield site investments are made in new communities without a previous tradition in pulp and paper production management is still dependent on experienced workers in older mills for giving guidance to new work crews. For instance, in one incident the workers of a mill refused to let new workers watch their work due to the frustration that the new investment was not situated in their mill site but abroad. Thus workplace level games concern the degree in which the workers' collectivity is willing to facilitate the transfer of skills, its speed, and reliability (cf. Grieco 1996).

For the management it is difficult to strike the balance between the benefits of local responsiveness of the semi-autonomous teams and the drawbacks caused by collective job ownership and the work culture related to it (cf. Matsumoto 1983; Hibino 1996). In the pulp and paper industry, the benefits and drawbacks are often temporally separated: the benefits are reaped especially at the early stages of the life cycle of the mill and the drawbacks in the more mature phases due to inertia and resistance to change. The same high level of worker commitment which puts a mill on track at the beginning converts to resistance to change at the end of a cycle. This contingency is especially relevant in decisions on new investments and their locations.

Secondly, within the forest industry corporation, intersite and interdivisional competition for resources happens under changing rules and power structures. These changes derive from mergers and acquisitions, from divestments of major divisions and from generation shifts at top level management. Local management and even divisional general managers are not involved in the decisions made in the dominant coalition at the top of the management structure. This is mainly due to the fact that major investments are very capital intensive and the whole corporation has to extend its resources when committing itself to a major expansion investment. Workers and the local management have shared, or at least overlapping, interests in the long-term growth of the mill combine and the mill community in the interunit competition within the corporation. Thus there is a chance of extending the bargaining agenda of the present with exchanges of favours which deal with the joint survival perspective.

The main area where the need for coordination between workers and managers occurs concerns the style of local collective bargaining and the nature of the industrial relations culture. High reliability of deliveries is one of the key success factors in the paper industry. Thus the nature of the pressuring tactics of the local trade union is one of the parameters which is considered by the corporate management when new investments are allocated. In order to have some substance for the argument of 'good' industrial relations workers have to abstain from the use of strikes at the core of the production process. The shutdowns of capital-intensive continuous production processes are extremely expensive. To preserve the image of 'good' industrial relations, even the local management has an interest in filtering information to the headquarters. This concerns short strikes or walkouts because there is also a chance that local management is blamed for their outburst and, whatever their cause is, they spoil the image of the worksite as a representative of 'good' industrial relations.

Third, workers' ability to mobilize external political and administrative resources is important in understanding why employees are drawn into discussions on strategic initiatives at the levels of the mill and profit centre management. This extends easily the bargaining agenda from the intra-unit system of collective bargaining and participatory system to cover also resource allocation in the local community and regional administration.

Local trade unions and shop stewards have a strong presence in the representative bodies of municipalities, especially in towns with few large employers. In some cases the working-class parties have a majority in the decision-making bodies. By adding the representation of other parties, it is not untypical that an employer has a very strong representation in the decision-making bodies of a municipality by its employees and management. Such a tight coupling of mills and municipality administration has been an explicit target of some dominant employers earlier (Koskinen 1987*a*) and the role of a general manager or a personnel manager contained often a responsibility to be available for political and administrative tasks in the local community. These linkages are important for directing resources of the municipality towards targets which converge with those of a large local employer. Even very direct support can be demanded from the local administration, e.g. as to real estate development, infrastructural investments (harbours, roads, railroads), educational institutions, etc. (cf. Kristensen 1994). When such decisions are partly dependent on the positions of workers' representatives this provides an opportunity to make implicit deals. When the bargaining agenda extends to different legal and institutional structures, explicit couplings cannot be made. It can only occur through informal understandings. Thus the moves which widen the bargaining agenda have to be made iteratively.

5. THE MULTIPLICITY OF KNOWLEDGE BASES

The social proximity of the shop stewards to the management at the local level provides the workers' representatives with an enormous amount of information. Workers and their representatives are capable of reading the implicit messages from the usage of raw materials, machines, capacity, and shifts in the orders. The constant interaction with the management contains also a considerable number of hidden messages. Laconic communication is the main source of tactical information during periods of open conflict (Grieco and Lilja 1996: 134). However, accumulating information and experiences beyond the workplace is necessary for understanding the functioning of the modern corporation and industry logics.

During the last ten years, the managements of Finnish paper industry firms have adopted a policy of openness which means that the employees are supplied with accurate economic information of their business units. Senior shop stewards have corporate wide meetings paid by the employer several times a year. Some of them represent workers in various managerial bodies, like the mill level management teams, divisional boards, and/or boards of the incorporated companies which jointly form the huge corporations. Thus the shop steward mechanism has penetrated into higher levels of the managerial labour processes at least from a monitoring point of view. This development has coincided with a dramatic reduction in the yearly number of unsettled local grievance pro memorias: they have dropped from about 120 to 20 in ten years. According to the interview of the research secretary of the Paper Workers' Union, the underlying reason for this drop is the increased understanding of managerial problems among the representatives of the workers (Niemi 1995). The understanding of the long-term goals of the corporations by the workers' representatives facilitates games in which immediate gains are traded for future gains.

However, these participatory mechanisms are not enough to explain why the shop steward system has developed an understanding of the conflicts between competing corporate actors and their implications for the strategic decisions of each of the corporations and their mill sites. One part of the explanation is the transparency of the corporate strategies from the point of view of the mill sites: the strategy is laid out by investments and depends on sorting out bottlenecks and on an explicit design of vertical and/or horizontal integration and economies of scale. The other part of the explanation is related to the interlinkages of the corporate strategies across the largest paper industry corporations in the world. Gaps in forecast demand and supply of specific products within some geographic area lead to a competitive investment race among the major players. Announced investment decisions by one competitor are often followed by competing investment decisions by others with an intention to scare the other competitors away from the business opportunity. Such a race typically leads into overcapacity and contributes to the cyclicality of the industry. This industry level dynamic is an important condition for the interest representation of the workers and thus it is no wonder that the shop steward mechanism is constantly developing and testing local theories of corporate and business level strategy. Because some of its features are very visible it is not uncommon that the local theories are very accurate and provide an opportunity to predict managerial action.

A complementary source of information on the national industry level game is an assembly of senior shop stewards. In the pulp and paper industry, the relatively small number of mill sites—about fifty altogether—has given birth to such an exceptional institution. It links the mill sites of the major corporations together and allows a comparison of the situations in each of the domestic corporations active in the pulp and paper industry. The assembly contributes also to the evaluation of the investment and employment prospects of the future: the future of the whole industry, of the corporations, of individual mill sites, production lines, and departments. It is an active agent for developing a situation specific theory of management and employer action in the Finnish paper industry. The yearly meeting of this group of local representatives of the workers is only part of its activities. There is lots of informal exchange of information between workplaces. This exchange maintains a collective memory of critical incidents across the whole country. Thus local conflicts occur always in the context of earlier conflicts and the policy-making process of the union develops within the collective experience and reflection of the assembly of senior shop stewards.

In the event that shop stewards need an external support in dealing with managerial problems of their corporations they can turn to the research department of the union. In the case of the Paper Workers' Union it is a small unit of two to three academic professionals who are important sources of advice on issues of corporate and business management due to their wide industry-specific experience. Even managers of the corporations take advantage of the opportunity to talk to the researchers/consultants of the unions. Their opinion is consulted and respected because they know how to 'sell' technological, administrative, and structural changes in the corporation and in the industry to the workers. Thus, knowledge resources of the workers can also be turned into the resources of management. Besides being able to communicate better with their workers, the management can even be empowered by the trade union movement to influence the regional and national bureaucracy and the government which have typically strong links with the social democratic party. However, such support becomes, on a longer perspective, an item for exchange in the negotiated orders of the corporatist mode of governance of Finnish society.

The information and knowledge bases described above provide an overview for workers' representatives of the developmental trends in the whole industry and of the local factors at the mill sites. The changing scale of the corporations have, however, created gaps in the knowledge base of the shop steward mechanism. The major Finnish paper corporations have become European and with aspirations to build global linkages. This transformation of the corporate scale is only very slowly being matched with the development of consultative institutions for the so-called European firms. The European Works Council directive (94/45/EC), accepted in September 1994, puts demands on corporate-wide information disclosure and consultation but it will take years before the employees and the shop steward mechanism is able to react to the changing structure of the corporations. Even the corporate management is not very well equipped to make use of the synergy potential in such a growth strategy. However, a first step to open up the internal market within the corporations (and even across corporations) is to compare productivity measurements of similar paper machines in different countries. Such benchmarking can be a source of organizational learning as well as a starting-point for internal competition for survival (cf. Ferner and Edwards 1995: 247–8).

6. CONCLUSIONS

In a small forest sector society, the shop steward mechanism of worker representation employed in the core forest industry firms is interlinked with formal governance mechanisms of the corporations, industry level bargaining, and local and national political processes. Access to these fields of action over recent decades has changed the habitus of the shop steward system. This change in ways of thinking and acting has occurred in connection with a variety of games played against and with the management of the forest industry corporations. We have described the conditions for this change in the habitus along three dimensions: the relevance of a variety of temporal contexts in the minds of actors, the duality of conflict and co-operation, and the multiplicity of knowledge bases needed in competent action. They are clearly interlinked, creating a virtuous circle.

Fieldwork in the pulp and paper mills sensitized the author to the different temporal perspectives that were present in the interactions of the shop stewards and the management. Though the day-to-day contacts could involve considerable tensions and open conflicts due to divergent interests, there were mechanisms to coordinate activities in dealing with joint interests related to the long-term development of the mill site. With the increasing emphasis on the long term in the habitus of the shop steward mechanism there is more space for a social orientation which emphasizes cooperation over conflict. The threads of shared interests across hierarchical positions in the social system of the mill are harnessed by external threats and uncertainty caused by the business cycle and changes in the structure and ownership of the corporations, and amplified by the strategic moves of competitors on the global scene. By opening the books and by increasing the participation of the shop stewards in the higher levels of managerial decision-making, management has supported the confidence of workers' representatives that they have a feel for the ongoing competitive game. Information about the strategic space of the mill combines fosters the capabilities needed to educate the constituencies of the shop stewards into taking a longer-term perspective. This creates an electoral climate for candidates to serve as shop stewards who have demonstrated skills in long-term strategic thinking and action.

The wider structural conditions for this changing pattern in the habitus of the shop steward mechanism are crucial. Though many of the institutional conditions have been the same for other industrial firms, for instance the general agreement on the shop steward institution and laws on workers' participation, similar developments in other sectors have been exceptional. In the Finnish paper industry, the need to coordinate policies with bargaining partners was recognized immediately industry level collective bargaining began. Due to the highly cyclical nature of the industry, the bargaining power of the parties shifts unexpectedly from one side to the other. The survival of firms requires that neither side of the bargaining table take too much advantage of the changing bargaining power. Of course, there is considerable variety in opinions as to what is 'too much'. The shared stakes in the community and its development have provided a wider ground for longer-term thinking. This has been supported by cycles of investments which have been persistent in the Finnish paper industry. Such a path-dependent consistency in the transformation of industrial life has been exceptional. At the same time other manufacturing industries have been subject to deep restructuring measures in Finland and elsewhere in Europe. Discontinuity and the hegemony of markets have dominated even in countries which have a developmental state and a commitment to corporatist regulation.

REFERENCES

Batstone, E., Boraston, I., and Frenkel, S. (1977), *Shop Stewards in Action* (Oxford: Blackwell).
Bourdieu, P. (1990), *The Logic of Practice* (Cambridge: Polity Press).

Chua, W. F., and Clegg, S. (1989), 'Contradictory Couplings: Professional Ideology in the Organizational Locales of Nurse Training', *Journal of Management Studies*, 26/2: 103–27.

Crozier, M., and Friedberg, E. (1980), *Actors and Systems* (Chicago: University of Chicago Press).

Daniel, W. W. (1973), 'Understanding Employee Behaviour in its Context: Illustrations from Productivity Bargaining', in J. Child (ed.), *Man and Organization* (London).

Edwards, P., Collinson, D., and Della Rocca, G. (1995), 'Workplace Resistance in Western Europe: A Preliminary Overview and a Research Agenda', *European Journal of Industrial Relations*, 1/3: 283–316.

Ferner, A., and Edwards, P. (1995), 'Power and the Diffusion of Organizational Change within Multinational Enterprises', *European Journal of Industrial Relations*, 1/2: 229–57.

Grieco, M. (1996), *Workers' Dilemmas: Recruitment, Reliability and Repeated Exchange* (London).

—— and Lilja, K. (1996), 'Research Note: Contradictory Couplings', *Organization Studies*, 17/1: 131–7.

Hibino, B. (1996), 'Transmission of Workplace Level Institutions in Human Resource Management'. Dissertation, Stanford University.

Koskinen, T. (1987a), 'Tehdasyhteisö', *University of Vaasa, Reports 123* (Vaasa).

—— (1987b), 'Herruutta, hallintaa vai vuorovaikutusta? Tehdasyhdyskuntien muotoja ja vaiheita Suomessa', *Hallinnon tutkimus*, 6/2: 101–5.

Kristensen, P. H. (1994), 'Strategies in a Volatile World', *Economy and Society*, 23/3: 305–34.

Laurila, J. (1995), 'Social Movements in Management', *Helsinki School of Economics, Series A-100* (Helsinki).

Lehtinen, J. (1995), 'Vienti on viiden varassa', *Talouselämä*, 39: 28–30.

Lilja, K. (1987), 'Workers' Collectivity at the Workplace as an Independent Organizational Mechanism', *Scandinavian Journal of Management Studies*, 3/3: 197–211.

—— (1989), 'Epics and Epochs: Organisational Learning and the Kaskinen Pulp Mill', Helsinki School of Economics Working Paper F-232 (Helsinki).

—— (1992), 'Finland: No Longer the Nordic Exception', in A. Ferner and R. Hyman (eds.), *Industrial Relations in the New Europe* (Oxford: Blackwell), 198–217.

—— Räsänen, K., and Tainio, R. (1992), 'A Dominant Business Recipe: The Forest Sector in Finland', in R. Whitley (ed.), *European Business Systems* (London: Sage), 137–54.

—— and Tainio, R. (1996), 'The Nature of the Typical Finnish Firm', in R. Whitley and P. H. Kristensen (eds.), *The Changing European Firm* (London: Routledge), 159–91.

Matsumoto, K. (1983), *The Rise of the Japanese Corporate System* (London: Kegan Paul International).

Niemi, H. (1995), Personal communication.

Purcell, J. (1981), *Good Industrial Relations* (Hong Kong: Macmillan).

Raumolin, J. (1984), 'Metsäsektorin vaikutus Suomen taloudelliseen ja yhteiskun-nalliseen kehitykseen', *Oulun yliopisto: Pohjois-Suomen tutkimuslaitos C 51* (Oulu).

PART 3

Changing Governance Structures, Managerial Strategies, and the Reorganization of Work Systems

7

Institutional, Sectoral, and Corporate Dynamics in the Creation of Global Supply Chains

FRANK MUELLER

RAY LOVERIDGE

1. INTRODUCTION

Over the last century industrial and developmental economists, historians, and political scientists have provided many descriptions of the institutional structures shaping national markets and these processes of governance. Origins have often been traced to national responses to randomly exogenous historical events or contingencies, including the role played by a national elite and national leaders. By the 1960s the debate among Western analysts had come to focus on the question of convergence across national systems. Processes of bureaucratic rationalization were seen to bring about a uniform web of rules requiring standard interpretation by a new global elite of professional managers. The basis of most versions of the 'convergence thesis' is the—essentially Weberian—assumption that the process of industrialization, in which the use of machines and an accompanying rationalization of public thought and procedure pervade all aspects of social life, has been and remains the impelling logic behind societal development. This assumption is now being challenged in so-called post-modernist approaches to the analysis of contemporary events. However, the indices of modernist 'progress' remain central to the operation of most organizations particularly those with a global brief such as the World Bank and UNO agencies. Since the days of the old League of Nations the economic and social performance of nation states has been measured, monitored, and classified into grades in which, until recently, Western countries made up a premier league of outstanding and exemplary achievers.

The concept of national business systems (NBSs) derives from a burgeoning body of literature that seeks to demonstrate that the institutional structures of industrialized societies are not only different, but likely to remain so. The reason for this apparent state of homeostasis is that particular configurations of institutions have shaped the conduct of business, or of market behaviour, within particular countries in a manner that provides them with a competitive advantage *vis-à-vis* firms in other nation states (Hollingsworth *et al.* 1994). Furthermore, it is suggested that the cultural or ideational foundations of institutionalized behaviours within NBSs are such that they cannot easily be reproduced in the form of codified techniques capable of being transferred (Hamilton 1983). Thus, it appears, that national culture or, more identifiably, its articulation in the form of normative structures can be seen as providing an idiosyncratic asset for successful NBSs. In terms of the opportunistic, oligopolistic struggle described by the New Institutional Economists, most notably by Williamson (1985), the internalization of this asset is, in any case, a consciously rational decision made on the basis of the relative costs of accessing and controlling the uses to which the asset may be put. That being so, it is supposed that convergence on a common mode of market behaviour across competing nations will be unlikely (Whitley 1994*a*, 1994*b*).

Whitley (1994*c*) offers an exploration of 'variations in market organization between institutional contexts' (ibid. 9) based on 'consideration of how "firms" are constituted as relatively discrete economic actors in different market societies' (ibid. 10). The outcome of his analysis is that (*a*) characteristics of the resulting relationship can themselves lead to a resulting internal tendency to instability/stability (ibid. Fig. 8.1) and (*b*) that the internal interdependence of organizations within a pre-existing institutional structure ensures its survival (ibid. 247–8). Arguably, the National Business Systems approach is put forward on the basis of an internal structural tendency towards either a benevolent or destructive condition of homeostasis, often expressed as a model of path dependency. In our view, there are two problems in the NBS approach: the first concerns their obvious and necessary functionalist perspective. What is required by their audiences is, as Whitley (1992) puts it, an explanation for the 'variety of effective forms of business organization and their interdependencies with key institutions, such as the state and the financial system' (p. 1). Business organizations are set up as intended modes of action and can be judged in these terms. The danger, however, is that both the complexity generated by the number of organized transactions and the nature of social transaction itself is accounted for in the outcomes of a—for certain purposes inadequate—systemic analysis. Secondly, systemic analysis is by definition static or comparatively static, unless there exists some underlying causal mechanisms or rules of aggregation to account for internal interdependencies and the direction in which the system is developing.

In his recent extension of this theory Kristensen (1996) has suggested that 'natural systems' arise from associations amongst individual actors— defined to include both private persons and corporate bodies—and provide intermediaries between the state and the location of the business activity. However, the relevance of this theory for East Asian countries is not clear: whereas a natural system of association in European countries is characterized by intermediaries having to seek legitimacy in terms that relate to well-established institutionalized interests, the executive authority of modern bureaucracies in newly industrializing countries is often isolated from factional interest, rooting its ultimate authority on broadly expressed national interest within a global arena.[1]

In this chapter we explore the contesting forces shaping the developing relationship between MNCs and the institutions that underpin National Business Systems. We focus our analysis on recent developments in the automobile sector and in the supply chains that service it. We suggest that the present intensive level of competition between MNCs among vehicle assemblers and the largest sub-assemblers has shaped the acceptance of similar strategies within the sector towards its ongoing rationalization. We argue that in spite of the particular characteristics of this sector it provides an example of the manner in which sectoral contingencies perceived by the negotiating agents, both national and corporate, can shape the arena in which their transactions take place as well as the sanctions available to them. This suggests that the immutability of national institutions and the impact of their ideas on the culture and aims of MNCs is not unidirectional, indeed it might appear that their influence is being eroded by current MNC strategies.

2. COMMITMENT AND COERCION IN THE RESTRUCTURING OF GLOBAL SUPPLY CHAINS

Complementing the globalization of automobile assembly, first-tier and direct suppliers of auto components have been pressured to follow the assemblers in localizing their production in close geographical proximity to the latters' assembly lines, and making a firm commitment to a promised level of quantity, quality, and reliability of supply. Along with this need to engage in higher levels of foreign direct investment, suppliers that have been successful in being retained by the largest MNCs—as one of a few 'preferred partners'—are, paradoxically, faced with the prospect of making a potentially crippling scale of investment in required production levels beyond anything hitherto attempted. For some British firms in which one of the authors has been carrying out research, the possibility of raising the required capital in the financial market has proved so costly that other product lines have been dropped in order to relocate internal resources to the processing of a single auto component. In another case the supplier firm has resisted the offer of sole supplier status for a decade or so but is currently aware that exclusion from programmes of centralization and

[1] See for example Vogel (1991) and Johnson (1982) for two of the several accounts of the imposition of modern institutions and their relationship to the emergence of NBSs in the global context defined by the 'Cold War'.

rationalization currently being carried out under, for example, 'Ford 2000' and its GM equivalent will leave the supplier firm dependent upon jobbing orders from other global assemblers.

In addition to these trends in interfirm relationships in the motor vehicle supply chain, there has been a return to the use of the internal market in MNC bargaining with national unions, works, and company councils. This issue became prominent in the 1970s when Ford (UK) trade union stewards played a leading part in convening meetings with their counterparts in other European countries in attempts to regulate management's planned dispersal and duplication of the internal sourcing of standard European models (Friedman and Meredeen 1980). Previously the International Federation of Chemical Unions was established in Geneva to prevent a repetition of cross-state wage competition conducted in that sector in the 1930s (Levinson 1972). The International Metalworkers Federation met first in Paris in 1959 and at successive conferences determined to set up World Auto Company Councils for all major MNCs. The first three for Ford, GM, and Chrysler met in Detroit in June 1966, the fourth (VAG-Mercedes) met at Wolfsburg in 1966. The subsequent success of both Ford and GM in dispersing component production across Europe taken together with the apparent ease with which, for example, Mitsubishi can now source its domestically assembled new vehicle from Australian suppliers suggests a level of global integration in supply chains higher than anything previously experienced.

By the late 1970s it had become evident to American and British manufacturers that control over the supply of bought-in components was a more significant factor in the growing supremacy of Japanese car assemblers than were internal cost advantages held at an earlier stage in their economic growth. In particular the Japanese assemblers had achieved the benefits of exercising a hierarchical form of authority over suppliers whilst maintaining a market-based mode of transacting at each stage of the supply chain. The origins of these relationships derived from the manner in which the large industrial groupings or *kyorkokukai* had either 'spun-off' specialized activities from the core task of the assembly of final products, that is devolved formerly integrated activities to autonomous enterprises, or had taken minority ownership interests in key component suppliers. The relational basis between the parties had developed as an obligational rather than adversarial one as in Britain and the USA (Sako 1992). Equally important was the establishment of supplier-clubs to provide both informational and relational ties reinforced by regular 'solidarity' events (Dore 1987).

However, both Sako and Dore might well be seen as *under*emphasizing the coercive pressures that complement the 'trustful' transactional linkages in Japanese supply chains. As Altmann *et al.* (1992) have suggested on the basis of their study of the German auto supply chain, pressures towards system-rationalization create a hierarchical dependency rather than a trustful clannish or, even, collegial relationship between final assemblers and suppliers. Arguably, buyer–supplier relations in the Japanese model are characterized by substantial dedicated investments with high asset specificity; stability in the relationship; the sharing of complex tasks; the sharing of confidential information; a high security and predictability of purchasing orders; the exercising of legitimate authority by the core assembly firm (e.g. Nishiguchi 1989). The presence of these characteristics would indicate a *hierarchical* rather than market relationship, and the introduction of often diffuse networking concepts does not help.

It is these features that led us to coin the phrase of 'externalization of coercion' (EoC) or 'externalization of hierarchy' (EoH). Thus, in the process of interfirm rationalization described there is little room for horizontal collaboration between craft-based suppliers in the manner envisaged by Piore and Sable (1984). Not only have relatively small British firms been victims of this rationalizing process. Over the last decade all of the German car producers have shown their impatience with long-standing domestic suppliers in reported public statements to the press. More importantly, they have placed major orders with British, Spanish, or French suppliers, or have invited companies outside the industry to bid for contracts. For example, Siemens bought the Michigan electronic (ECU) plant of Allied Signal having been promised business by GM and BMW that would previously have gone to Robert Bosch (authors' interviews in Siemens USA, Southbend, Michigan, August 1990). The major problem with the cooperation/obligation model of buyer–supplier relations is that it cannot explain this global search for suppliers. In the former model the preservation of close trust-based links to regional or national suppliers should have overriding priority, but this point of view belittles the relentless pressure for rationalization which requires a global search for low cost, high-quality, and highly reliable suppliers (Mueller and Loveridge 1995). Arguably, these pressures are better captured by a commitment-coercion model.

3. RESTRUCTURING THE SUPPLY CHAIN IN THE AUTOMOTIVE SECTOR: THE EXTERNALIZATION OF HIERARCHY

The systemic features of the so-called Japanese model of production quickly became incorporated in a prototype for the reorganization of the automobile industry (Womack *et al.* 1990; Lamming 1993). First the tiered nature of the supply chain was to be explicitly recognized by attributing 'favoured' or 'preferred' supplier status on certain sub-assemblers and the specialist component manufacturers. The latter were to be orchestrators of most of the supply of semi-finished commodities constituting several thousand small jobbing firms further down the chain. An extension of the role of the sub-assembler is that of working with the product development team of the assembler in the creation of the specification of subsystems within new models. Often assemblers force suppliers to adopt certain standards, just as these first-tier suppliers force lower-tier firms to adopt certain standards. Consequently the possession of compatible IT systems, particularly CAD and the ability to network such systems was a necessary condition for occupation of this enhanced role. This, together with a permanently heavy commitment to investment in design and development, made it difficult for small suppliers to offer these services. It was not perhaps surprising, therefore, that the 1980s saw a new wave of acquisitions by larger suppliers across Europe and a movement among these firms towards 'focus' in their portfolio of activities. In both the USA and Britain engineering conglomerates such as BRD, BBA, GKN, TI, and others chose to focus on motor vehicles along with one or two complementary activities (most often in 'Defence' related supply). Concomitantly they brought their dispersed subsidiaries into a much more tightly knit divisional structure bearing the corporate logo. (See, for example, the annual reports of the above-named companies together with their large German and French counterparts e.g. KKK and Valeo.) The 'tight-loose' links with operating units were greatly facilitated by the use of centralized monitoring by means of communications and information technology (CIT).

Thus, the boundaries of supplying firms have become much more opaque as buyers assert a right to much higher levels of internal scrutiny. From the early 1970s assemblers in the UK and USA had attempted to conduct an industrial relations audit on their suppliers. Neither their credibility nor capability in the field of human resource management, however, allowed the practice to gain any degree of authority. Still, by 1986 Rover was able to successfully intervene in an internal dispute within a supplier (Turnbull 1986). Subsequently the accent on quality and maintenance of supply has involved customers in rigorous audits of the suppliers' capacity at all levels. In surveys conducted in the late 1980s suppliers who had achieved preferred supplier status (PSS) commented favourably on the new monitoring system. The longer-term benefits had become obvious to many. Acceptance by an assembler such as Ford or Nissan could be regarded by other major assemblers as 'certification' as a good supplier and could therefore lead to further business.

The achievement of the same vertical structure of coercive-commitment relations has become a well-publicized goal of Western assemblers, both in Germany and Britain. Rover, whose share of the UK market slipped from 40 to 14 per cent by the middle of the 1980s, has been at considerable pains to demonstrate that it has adopted all aspects of the Japanese model in its approach to suppliers. Other European sourced assemblers including Ford, GM, Toyota, Nissan, and Honda, have also imposed JIT conditions on suppliers. In most European assembly plants the numbers of regular suppliers are said to have been reduced by a factor of at least ten, and this trend has been complemented by a growing element of devolved responsibility to preferred suppliers (or sub-assemblers). Respondents in a survey conducted by Turnbull (1988) balanced the value of recognition given by a major assembler against the overhead costs of meeting the requirements of a JIT system. This appeared particularly difficult for small jobbing suppliers and for materials producers at the end of the supply chain, both of whom had been forced into the retention of *higher* levels of stocks in order to supply the short-lead times of sub-assemblers and assemblers. To a large extent this appeared to be a function of scheduling changes by the latter; even Nissan forced suppliers to meet irregular changes in demand, while Rover had established warehouses close to production lines which suppliers were forced to keep at cost to themselves. Many of Turnbull's respondents appeared to greatly resent the additional overheads created by the adoption of JIT.

It is, indeed, evident that a major attraction in the adoption of JIT systems by many upstream specialist component manufacturers and sub-assemblers is the cost-saving gained in terms of reduced costs. It seems equally true that its adoption by many small metal or plastic shapers and other jobbing concerns is relatively rare. There are a number of reasons for this. In many JIT configurations machines are duplicated between groups. In order to make up for the large proportion of down-time in such equipment, stock savings and quality improvements must be very high. Similarly, materials suppliers will only offer deliveries JIT to economic quantities. Without sufficient economies of scale or scope kan-ban systems are not practicable. Even in Japan no more than 50 per cent of suppliers are able to implement this system (Rutherford *et al.* 1988). Equally importantly the disruption within the prevailing social and logistical organization of work could be crippling for a small business that has grown out of the skills structure of the local labour market.

Most small European engineering firms continue to reproduce a shop-floor hierarchy built on a previous craft structure. While not now recognized in the newly modularized systems of formal apprentice being introduced within EU member nations it is nevertheless stubbornly maintained in local custom and practice. Even within the large sub-assemblers the ability of management to bring about the multi-skilling of crafts people and their incorporation into kan-ban modules has often been difficult to achieve. The UK electronics components supplier Lucas Industries, was a pioneer of Japanese methods of production engineering in 1982 but has failed to achieve the desired devolution of all services to the 'natural group' module and complete flexibility between tasks in all cases (see Elger and Fairbrother 1990; Loveridge 1993). The further implications of the integration of work practices include a drastic reduction of functional divisions between departments. The impact of these changes extends all the way to

the specialized roles of unit and company board executives. It is evident
that while collaboration between functions has improved, the level of dis-
mantlement of these internal vertical specializations is only slowly taking
effect in Western firms (authors' interviews).

One of the important effects of the processes described so far is that firms
along the value chain will become increasingly dependent upon each other,
but particularly dependent upon the focal or core firm which organizes the
intercorporate production (or value adding) processes in order to appropriate a large share of the resulting gains. Given this enlarged reach across
corporate boundaries exercised by the core firm it is also more readily prepared to use plants belonging to other corporate entities; this increased
readiness can be used to pressurize in a market-like way internal operations into increasing their effectiveness in contributing towards corporate
goals. Clearly, there are high costs of adaptation which have to be undertaken in the process of establishing the external hierarchy. In most cases
these costs have to be absorbed by suppliers to original equipment manufacturers. As a consequence of this there has been a growing movement
towards mergers and rationalization at different points of the supply chain.
This rationalization process has in turn led to a growing polarization
between large and small craft-based suppliers. In the case of the larger firms
a more equal bargaining situation exists between large-scale sub-assemblers
like Robert Bosch GmbH and Allied Signal and their customers among
auto assemblers. For small-scale suppliers the position is much more coercive and their future much less certain. This process might well be seen as
eroding the associational solidarity which has hitherto characterized
sectoral relationships within the German automobile industry.

4. THE INTERNALIZATION OF MARKETS (IOM): CONDITIONS AND PROCESSES

In the previous section, we looked at the EoH which, however, is only one
side of the coin, because the other side is represented by the IoM. Corporate
boundaries thus become permeable in two directions: the hierarchy principle is extended outwards, the competition mechanism is extended inwards.
The latter refers to the development that operating units are not only
increasingly contesting each other for new investment, they also face the
competition of corporate entitities from outside. There is, arguably, an
increasing interdependence between the nature of extended external hierarchies and the systematic use of the 'competitive tendering' leverage by
corporate decision-makers. The reorganization of the workplace can be
driven forward through rationalization strategies applied within a wider,
often global, arena (Hirsch-Kreinsen 1994). The 'Western' pattern of IoM

is not in contradiction to but, rather, complements the Japanese principle of EoH.

Indeed, because of the increasing use of instruments of competitive tendering in *intra*corporate affairs, plants are under continuous threat that some of their production output will be given to a competing sister plant at home or abroad, or that it will be outsourced to another firm altogether. Such threats have shown themselves to be tremendously instrumental in gaining agreement to important aspects of workplace change, such as teamwork arrangements, weekend working arrangements, and longer machine running time. This type of 'corporate investment bargaining' typically takes place between corporate management and national/local trade union or worker representatives. Also, certain organization design, internal labour market (ILM), and human resource management (HRM) features are *prerequisites* for making more extensive use of the shifting of workplaces abroad. For example, present threats are more credible if things worked out in the past. Internalized career systems and functional skill formation mechanisms are often crucial for making things 'work out'. For example, Bosch in Wales and Volkswagen in Spain used training and development systems that were closely modelled upon their German systems. In turn, managerial mobility is required in order to smooth this transmission process which means that a highly developed managerial internal labour market is clearly advantageous.

It is, perhaps, significant that the most overt use of intracorporate leverage by European auto manufacturers appears to be currently taking place across German corporations rather than within Anglo-Saxon groups. This might be taken as an indication that shareholders of German companies are increasingly asserting their right—in conjunction with their management agents—to decide *alone* about the allocation of corporate assets. If this is true, then German stakeholders face the prospect of gradually losing perhaps not their legal right but probably their factual power to have a significant say in corporate investment decisions (Mueller 1996). The reason can partly be seen in the delayed response of German manufacturers due to their insulation from the immediate effects of global competition in the early 1980s. Another explanation, however, would be to argue that certain features of the German NBS have made the adoption of this organizing principle less pressing. According to the comparative industrial relations literature, it is the existence of consultative and co-determination institutions and procedures which has provided a sufficiently capable forum for continuous productivity bargaining within a broad consensus-based framework. These have often been regarded as successful substitutes for much cruder Anglo-American concession bargaining.

In general the growth rate of German auto component manufacturers slowed from 10 per cent to around 3 per cent over the 1980s, declining rapidly until even firms like Robert Bosch incurred losses in 1991 and 1992. Since the establishment of Bosch's first workshop in 1886 this organization has sought to establish a reputation in human resource management pioneering high day wages, the eight-hour day, and the five-and-a-half-day week before the First World War. It did not, however, attempt to introduce either team working or continuous improvement until 1990. (When they did so, Bosch management adopted a quotation from their founder as the underlying precept for the new system rather than acknowledging its Japanese origins!) Production on a team-working basis was first introduced into a purpose built plant in South Wales, its first British based factory. Subsequently Bosch has made it clear to all subsidiaries and plants that any new investment cannot be taken for granted but has to be *earned*.

In order to make its threats credible, between 1990 and 1992, Bosch invested DM 600 million in France and DM 300 million in each of Britain and Spain. As a result of two subsequent concrete investment decisions in favour of Cardiff and Treto (Spain), employment estimated at 1,060 jobs was created outside Germany. In February 1993, Bosch management decided to invest DM 200 million in the existing Reutlingen (Southern Germany) plant, after the IG Metall negotiators had conceded that an agreed 3 per cent wage increase would only apply to the basic wage. Without this concession, management had threatened to transfer production abroad. A similar bargaining and negotiation took place over a planned semiconductor plant at Stuttgart, for which Bosch needed agreement for Sunday work. Only after it had received this agreement was Bosch management prepared no longer to pursue the Scotland option (*Financial Times*, 3 September 1993). However, Bosch management made a different decision with regard to the location of a plant for the manufacture of electric power tools which was given to Malaysia to complement Bosch's continuing operations in Leinfelden-Echterdingen (near Stuttgart).

Another illustration of the utilization of internalized competition by a German MNC can be provided from Daimler-Benz. The largest German automobile assembler, Daimler-Benz, suffered a set-back to its corporate reputation through the rather opaque use of its assembly methods in comparisons with those of more effective Japanese assemblers in the Womack *et al.* (1990) study. In summer 1992, improvements in absenteeism and adoption of team-based work organization were made preconditions for continuation of investment at Rastatt, Southern Germany by Daimler-Benz senior management board. The overall unit cost situation in Germany was considered highly unsatisfactory by management, and more foreign investment anticipated. Local union leaders at Rastatt promised a fight over the investment, and criticized management's apparent strategy of utilizing new investment in order to end existing wage agreements. Among Mercedes management's list of demands was the abolition of night shift allowances and break periods, and a cut in Christmas bonuses, which are currently equivalent to half of one month's wages. In order to make credible the threat to the unions, alternative sites in the Czech Republic, France, and Britain were actively considered by management for production of the new 'Minimerc'. The threat gained in credibility because of management's previous decisions to build an all purpose vehicle at the new US plant. The chairman of the employee company council at Daimler-Benz described management's strategy at Rastatt as 'effectively blackmail' in forcing unions to agree to cost saving measures aimed at closing the apparent DM 200 million cost gap in favour of the potential Czech site. However, the employee company council probably made an underestimation by viewing it as bad management style, rather than acknowledging it as a systematic management lever. In December 1993, as a way of concession, the central works council offered to forego 1 per cent in wage rise in each of the two following wage agreements—to be borne by all Mercedes-Benz workers— and furthermore to agree to one shift being worked at a normal rate on Saturday. Works councils at Mercedes-Benz also gave promises of more flexible working arrangements. In the final agreement, management accepted union concessions as sufficient to decide in favour of Rastatt, and was prepared to guarantee that in no plant would involuntary redundancies take place. Subsequently, at Mercedes-Benz's plant in Bremen the works council was threatened that 3,000 jobs would be lost, unless it agreed to nine-hour shifts.

The IoMs can, of course, also be practised even if all operations are within the same national borders. After experimenting with it at its Regensburg factory, BMW introduced a four-day week working time model into its Munich plant (*Frankfurter Allgemeine Zeitung*, 17 September 1991). Although different from the Regensburg model, where it was used to implement an extension of machine running time to six days per week, the new regime will also facilitate some—although not regular—Saturday working at the Munich operations. However, BMW management did manage to introduce a flexible shift system at its Dingolfing plant which will include Saturdays and be similar to the Regensburg plant system. This exposed BMW management to union accusations that it was systematically blackmailing the workforce into accepting Saturday working. The IG Metall has great difficulties with BMW's plant agreement at its Regensburg plant, because there the Saturday has become a 'normal' working day. The IG Metall sees this not as primarily gaining flexibility but extending machine running time, a case where company interests have come to completely dominate over employee interests. In contrast, the IG Metall supports the type of plant agreement that has been struck at Opel Rüesselsheim which came into effect on 20 August 1995: according to the agreement the Saturday is not a *regular* working day, but is available as a buffer for necessary repair and maintenance work.

Clearly, multinationals like GM with a so much wider geographical spread have an even stronger bargaining hand *vis-à-vis* the unions, given their higher potential to threaten relocation of future investment. From the mid-1980s, a strategic approach 'emerged' at General Motors Europe that can partly be interpreted as a forcing and fostering strategy based on the internalization of market relations. Instead of linking new investment to external market developments only, management in a way 'discovered' that it could in fact be used to achieve change in the established workplace regime.[2] The forcing effect took place in the form of a domino effect: six-and-a-half or seven-day, near continuous shift production in capital-intensive operations was introduced in Zaragoza, Spain in early 1988, in Kaiserslautern, Germany, in March 1988, in Bochum and Rüsselsheim in September and December 1988 respectively. In each case, agreement at one plant increased the pressure on the others, a domino effect which made even large plants with strong union organization—like the plants in Bochum and Rüsselsheim—finally give in to management demands. A year later, General Motors started a review of labour relations and work organization in its European plants. Radical changes were first introduced at GM's plant at Antwerp, Belgium, with two ten-hour shifts and best working practices. But unlike a relatively straightforward matter like machine utilization, best working practices involved not only forcing but also fostering employee involvement and commitment.

At the same time changes could be sold to trade unions as holding the promise of job enrichment and greater participation. In 1990, far-reaching concessions on workplace reform, flexibility, and productivity improvement were reached at GM's British Vauxhall Ellesmere Port plant, an agreement substantially influenced by practices already in use at GM's German and Belgium plants. The agreement was reached after US management had given the British unions a quasi-ultimatum: to agree radical new working practices or face the loss of new investment. The Ellesmere Port agreement secured the start of engine production on Merseyside after a break of six years. The agreement included teamworking with practically no restrictions on flexibility and labour mobility, a new dispute procedure, the option to use temporary personnel, and a reduction in the number of employee classifications from thirty to eight. General Motors did not require a single union deal. Instead they insisted on single table bargaining, which was agreed upon between the three unions involved, namely the AEU, the TGWU, and the MSF. Whilst agreement on twenty-four-hour production was a prerequisite for the investment in the new engine plant being built at Ellesmere Port, GM subsequently attempted to transfer the new regime to the existing operations at the same site. In order to make full use of expensive capital machinery, General Motors also considered the intro-

---

[2] This paragraph is based on Mueller (1991).

duction of three-shift working on some of the existing operations at its Luton and Ellesmere Port plants. New investment decisions can be effectively employed to keep up the pressure and make people prepared to embrace radical change.

In 1992–3, the Kaiserslautern engine plant made substantial concessions in terms of shift arrangements and new working practices, which allowed machines to be operated for 120 hours per week without interruptions for shift changes. The works council also agreed to maintenance work on Saturdays without extra pay, but instead with compensation in time off during the week. For these concessions, the Kaiserslautern engine plant was 'duly rewarded' with major new investment. Subsequently, it turned out that management had made the acceptance of lean production methods a precondition for the investment. Some of the new concepts desired by management include synchronous plant layouts, lean manufacturing, lean organization including direct lines of communication and self-directed work groups, and use of advanced material flow concepts including kan-ban cards (*Frankfurter Allgemeine Zeitung*, 18 August 1993). More recently, Opel management achieved agreement to have separate company-level negotiations with IG Metall. At Opel, pay rises will be kept to two-thirds of the industry-wide settlement if the pay rise is above 2 per cent. Furthermore, there will be joint efforts to reduce absenteeism, and the traditional thirteenth month of income will be subject to productivity increases. Opel is also adopting more flexible working arrangements. At a new part in the Kaiserslautern engine operations the company has agreed with the factory committee the introduction of a Saturday shift, which will be evened out by time off during the week and not by additional payment—i.e. it will in effect be cost free. Through these measures Opel, just like BMW before, have now gained the capacity to increase the running times of their machines.

In summary, corporate management cleverly employed new investment decisions and left the plant level actors in different national localities little choice but to embrace radical change. Learning was accelerated because of the force exerted through the internalization of competitive markets thus *disrupting* existing institutional settlements. In all the cases described, our data were such that workers' responses were only discernible through the actions of worker representatives. However, to what extent those actions are in fact *representative* of workers' attitudes and opinions is subject to an ongoing, but separate debate (e.g. Edwards *et al.* 1995).

5. DISCUSSION

The preceding discussion has shown that there have been a range of contingent impediments to the adoption of Japanese style modes of contracting along hierarchically structured supply chains and concomitant modes of US-style internalized 'competitive tendering'. These impediments include the constraints imposed by the high financial costs of conversion to IT-based modes of communication and collaboration and the technological capabilities of participant organizations. Furthermore, there can be little doubt that in Anglo-Saxon countries—where the rhetoric of 're-engineering' solutions has been greatest among corporate executives—the adaptation of shop-floor behaviour and, perhaps more importantly, of line managers' attitudes has been part of a long learning process. By the end of the 1980s, and almost a decade behind British and American firms, major auto assembly and component firms in Germany began a concerted campaign to introduce new forms of organizational control, chiefly by abandoning long-established domestic supplier relations (Mueller and Loveridge 1995). Their reasons have been related to an apparent break-down in the confidence held by assemblers in their major collaborators among sub-assembly providers and a growing propensity to place new design development and production contracts with French, British, or US firms.

Politically this process of corporate restructuring has been difficult to accomplish in the highly regulated framework of trade and employers associations in which German assemblers have (in some aspects by statutory law) to work. Large British and US firms have, in the past, generally been able to control their fragmented supply chains through frequent market-based actions for short-term contracts. Over the last two decades this mode of market control has shifted to an attempt to impose an external hierarchy for loose-tight relations. Paradoxically this appears to have brought about a somewhat more balanced system of leverage within supply chains in these countries but only at the level of first-tier suppliers. For many small suppliers, for example of metal and plastic stampings and extrusions, their commercial viability still depends on flexible specialization, but now this can often only be achieved through heavy up-front investment in automated machinery.

These, sometimes apparently contradictory, trends in what have often been seen as polar ideal types of NBSs, i.e. Germany and USA/UK, appear to be symptomatic of an *ongoing process of rationalization within a continuously globalizing sector*. With their ability to orchestrate their supply-chain relationships with suppliers and distributors, MNCs in the automobile sector have acquired the ability to impose standards of quality, operational predictability, and costs to a degree that was formerly not possible either within the arms-length, market-based, relations normal in Anglo-Saxon countries or within the bureaucratically regulated arenas of sectoral and federal structures of German associations. This may be illustrated by the prominence among senior managers that has been recently acquired by new systems engineers such as Lopez, whose success has consisted in the imposition of practices and standards on suppliers, first from his position at GM then at Volkswagen. At the same time change that is sought within both suppliers' organizations as well as that of its MNC orchestrators consists of moving towards an information-rich network of trust-based whilst simultaneously competitive relations.

In this vein, the 'Theory of Strategic Negotiations' of Walton *et al.* (1994) became pertinent to our analysis. These authors suggest that significant differences exist between the routes taken by firms in different *industries* in introducing change in the workplace. Where equipment is very expensive and capital utilization is crucial, *fostering* (aimed at maximizing commitment by the workforce) might yield most benefits in so far as it succeeds in making the workforce work harder and smarter (e.g. pulp and paper manufacturing). Where payroll and other staff costs are very significant, *forcing* strategies (aimed at achieving changes in employment conditions) might be more appropriate, in so far as they would change work organization and costs (e.g. railroads). In the intermediate cases (e.g. auto parts) both fostering and forcing might achieve benefits. What is suggested by our research, and by the cases briefly described above, is that the work processes in auto components firms have been highly fractionated, in the German case by the federally regulated hierarchy of formal vocations, in the Anglo-Saxon case by the largely informal workings of the internal market. Restructuring both the internal and external couplings in the value chain between firms supplying the automobile assembler has demanded the use of 'force' or market coercion. By this means the major MNC seeks to create a more rational *external* and *internal* hierarchy of relationships across the globe. At the same time the appropriation of the idiosyncratic knowledge of those contributing value to the design and development of innovative products within a fiercely competitive global market has necessitated a *fostering* of high commitment to this objective at every stage and level of the supply chain. Thus the emergent survival strategy adopted by automobile manufacturers has aspects of both forcing and fostering (F&F) in the shaping of a new architecture of relationships.

As we have indicated in our analysis the F&F strategy is one whose success in converting the prevailing cultures of local plants or firms is by no means ensured. However, the pressures of oligopolistic competition across the globe does provide a threatening, or as Child (1972) described it, 'illiberal', environment in which a shared perception of contingencies facing component suppliers across disparate national cultures is likely to trigger similar responses. This being so one might anticipate some convergence in the patterns or new structures of operating and doing business within this sector. Thus the institutionalized structures of industrial relations in each country are being put under great strain, in part because of the anxieties of the national leaders themselves to retain the patronage of MNCs, whether domestic or foreign based. At the same time the internal restructuring of tasks and skills is being brought about by F&F strategies.[3]

However, the Walton *et al.* study (1994) seems to warn against universalistic judgement and suggests instead that MNCs' actions must be set against the operating contingencies that apply within each sector in which each company, division, or subsidiary carries on its business. In selecting the auto components sector the authors were aware of the conditions that have made the motor vehicle industry the archetypical model for the mass marketing of consumer durables and, more particularly, made the possession of a motor car the twentieth-century cultural symbol of the economically emancipated citizen of developing countries. The important multiplier effects on employment and acceleration of associated investment have made motor manufacture a keystone in the national economic strategies being pursued by the governments of many newly developing countries (NICs). As a consequence the major assemblers have been both threatened by ever increased competition from new entrants from NICs whilst being wooed as partners by the latter. In these conditions F&F strategies have not only been pursued in favourable labour market conditions by 'opportunistic' Anglo-Saxon employers, but also seen by German employers to be of such advantage as to erode their commitment to well-established regional and federal corporate structures of governance.

On the basis of this evidence we therefore suggest that the assumption that 'prevailing' institutional configurations, described as national business systems, are uniquely immutable and unidirectional in their effect, should be treated with a measure of scepticism. It is likely that global market conditions within sectors, both emergent and mature, will affect the manner in which socio-political factors shape the success of such systems and the MNCs that arise within them. What is perhaps required is that the interaction between the MNC and the key institutions isolated by NBS/NIS theorists should be studied in greater depth in its local context and across a range of sectors as well as a number of levels of corporate activity. The political and methodological difficulties involved in such research are evident to all who have attempted it.

6. CONCLUSIONS

There has recently been a revival of the attempt to explain the economic success of firms trading across national boundaries in terms that ascribe

---

[3] Pressure is therefore placed on higher education in Western nations to work with firms in modifying their curricula to reflect the latter's need for specific 'competency' based training. (In recent academic research authors have tended to imply that the closer a nation's education system comes to meeting the specific needs of *particular* large employers the more 'effective' is the education provided.)

causal inference to the national institutions of their country of origin. While not discounting the shaping effects of national institutions this chapter has attempted to assert the power of sectoral perceived contingencies in bringing about a global convergence in strategies currently being pursued by firms in the automobile industry, and in particular by final assemblers of motor vehicles *vis-à-vis* component suppliers and shop-floor employees. The contingent-related analysis of strategies—labelled as 'forcing' and 'fostering'—has been adopted from the work of Walton *et al.* (1994) to describe the elements that go towards shaping the attempts to rationalize the value chain in the latter sector.

Taken together the two trends might appear contradictory. What is suggested in this chapter is that the two strategies may be seen as being simultaneously employed by MNCs. Trading partners, both internal (i.e. employees) and external (i.e. subcontractors) are *simultaneously* offered benefits for increased commitment, including influence in operational implementation (empowerment). At the same time they are being coerced through the willingness of national stakeholders i.e. trade unions, to compete for the location of these benefits within their own territories (Mueller 1991; Mueller and Purcell 1992). Hence institutionalized constraints that have shaped employer–employee relations within each separate nation state can be seen to be threatened by the ability of the MNC to orchestrate such pressures. It is suggested that both the competitive pressures to apply such strategies and the leverage that they afford to the MNC are significantly greater in the automobile industry than elsewhere. It remains true that forcing and fostering appears to be widely used by the MNCs in a manner that coopts national institutions to projects that are likely to undermine their own efficacy and, perhaps ultimately, lead to their own demise.

REFERENCES

Altmann, N., Kohler, C., and Meil, P. (1992), *Technology and Work in German Industry* (London: Routledge).

Child, J. (1972), 'Organization Structure, Environment and Performance: The Role ot Strategic Choice', *Sociology*, 6: 1–22.

Dore, R. (1987), *Taking Japan Seriously* (Stanford,Calif.: Stanford University Press).

Edwards, P., Collinson, D., and Della Rocca, G. (1995), 'Workplace Resistance in Western Europe: A Preliminary Overview and a Research Agenda', *European Journal of Industrial Relations*, 1/3: 283–316.

Elger, T., and Fairbrother, P. (1990), 'Inflexible Flexibility', Annual Conference of British Sociological Association, 3 April.

Friedman, H., and Meredeen, S. (1980), *The Dynamics of Industrial Conflict: Lessons from Ford* (London: Croom Helm).

Hamilton, G. (1983), 'Capitalist Industrialisation in East Asia's Four Little Tigers', *Journal of Contemporary Asia*, 13: 35–75.

Hirsch-Kreinsen, H. (1994), 'Die Internationalisierung der Produktion: Wandel von Rationalisierungsstrategien und Konsequenzen für Industriearbeit', *Zeitschrift für Soziologie*, 23/6: 434–46.

Hollingsworth, J. R., Schmitter, P. C., and Streeck, W. (1994) (eds.), *Governing Capitalist Economies: Performance and Control of Economic Sectors* (New York: Oxford University Press).

Johnson, C. (1982), *MITI and the Japanese Miracle: The Growth of Industrial Policy 1925–1975* (Stanford, Calif.: Stanford University Press).

Kristensen, P. H. (1996), 'National Governance and Managerial Prerogatives in the Evolution of Work Systems: England, Germany and Denmark compared', Paper presented to EMOT Theme 1 Workshop 24–8 January 1996, Barcelona.

Lamming, R. (1993), *Beyond Partnership* (London: Prentice Hall).

Levinson, C. (1972), *International Trade Unionism* (London: George Allen & Unwin).

Loveridge, R. (1992), 'Crisis and Continuity: Reviewing the Past to Preview the Future', in S. Srivastva and R. E. Fry and Associates, *Executive and Organizational Continuity: Managing the Paradoxes of Stability and Change* (San Francisco: Jossey-Bass).

——(1993), 'The Evolution of Qualification Networks in Three MNCs', 11th EGOS Colloquium, Wissenschaftszentrum, Berlin.

Marshall, A. (1961), *Principles of Economics*, 9th edn. (London: Macmillan).

Mueller, F. (1991), 'The "New Employee Relations": A Comparative Study in Automobile Engine Plants in Germany, Austria, Britain and Spain'. Unpublished D.Phil Thesis, University of Oxford: Faculty of Social Studies.

——(1996), 'National Stakeholders in the Global Contest for Corporate Investment', *European Journal of Industrial Relations*, 2/3.

——and Loveridge, R. (1995), '"The Second Industrial Divide?": The Role of the Large Firm in the Baden Württemberg Model', *Industrial and Corporate Change*, 4/3: 499–526.

Mueller, F., and Purcell, J. (1992), 'The Europeanisation of Manufacturing and the Decentralisation of Bargaining: Multinational Management Strategies in the European Automobile Industry', *International Journal of Human Resource Management*, 3/1 (Spring), 15–34.

Piore, M. J., and Sabel, C. (1984), *The Second Industrial Divide* (New York: Basic Books).

Porter, M. E. (1990), *The Competitive Advantage of Nations* (New York: Free Press).

Rutherford, T., Imrie, R., and Morris, J. (1988), 'Subcontracting Flexibility?' Cardiff Business School Japanese Management Research Unit Working Paper, No. 5.

Sako, M. (1992), *Prices, Quality and Trust: Inter Firm Relations in Britain and Japan* (Cambridge: Cambridge University Press).

Turnbull, P. (1986), 'The Japanisation of Production and Industrial Relations at Lucas Electrical', *Industrial Relations Journal*, 17/3: 193–206.

——(1988), 'The Limits to Japanisation: Just-in-Time, Labour Relations and the UK Automotive Industry', *New Technology, Work and Employment*, 3/1 (Spring): 7–20.

Vogel, E. F. (1991), *The Four Little Dragons: The Spread of Industrialization in East Asia*, Cambridge, Mass.: Harvard University Press.

Walton, R. E., Cutcher-Gershenfeld, J. E., and McKersie, R. B. (1994), *Strategic Negotiations: A Theory of Change in Labor-Management Relations* (Boston: Harvard Business School Press).

Whitley, R. (1992), 'The Comparative Study of Business Systems in Europe: Issues and Choices', in R. Whitley (ed.), *European Business Systems: Firms and Markets in their National Contexts* (London: Sage).

——(1994*a*), 'The Internationalization of Firms and Markets: Its Significance and Institutional Structures', *Organization*, 1/1: 101–24.

——(1994*b*), 'Dominant Forms of Economic Organization in Market Economies', *Organization Studies*, 15/2: 153–82.

——(1994*c*), *Business Systems in East Asia* (London: Sage) (1st edn. 1992).

Williamson, O. E. (1985), *The Economic Institutions of Capitalism: Firms, Markets, Relational Contracting* (New York: Free Press).

Womack, J. P., Jones, D. T., and Roos, D. (1990), *The Machine that Changed the World* (London: Macmillan).

8

The Transmission of Work Systems
A Comparison of US and Japan Auto's Human Resource Management Practices in Mexico

BARBARA HIBINO

1. INTRODUCTION

A major issue that many multinational firms face in setting up subsidiaries abroad is whether to transfer practices from headquarters 'as is', adapt practices to local circumstances, or alter the practices into a third, hybridized form. In some cases, the firm can transmit globally standardized work systems across institutional contexts, as discussed by Muller and Loveridge in this volume. However, there is also considerable evidence that organizations owned by multinationals cannot easily implement new managerial interventions and forms of organizing work since the local environment can be also highly influential in transfer outcomes.

This chapter attempts to elaborate on how both global and local influences (Prahalad and Doz 1987) explain the transmission of human resource management practices to Mexico. The author examined factories manufacturing car engines in very different national environments. These factories were those of a US company operating in both the USA and Mexico (UA and UM), and of a Japanese company operating in both Japan and Mexico (JA and JM). The study assumed that any differences between the firms, because they were engaged in the same task of engine manufacture, were largely attributable to differences in institutional environments (Bendix 1956). This approach is similar to that of sector theorists who recommend theorization by industry or sector (Lilja *et al.* 1992). Examination of Mexican subsidiaries alongside plants at headquarters could indicate how institutional environments affect work organization by revealing the effect of lifting the institutional environment of headquarters and imposing the same, third Mexican environment.

In both the US and Japanese firms, some aspects of human resource management were transmitted to Mexico and were 'global'. These 'global' practices differed from each other but resembled governance structures in the headquarters environment. For example, the teacher–student relation of the educational system constituted a habitualized social relationship which differed between countries and was reflected in the workplace. In the US, the teacher–student relationship was one that assumed student talent and encouraged independence in action. In Japan, the teacher–student relationship assumed that students needed to be carefully introduced to experiences to develop skill, and encouraged dependence on the corporate system to cultivate such talent. These relationships in the public school system, were reflected in the workplace. Therefore, the teacher–student relationship played a role in the social construction of natural governance systems in the USA and Japan and in their companies. In this chapter, these mirrorings of governance structures at the workplace level are referred to as institutions. One of the main findings of this chapter is that certain aspects of the habitualized social relationship, in particular, the student–teacher relationship, transmitted very well to Mexico. In the Mexican subsidiaries, the employment relation resembled that of the US in the US subsidiary and that of Japan in the Japanese subsidiary.

However, just as there is some evidence that global systems can be implemented despite institutional contexts, there is also evidence that the contrary is true: new managerial interventions and forms of organizing work cannot be simply implemented in organizations owned by multinationals since the local environment is also highly influential in transfer outcomes (Prahalad and Doz 1987). For example, a 'societal effect', that influences work organization differentially across different societies, has been well established (Maurice *et al.* 1980; Rose 1985). It has also been shown that in Europe as well as in many other countries, multiple institutions simultaneously affect work organization and that these simultaneous effects produce 'business systems' that become particular to each country or region (Whitley 1992). As Schienstock has shown in a previous chapter, innovations are not always easily implemented because of such institutional contexts. Lock-in to previous systems may prevent effective adaptation. It has been subsequently theorized by Kristensen in this book that governance structures permeate institutions as well as work organization and regulate economic and social action. These governance structures habituate people to act in a certain way, such that actions become taken for granted and other courses of action are not even considered. Structural factors, such as whether a plant is a greenfield or a brownfield site as Sharpe has shown, also work to influence the formation of governance structures that can vary even within the same production site. The societal effect, business systems, governance systems, and patterns of habituation all work to complicate transmission of workplace practices to different country contexts.

'Global' versus 'local' approaches to explaining transmission are neither mutually exclusive explanations nor mutually contradictory. Both approaches were found to be valid in the data. 'Local' effects were found to predominate in areas of human resource management linked to the system of labour relations, and prevent transmission. 'Global' effects were found to be transferred in areas of human resource management linked to the habitualized student–teacher relationship in the different countries of origin for transfer.

The effect of the system of education on human resource management

The similarity between human resource management in firms and education in public schools has been pointed out by Scott and Meyer (1991), who describe the resemblance as 'striking'. The roots of this relationship are historical and long-standing. In the US, it appears that various sources of diversity have led to difficulty in forging consensus about curriculum and other aspects of education. Because of the lack of consensus, these decisions have been relegated to localities, to school districts within states. Weak central control has led to a diverse offering of curriculum within the US. By contrast, militarism in pre-Second World War Japan and MacArthurism after the war, accustomed the country to centralized control of education and a national curriculum. The effect of centralized control is that in any district in Japan, within the same grade grouping, students are studying the same curriculum at the same time. With centralized control of education, the government held greater responsibility for educational outcomes than in the decentralized system of the US, where educational outcomes were more diverse and difficult to control (Stevenson and Stigler 1992). These appear to be the historical roots for the different governance systems which for the purposes of this chapter, in the US is labelled 'talent' and in Japan is labelled 'experience'.

US Auto (UA) and US education can be characterized as being driven by a 'talent' model of education. The 'talent' model assumed that individuals are 'talented' and did not need much guidance, but only an opportunity to flourish. Instruction emphasized theory. Practice was left to 'talented' individuals to figure out applications on their own. Education and human resource management were considered low-status activities because they were really ancillary functions for 'talented' individuals. As at UA where human resource management was decentralized to each individual plant, the organization of US education was decentralized so that 'talented' individual districts could fashion curriculum based on their own needs. Each school district was responsible for fashioning its own curriculum, and teachers within each district were responsible for participating on curriculum selection committees. As a consequence of decentralization, curriculum was subject to much innovation. It was cut up in distinct units and varied from school district to school district much like the curriculum at UA which varied from plant to plant (Stevenson and Stigler 1992).

The 'talent' system was reinforced by the system of teacher training and job placement, which paralleled the placement of line managers at UA. Teachers often learned their jobs on their own through trial and error rather than by receiving guidance. Job placement was primarily through seniority. More senior teachers had a greater say in placement than less senior teachers. It should be noted that, this did not indicate an experience governance system, because an experience system would determine placement based on how it would affect skill development rather than using experience solely as a queuing system. As a consequence, there has tended to be a greater concentration of more experienced teachers in the more desirable suburban schools rather than urban schools. In parallel, seniority was influential in the concentration of more talented employees in newly established plants. Instruction was potentially uneven in US public education (Stevenson and Stigler 1992) as it was on the factory floor at UA. The greater diversity of the student body also created greater problems in instruction in the US, reinforcing the idea that the teacher's and line manager's role was to present material and leave interpretation up to students/workers.

Likewise at UA, there was an emphasis on theory; much innovation in curriculum; teachers (line managers) learned their work on their own; and the pressures of decentralization reinforced 'talent' assumptions. Educational models apparently affected these aspects of human resource management at UA as UA employees often reiterated the beliefs in decentralization and individual autonomy present in the educational system in its organization, the structure of curriculum, and pedagogical assumptions. The student–teacher relationship habitualized in schools appeared to affect corporate curriculum, pedagogy, and on-the-job training.

Similarly, the organization of Japanese education resembled the 'experience' model as at JA. In the 'experience' model, it was assumed that learning was based on guidance from a more informed, more experienced party, and that individuals were helpless without such informed guidance. In an 'experience' system, the burden for learning was placed on the teacher because the teacher was considered the more experienced party whose instruction would lead students along. To illustrate the implications of this idea, in Japan, national universities faculty meetings often focus on the students who are failing and discuss faculty actions to ensure that students can pass examinations. In the US, by contrast, faculty meetings are rarely over student performance—meetings are more likely to deal with programmes, curriculum, and budgetary issues (Stevenson and Stigler 1992).

As a result, curriculum formation was taken very seriously in Japan. Curriculum was centralized and standardized into a national curriculum and national certification system. It was organized in subjects that were repeated over time as a 'well developed plot' (Hibino 1993; Rohlen 1994). This curriculum assumed that gaining experience in problem-solving was key, and therefore, emphasized practice. Because the expectation was that learning takes time, the emphasis was also on effort, not ability (Rohlen 1994).

The 'experience' governance structure was also at work in teacher training and resembled training for production employees at JA. Training was primarily through job placement and rotation. Job placement was designed to encourage teachers to learn how to teach a range of subjects, and teacher placement was controlled for optimal distribution across school districts. The district's intent was to make sure that more and less experienced teachers were evenly distributed across schools. Less experienced teachers were carefully introduced to teaching by more 'experienced' teachers. Japanese teachers spent less time in the classroom than US teachers, but had more time to prepare for lessons, learn from other teachers, and take steps to show concern with students by writing notes to the families involved (Stevenson and Stigler 1992). The lines between personal and professional lives of teachers were blurred since teachers were expected to serve as moral guides and often made visits to student's homes (LeTendre 1994) in much the same way as managers at JA.

JA's human resource management system mirrored Japanese education. JA's structure of human resource management emphasized standard operations (analogous to a national curriculum); its training of line managers stressed years of experience and guidance by those more senior (analogous to teacher training); its system of job placement was based on similar system-wide considerations; and it placed a focus on repetition and problem solving.

The resemblance between business human resource management in companies and public education in schools appears to be a natural outcome of the extensive contact between the two sectors, and of the long process of habitualization occurring in public schools. Employees naturally bring with them concepts of education to human resource management because exposure habitualizes them to teaching methods so that employees were teaching in much the same way they were taught. Public education habitualized employees to a particular type of the student–teacher relation and these relations are re-evoked in new settings.

This treatment of public education augments that of the societal effects theorists, which considers public education as influencing organizational shape through the formation of 'professions' that then influence the acquisition of competence within the firms, and organizational shape (Maurice *et al.* 1980). The data in my study indicate that public education also affected the actual practice of human resource management in ways that are important. Public education appeared to affect human resource management in the firm by habitualizing employees to ways of organizing curriculum and pedagogy.

When both firms transferred those aspects of human resource management with parallels to education—organization of curriculum (centralization, standards, coherence, amount of innovation), and pedagogical methods used in training (for line managers and for employees), the general flavour of human resource management transmitted to Mexico. For example, in Japan Auto's Mexican subsidiary, employees experienced some of the same centralized curriculum as in Japan, and were taught using the same pedagogical methods of 'show student—have student demonstrate skill—correct student' sequence. In US Auto's Mexican subsidiary, employees experienced a decentralized curriculum as in the US, and were taught their jobs as in the US, through a 'buddy' system that paired inexperienced with experienced employees for a short period of time.

The effects of labour relations systems on human resource management

National labour relations systems also affected human resource management practices because they caused the firms to face different constraints. The firms faced differing levels of flexibility in their ability to change practice and to determine how practices are carried out. In the Japanese automobile industry, unions were organized by each company and changes in work rules required the approval of the company unit. Changes in the Japanese system were relatively more easily made than in the US automobile industry, where unions were organized by industry and changes required the consent of a much larger group, of employees from multiple companies in the industry.

These differing levels of flexibility were actively manifested in the actual work sites. At UA, hiring was restricted to a pool of employees laid off from other plants. Placement was also restricted since the main criterion for placement was seniority, or years of experience with the company: the greater the seniority, the greater the voice of an employee in placement. This system was distinct from the 'experience' governance system which fashioned placement but around the corporation's need for certain kinds of experience. UA also could not control the training of blue-collar employees beyond orientation, nor could the company test employees. The system of pay and promotion for blue-collar employees was also regulated by agreements with the union. Employees were paid hourly and received higher pay when moving from assembly to machining, and from machining to the skilled trades areas, forestalling development of area-specific skill.

UA had more control of human resource management of white-collar employees, for whom the company faced fewer restrictions on hiring, firing, training, placement, job rotations, and pay. Hiring was largely through interviews; job placement was flexible and depended on the coincidence of opportunity and employee experience; training was done on an 'as needed' basis. However, because of the relatively freer labour market in the US, employees could 'job hop' and easily find positions in other firms. As a result, the company had little control over employee career paths and over the longer-term development of human resources within the firm. UA's relative lack of control over human resource management complemented the 'talent' system because the company was required to rely on the employees as given, because relatively little control over employee development was possible. Orientation training was intensive, but after orientation employees regulated training largely on their own.

At JA, the enterprise union system of labour relations allowed the company greater control over the career paths and long-term development of human resources for both full-time blue- and white-collar employees. These employees were an elite group, comprising as little as one-third of the labour force (Taira 1982). Selection of this elite was thorough, and included detective work on employee candidates (Taira 1982). Part-time employees aspired to full-time status and worked hard to prove themselves worthy of selection. With benefits such as pension plans and sick pay that are typically accorded to white-collar employees, the system for blue-collar employees has been called 'welfare corporatism' by Dore (1973).

Hiring was company controlled since blue-collar employees were hired on the basis of performance on tests; and white-collar employees were hired on the basis of interviews and background checks. The company also had relatively greater control over job definitions since changes in job definitions were easily made. Company control was also exercised over job placement since employees had little say in job placement. In some cases, employees could be 'loaned' to other companies, while in others, employees were required to be stationed overseas and could be separated from family for years. White-collar employees with greater promise were rotated among critical functions (Pucik 1988). Rotation was also used to enhance communication within and across departments (Tachiki 1992). Promotion requirements were also relatively easily changed since company/union agreements could specify the skills in employees needed for promotion, and formulate a grading system for employees' performance (Inagami 1988). At JA, these were so flexible that grading was revised every year to determine the progress in employee skill development, their yearly increments in salary, and promotion to higher job grades (Koike 1989; Tachiki 1992; Ogawa 1989). Thus pay was also under company control and linked with performance. Human resource management in Japan was company controlled.

The enterprise union system of JA complemented the 'experience' governance system because it unified blue- and white-collar employees in career ladders based on experience. Both were placed on the job with someone more senior than them who oversaw their work. The chain of supervision in the company was based primarily on experience since experience was the first criterion used for consideration to promotion. Control over job definitions was also central for the experience model to be workable, since an experience model to some extent required that the delineations between various kinds of work remain ambiguous so that responsibilities could be slowly handed over to more junior employees as they grew in capability. Another requirement of the 'experience' model was that employees needed to be motivated to follow the company programme because placement was in the hands of the company and often meant subordinating individual wishes for placement.

The company was able to form incentives because income was flexible, based on a livelihood wage, age, experience, company, group performance, individual performance, and family circumstances (Koike 1990; MacDuffie and Pil 1994; Takezawa and Whitehill 1983; Tachiki 1992; Cole 1971). Workers also had greater incentives to remain with the company because pensions grew large over time, building an attachment to the company (Cole 1971). The 'experience' model was also possible in a context of long-term employment (until age 55) in which more senior employees' own jobs were not threatened while training other employees. Decisions were made jointly and frequently with the union about compensation and benefits, the structure of the career ladder, changes in job content, training requirements, and production strategy (plant openings and closings) (Inagami 1983; MacDuffie 1993).

The transfer to Mexico of HR practices associated with labour relations

In Mexico, this flexibility changed because some of the 'constraints' faced at home would be lifted and new 'constraints' could be placed because of the new, Mexican labour environment. However, the Mexican environment did not present the same kind of difference to both companies because the two companies approached Mexico from different flexibility starting-points. As a result, the adaptations that the companies needed in Mexico were relatively different. For example, for UA, Mexico was relatively more flexible, while for JA, the same environment may be relatively more inflexible. To emphasize this point, relative flexibility implies that the salient aspect of institutions is not their flexibilities in and of themselves, but their flexibilities in relation to the environment of transfer. To understand transmission of workplace level institutions, the interface between two institutional environments—the source and the receiving end—needed to be examined.

In Mexico, both sites were influenced by the 'government' union (Meyer and Sherman 1983) with a historically symbiotic relationship between the two sectors: the government depended on the unions to rally political support and to control wages; in turn, the government allotted government positions to the officials of the National Confederation of Mexican Workers (CTM), supported its activities through subsidies, and encouraged its organization in the country (Meyer and Sherman 1983). Government involvement also enabled the unions to have a larger voice in policy while the unions also provided mechanisms for government control over labour (Meyer and Sherman 1983).

The Mexican government union system presented relatively different situations for the two companies in terms of flexibility and adaptations needed for practices to be viable in Mexico. The Mexican government union system was more flexible than the US industrial union system since it gave the company control over classroom training, on-the-job training, testing, placement, rotation, and formation of career ladders. The Mexican hourly rate system was also more similar to the hourly system in the USA, and the turnover rate caused UM to have a system of placement and career paths that was much like that in the US.

On the other hand, it was more inflexible than the Japanese enterprise union system since it controlled selection, promotion, and discipline and required hourly pay. In Japan, these aspects of human resource management—especially pay—were under company control and used to encourage employees to develop skill. At the time of the interviews, Mexico was in a period of economic growth with a government-imposed wage freeze, causing high turnover at both sites. It caused JM to have to contend with a constant churning in personnel that made it difficult to control placement and career paths unlike circumstances faced in JA. However, as in Japan, Mexico allowed some degree of alteration of the career ladder.

From UM's perspective, this new control over human resource management gave plant management a new lease on life in terms of personnel management (Shaiken and Browne 1991). UA managers described Mexican workers as having undergone a tougher selection process, selecting workers that were younger, hardworking and motivated, and with better formal educational backgrounds. The US counterparts were described as more experienced and skilled. The Mexican management had a newfound control in assigning workers to tasks (Shaiken and Browne 1991) enabling them to experiment with personnel rotation systems, systems of testing before promotion, and a system of promotion that allowed blue-collar employees to have a higher ladder to climb. These measures apparently placed a greater emphasis on skill development and a higher level of motivation among blue-collar employees despite facing similar pay systems.

From JM's perspective, the same Mexican workforce was relatively less flexible. The lower level of average education (primary school), and the more varied educational experiences of engineers, was said to hamper communication. An area manager in Japan related that at one point, the company had tried to transfer more automated systems for checking engine quality, but encountered difficulties in training employees on repair of this machinery. As a result, the company found it much easier to use less automated systems. From JM's perspective, the workers were relatively less motivated than in Japan. Motivation was a major problem because of the routinized nature of manufacturing work, and compensation by hourly pay. The hourly pay system apparently caused similar problems for JM as UA faced in the USA.

Another pattern was ascertained in the data. In the case of every work practice examined, for JM the Mexican environment was either similar in flexibility to Japan, or more restrictive. By contrast, for UA, Mexico was in all cases, similar in flexibility to the USA or less restrictive. This finding is consistent with other studies comparing US and Japanese transfer to other countries. These studies have also found transfer for Japanese companies to be more difficult than for US companies (Putti and Chong 1985; Westney 1987; Kopp 1994). This study comes to the same conclusion, but through a different route of depicting the systems of labour relations in terms of flexibilities between headquarters and subsidiary environments.

Influences on human resource management practices in Mexico, then, are neither purely 'global', i.e. faithful transmissions of headquarters; nor purely 'local' i.e. completely altered by the environment. Rather, they are a combination of both global and local influences which, in the cases examined, fall into clear patterns. Those human resource management practices associated with the teacher–student relation of the educational system transferred with fidelity. Those practices associated with the system of labour relations altered. The alterations also indicated patterns, depending on the flexibility of the Mexican environment in relation to headquarters environments.

With respect to public education, future studies can examine if, in addition to professionalization, public education affects the actual practice of human resource management by habituating employees to certain ways of organizing curriculum, implementing pedagogy, and emphasizing different training vehicles—on-the-job or in classrooms. It can also examine if HR practices related to public education are successfully transferred; and HR practices related to labor relations are altered in accordance with the patterns discovered of relative institutional flexibility.

This research could also be extended in directions suggested by the 'national business recipes' school of thought which establishes in greater detail the linkages of organizational variation to 'nationally specific features of economic action' (Whitley 1992); as well as to more sociologically based institutions, including the role of the state, financial system, training, business associations with education and system of industrial relations

(Kristensen 1996). Future research can broaden the scope of external, society-based institutions examined that reinforce and reflect internal, company-based institutions of 'talent' and 'experience' found at US and Japan Auto.

  Further investigations can additionally examine how companies may view different regions as environments that offer different bundles of HR flexibility. Both US and Japanese firms have been engaged in this kind of location bargaining strategy. In some cases, Japanese firms have been known to relocate entire production complexes because of labour strife, e.g. the movement of Nissan's production complex from Cuernavaca to Aguascalientes. In other cases, they have chosen location, particularly in the US, based on the absence of unions or with promises to reshape labour relations in a way that is more flexible than is typical in the USA (Florida and Kenney 1991). Ford, for example, has played off location in Spain for location in the UK because of the promise of more flexible labour contracts than previously possible in the UK. Flexibility in this context is not a constant, because corporations can shape their environments. In Mexico as well, the system had been made more flexible over time due to pressures from the private sector, effected particularly during economic downturns (Carillo, undated). The growing dominance of the corporation as an institution is a force that will need to be contended with internationally and will continue to affect transitions in European work systems, organization, and management as it will do so also in the rest of the world.

REFERENCES

Bendix, R. (1956), *Work and Authority in Industry* (New York: Wiley).
Carillo, J. V. (undated), 'The Restructuring of the Car Industry in Mexico', *Working Papers of the Mexican Center, Institute of Latin American Studies*, 90-05 (Austin: University of Texas at Austin).
Cole, R. (1971), *The Japanese Blue Collar* (Berkeley: University of California Press).
Dore, R. (1973), *British Factory, Japanese Factory: The Origins of National Diversity in Industrial Relations* (Berkeley: University of California Press).
Florida, R., and Kenney, M. (1991), 'Transplanted Organizations: The Transfer of Japanese Industrial Organization to the US', *American Sociological Review*, 56/3: 381–98.
Hibino, B. (1993), 'The Making of Engineers at Ford-Romeo and Nissan Yokohama' *International Journal of Engineering Education*, 9/1: 104–12.
Inagami, T. (1983), 'Labor-Management Communication at the Workshop Level', *Japanese Industrial Relations Series*, 11 (Tokyo: Japan Institute of Labor).
——(1988), 'Japanese Workplace Industrial Relations', in *Japanese Industrial Relations Series Number 14* (Tokyo).

Koike, K. (1989), 'Human Resource Development on the Shop Floor in Contemporary Japan', paper delivered in a conference held by the International Labor Organization on Japanese Employment in the Context of a Changing Economy and Society (Paris).

——(1990), *Understanding Industrial Relations in Modern Japan* (Hong Kong: Macmillan).

Kopp, R. (1994), 'International Human Resource Policies and Practices in Japanese, European, and United States Multinationals', *Human Resource Management*, 33/4: 581–99.

Kristensen, P. (1996), 'Variations in the Nature of the Firm in Europe', in R. Whitley and P. Kristensen (eds.), *The Changing European Firm: Limits to Convergence* (London: Routledge).

LeTendre, G. (1994), 'Nudge them on: Teaching, Hierarchy and Social Organization in Japanese Middle Schools', in T. Rohlen and G. LeTendre (eds.), *Learning and Teaching in Japan* (Berkeley: University of California Press).

Lilja, K., Rasanen, K., and Taino, R. (1992), 'A Dominant Business Recipe: The Forest Sector in Finland', in R. Whitley (ed.), *European Business Systems: Firms and Markets in their National Contexts* (London: Sage Publications).

MacDuffie, J. (1993), 'Human Resource Bundles and Manufacturing Performance: Flexible Production Systems in the World Auto Industry', draft, Aug. (Pittsburgh).

——and Pil, F. (1994), 'Transferring Japanese Human Resource Practices: Japanese Auto Plants in Japan and the U.S.', draft, Jan. (San Francisco).

Maurice, M., Sorge, A., and Warner, M. (1980), 'Societal Differences in Organizing Manufacturing Units: A Comparison of France, West Germany, and Great Britain', *Organization Studies*, 1: 59–86.

Meyer, M., and Sherman, W. (1983), *The Course of Mexican History* (2nd edn.) (Oxford: Oxford University Press).

Ogawa, E. (1989), *Modern Production Management* (Tokyo: Asian Productivity Organization).

Prahalad, C., and Doz, Y. (1987), *The Multinational Mission: Balancing Local Demands and Global Vision* (New York: St Martin's Press).

Pucik, V. (1988), 'Managerial Career Progression in Large Japanese Manufacturing Firms', *Research in Personnel and Human Resource Management* (Greenwich, Conn.: JAI Press).

Putti, J., and Chong, T. (1985), 'American and Japanese Management Practices in their Singapore Subsidiaries', *Asia Pacific Journal of Management*, 2/2: 76–94.

Rohlen, T. (1994), *Learning and Teaching: A Japanese Landscape* (Berkeley: University of California Press).

Rose, M. (1985), 'Universalism, Culturalism and the Aix Group: Promise and Problems of a Societal Approach to Economic Institutions', *European Sociological Review*, 1/1: 65–83.

Scott, W., and Meyer, J. (1991), 'The Rise of Training Programs in Firms and Agencies: An Institutional Approach', *Research in Organizational Behavior*, 13: 297–326.

Shaiken, H., and Browne, H. (1991), 'Japanese Work Organization in Mexico', in G. Szekely (ed.), *Manufacturing Across Borders: Japan, the US and Mexico* (Center for US–Mexican Studies, San Diego).

Stevenson, H., and Stigler, J. (1992), *The Learning Gap* (New York: Summit Books).
Tachiki, D. (1992), 'Total Quality Control: The Japanese Approach to Continuous Product Improvement', paper delivered at the Kvalitetsdagane I conference (Stavanger, Norway).
Taira, K. (1982), 'Labor Productivity and Industrial Relations in the U.S. and Japan', Proceedings of the 35th Annual Industrial Relations Research Association Meeting (New York).
Takezawa, S., and Whitehill, A. (1983), *Work Ways: Japan and America* (Tokyo: Japan Institute of Labor).
Westney, D. (1993), 'Institutional Theory and the Multinational Corporation', in *Organizational Theory and the Multinational Corporation* (New York: St Martin's Press).
——(1987), *Imitation and Innovation: The Transfer of Western Organizational Practices to Meiji Japan* (Cambridge, Mass.: Harvard University Press).
Whitley, R. (1992) (ed.), *European Business Systems: Firms and Markets in their National Contexts* (London: Sage).

9

Compromise Solutions:
A Japanese Multinational Comes to the UK[1]

DIANA ROSEMARY SHARPE

I. INTRODUCTION

A number of recent studies examine the ways in which internationalizing organizations' evolving management practices in foreign subsidiaries are shaped by the local environments in which they operate (see for example Hibino in this volume, Botti 1995; Kristensen 1994; and Graham 1993). Kristensen (1996 and in this volume) suggests that whilst global pressures may provide similar challenges to organizations in different countries, how organizations deal with them depends on the social and institutional frameworks in which they developed and operate. Detailed case-studies provide a means to examine such events through in-depth studies (see for example Burawoy 1979; Gottfried and Graham 1993; Kleinberg 1994; Delbridge 1995; Botti 1995) of the processes taking place in specific contexts.

Drawing on research conducted in two British subsidiaries of a Japanese multinational over a period of fifteen months this chapter analyses the tensions that emerged in attempts to implement change on one shop-floor on a site previously under British ownership but then bought by a Japanese parent. This is an unusual research case as most studies of Japanese shop-floor practices have focused on greenfield sites and have analysed the nature of systems being transferred from the parent organization rather than the nature of processes on the shop-floor being influenced by and shaping management practices. By working on the shop-floor and adopting an ethnographic approach, it has been possible to focus on the implementation of management practices and social interaction on the shop-floor in

[1] The author would like to thank Richard Whitley for his supervision of the doctoral research on which this chapter is based. His support and guidance during the research was much appreciated. The research was made possible by a scholarship kindly provided by Manchester Business School. The author is also grateful for the helpful comments provided by participants in a workshop on 'Dominant Institutions, Governance Structures and Work Systems' in the European Science Foundation programme on European Management and Organizations in Transition held in Barcelona, 25–7 Jan. 1996.

a way that has not been accessible through studies using interviews and questionnaires.

The chapter analyses three interconnected management initiatives on the shop-floor: (1) a change in authority relations on the shop-floor, (2) a change in the nature of the job grade structure, (3) the push towards multi-tasking and increased flexibility of workers across jobs.

2. THE CASE ORGANIZATION: HISTORICAL BACKGROUND TO THE STUDY

Hano Japan, a leading manufacturer in the car industry, bought out a local UK manufacturer in the industry in the 1980s as part of its strategy to serve its major Japanese customers in Europe. In the early 1990s this organization, Maynard, became part of an international joint venture between the Japanese parent and a European multinational which was also a leading player in the industry. The Japanese parent organization maintained a majority shareholding in Maynard. Further to the joint venture agreement a second UK leg to the venture, Machine Co., was established on a green-field site. A majority shareholding was also held in Machine Co. by the Japanese parent organization.

The British organization renamed Maynard had a long history. One of its two manufacturing activities dates back to the early 1920s, the other to the 1950s. The only change made on the Maynard board of directors following the acquisition was that a Japanese chairman was appointed. The management style of Hano Japan following the purchase was characterized by a consultative and approving role rather than a directive one. This was largely seen to be due to the fact that most of Maynard's business was with non-Japanese customers. A British director in the organization suggested that the Japanese parent company did not want to become involved in the historical business of Maynard. Another local director suggested that when Hano Japan bought Maynard their idea seemed to be that the company would run itself:

They could bolt a little on the end that would make products for the Japanese customers that they would be involved in maintaining and supporting and it would just go along like that.

The timing of the acquisition, however, was bad. The market had declined and sales of the organization reflected this, leading to the introduction of more Hano Japan expatriates shortly after the acquisition. The Maynard board of directors therefore changed composition during the first couple of years of Japanese ownership from being composed of five British directors to having five Japanese directors, one director from the minority European investment in the venture, and five British directors. A further five Japanese expatriates were brought into the organization including a senior design manager and four co-ordinators in the areas of manufacturing, production engineering, maintenance, and company planning. Each co-ordinator's role was to work alongside the local managers in a training and advisory capacity during the implementation of new management systems and practices in the organization. Approximately 1,000 people were employed across the two sites. The larger site, on which this chapter is based, employed over 850 people. At the time of the study the directors in the organization were facing pressure from the parent organization in Japan to move the organization into the black.

The factory studied had three sections. The press shop was the first section of the factory to be built and dates back to the 1950s. Some of the workers in the press shop had worked there for over twenty years. As part of an ethnographic study of control systems and work cultures, I spent four months working as a general operator in the press shop.

The press shop supplies parts to the rest of the factory, which is involved in the manufacture and assembly of car components. Eighty-two people were employed in the press shop across three shifts. Of these ten were considered as 'staff' and the remaining as 'hourly paid workers'. 'Staff' were generally defined by everyone in the organization as those who were 'salaried', not hourly paid. On the shop-floor the teamleader, section leader, and cell manager were also salaried 'staff'. Across the three shifts that operated in the press shop there were approximately sixty-seven men and five women hourly paid workers. The predominance of men amongst the hourly paid workers in the press shop was replicated amongst the staff positions also. There were no women acting as teamleaders, section leaders, or cell managers. At the time of the study there was no woman on any grade above the lowest grade, Grade III. The press shop can be considered to be a traditionally male-dominated shop in British factories. Many workers in the press shop had worked there since the 1970s and had worked in an engineering, textiles, or mining environment in previous jobs. The conventions and traditions of the press shop have influenced workers' current response to change initiatives by the management as can be seen through the examples of work group responses to changing authority relations, changes in the grade structure, and multi-tasking.

3. CHANGING AUTHORITY RELATIONS: THE TEAMLEADER

The quiet authority, unassertive leadership, and acceptance of hierarchy which has been seen as characteristic of Japanese organizations (see for example Dore 1994) was echoed amongst the Japanese expatriates in the two sites studied. This contrasted greatly with the authority relations between the British employees in Maynard where relations between the British shop-floor workers and British managers were often confrontational. The organization rearranged work roles and authority relations shortly after the purchase by the Japanese parent. There was a decision to move away from the traditional structure typical of many engineering shop-floors in the UK (see Figure 9.1) to one providing more emphasis on the management of work teams on the shop floor.

The previous authority hierarchy in the press shop consisted of superintendents, supervisors, and hourly paid workers. The superintendents reported to the factory production manager and were responsible for all activities in the factory across one shift. The factory ran on a three-shift system. One of the problems experienced with this structure was that there was little continuity across shifts in terms of management practices. Superintendents basically sought to manage their own shift and had little communication with or feedback from their counterparts on other shifts. Supervisors would head a section of the factory shop-floor, for example the press shop, typically across one shift. The structure provided a comparatively wide span of control over the hourly paid workers with around twenty to twenty-five hourly paid workers typically reporting to one supervisor.

In the new structure shown in Figure 9.2 the most significant change in formal authority relations to take place was the introduction of the teamleader position. A teamleader was intended to have ideally between seven and eight people working below him or her on one shift. In the press shop the teamleader was, however, responsible for almost twice this number of people. There were three teamleaders in the press shop each responsible for one shift. The teamleaders were the first level of staff in the organiza-

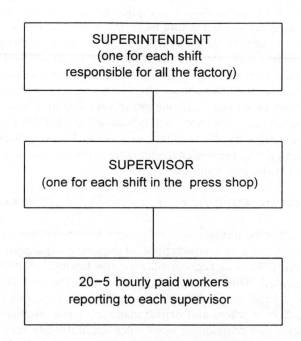

FIG. 9.1.   Authority relations in the press shop prior to 1993

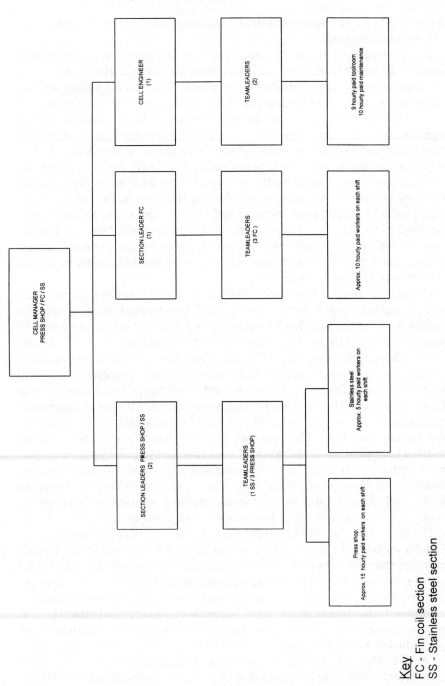

Key
FC - Fin coil section
SS - Stainless steel section

FIG. 9.2. Authority relations in the press shop

tion and played an important role in mediating relations between workers and the management.

The introduction of a teamleader position has provided an interesting situation in which traditional authority lines are revised. The literature on comparative authority relations in Japanese and British organizations (see for example Dore 1973) has portrayed the significant differences in the role of the foreman in UK organizations compared to the teamleader in Japanese organizations. Whereas in Britain the foreman has traditionally been perceived and acts as someone set above the work group, in Japanese organizations the teamleader is perceived and acts very much as a member of the group. This contrast in the nature of shop-floor authority relations was very evident in the press shop following the introduction of the team-leader role. The traditional foreman in British industry was brought up in the hard practical school of manual work. Traditionally 'the old type of foreman neither planned, nor delegated authority, nor trained under-studies, and discipline in his department was often secured largely by threats of dismissal' (Burns Morton 1945).

The span of control was significantly reduced in Maynard with the addi-tion of a third rung of 'staff' between the hourly paid workers and the section leaders. The teamleader's position was the first on the rung of staff positions in production. The teamleaders were selected from the hourly paid workers on the shop-floor. They therefore moved from what was called 'payroll' to 'staff', which represented a major change in perceived status and affiliations according to the traditions and conventions that had existed in the organization. The teamleader had a crucial role to play in the imple-mentation of the new managerial practices being developed by the direc-tors for the shop-floor. This included the fostering of a shop-floor culture where a commitment to the work of the team and to continuous improve-ment activities existed. The teamleader was encouraged during in-house training, which involved shadowing other teamleaders over a period of weeks and participation in off-the-job training courses, to manage by example in this area in order to convey a similar set of core values to the rest of the team. This was apparent from discussions with the teamleaders. Regular meetings held by the teamleader with his or her team were intend-ed to provide a means of fostering such a culture through the teamleader communicating not only performance and progress reports to the team but also by developing a sense of commitment and motivation in the team.

However, the ability of the local teamleader to carry out this role was greatly influenced by conventions existing in the wider social context of the UK industry where authority relations have not been traditionally based on an ideology of worker involvement and commitment (Cole 1979; Leibenstein 1984). The long tradition of a 'minimum involvement' philoso-phy and of a purely contractual approach by both sides of industry (Lane 1992) proved difficult to change in the press shop. A central aspect of the workers' orientation was the unwillingness to become involved in what they considered to be 'management's responsibilities'.

One example of this concerns responsibility for quality. The teamleader had the job of changing attitudes and practices amongst the team about work quality of the operatives. Previously, quality was something considered to be the domain of the inspector and the 'managers' not the operatives. The setters, who had the role of preparing the presses and the tooling for the operators were now given more responsibility for inspection. In the press shop the inspector commented:

... before the inspector used to have more status in the company. Everything had to come through the inspector. But now well, with the Japanese, but I suppose it is changing everywhere, they have given the setters more responsibility for checking quality so the inspector is really having a much smaller role now and is pushed into a corner although they do still do checks.

The teamleaders were also expected to change old ways of thinking regarding start and finish times and flexibility in lengths of breaks, creating a disciplined attitude in the workers that was quite different to the existing casual informal approach to breaks and finish times. In the newest section of the factory it was easier to implement management practices such as working from buzzer to buzzer. As one teamleader there mentioned:

it's because people have been recruited to work in here from outside and they are told this is the way we work in here. So they seem to accept it.

In the press shop it would have been difficult to introduce the practice of working from buzzer to buzzer. Any comments to keep on working would have gone against the informal understandings that existed on the shop-floor. The teamleaders turned a blind eye to the workers' informal practice of stopping work a few minutes early. This informal understanding appeared to suffice in that the teamleaders were satisfied as long as productivity and output figures were up to the targets set by management. Workers in the press shop operated with the notion of the previous bonus system in their mind and would often comment that they had reached their bonus output level so they could stop. The bonus system had been removed several years earlier and a flat hourly wage rate was now offered. However, the workers still operated with this idea of a bonus. This was partly because productivity levels of workers were monitored as a means of controlling output. In this way workers would stop work early if they knew that their productivity level for the day was reaching acceptable levels.

The use of the teamleader to convey a new value system and orientation to work has proved difficult given the tradition and convention that existed in the press shop. Compromise solutions have emerged as the influence of local custom, tradition, and practice has limited the extent to which day-to-day authority relations on the shop-floor have actually changed in practice. For example, team meetings were held but little was said. Multi-tasking existed in theory but in practice demarcation lines still existed in spirit between such groups as the servicemen, press operators, and the setters. The development of a consensual team spirit and shared commitment to the formal work objectives, an important element of the parent organization's social means of control on the shop-floor, has proved elusive in this particular context.

In contrast, at the second, greenfield, site of Hano in the UK there was an opportunity to recruit workers who were less influenced by established custom and practice in the UK industrial context. The location of the site in a new town away from traditional manufacturing and unionized areas meant that the local workforce were entering the factory with fewer pre-conceived ideas about shop-floor authority relations and work roles than the press shop on the brownfield site. This was most evident on the assembly lines on the greenfield site. The study of the greenfield site also showed that establishing a factory with a carefully selected workforce, comparatively less experienced in working on British manufacturing shop-floors, enabled the implementation of new management practices with fewer challenges and resistance. The assembly line workstations, in contrast to the discrete workstations in the press shop, also facilitated the implementation of the teamleader roles. The assembly line was more conducive to a sense of interdependence and co-ordination of effort which increased the sense of working together as a team.

However, it should be noted that the greenfield assembly line studied also indicated that those in positions of authority on the line would sometimes adjust and revise their role in times of pressure in attempts to meet the targets they had been given. This suggests that the more traditional British shop-floor authority relations based on exercising power over workers through threats and blame were resurrected under pressure. Changing established routines remains difficult even in greenfield locations.

4. WORK GROUPS IN THE PRESS SHOP AND THE IMPACT OF A CHANGING GRADE STRUCTURE

Similar compromises occurred over the changing grade structures and initiatives for multi-tasking. Work groups in the press shop identified with the craft or job that they were doing, resulting in resistance to changing grade structures and initiatives for multi-tasking. The identification of British workers with their craft or job has been extensively discussed in the literature. For example, Lane (1989) following Maurice *et al.* (1980) has discussed the high horizontal differentiation that exists between operators and maintenance, staff and line, and production and technical services in British organizations and has outlined how this may be based on an underlying contractual attitude about the nature of work in which there are strict limits in the mind of the contractee concerning the activities involved in the job.

The clear-cut notions of the boundaries of a job which have traditionally been supported by the unions in UK manufacturing contrast sharply with the way Dore (1973) and others characteristically analyse worker orientation in large Japanese organizations operating in Japan where studies have indicated a more generalized commitment to the firm rather than to a job (Cole 1979). This commitment to the firm in large Japanese organizations is usually explained by the existence of an internal labour market and long-term career opportunities in many (though not all) such organizations (Kumazawa and Yamada 1989). Clark (1979: 260) has referred to the way that the authority of superiors has been acceptable to those they commanded in Japanese organizations, because their subordinates, given time and the acquisition of merit, could expect to have their own term in office.

In addition to the changes implemented in formal authority structures, two other associated changes affected shop-floor social relations in Maynard. These included the compression of the hourly paid workers' grade structure and a push towards multi-tasking in the workforce. Whilst these changes were taking place the basic nature of the work process in the press shop remained relatively unaltered with little investment in new technology having been made. From time spent on the shop-floor in different sections outside the press shop it appeared that where new technology had been introduced workers were faced with learning new ways of doing things. This in itself appeared to support other changes in work organization and practices. In the press shop, however, workers were being asked to redefine the nature of their work and work relations without any change in technology.

Traditionally at Maynard there was a grade structure which classified the hourly paid shop-floor workers into seven grades. This was gradually compressed down into a grading structure of four levels as part of a strategy to increase the flexibility of workers on the shop-floor through multi-tasking. The four levels in the revised grading structure included workers being classed as grade D servicemen and fork lift truck drivers, grade C general operators, grade B setters and setter-operators, and grade A skilled workers. The terms used to describe these grades varies by people according to how long they have been in the organization and generally where they have worked before.

I found that many workers in the press shop still identified themselves with the craft or job that they were doing rather than with the grade. For example, workers identified themselves as a spot welder or press operator rather than as a skilled worker or a general operator. In this way they identified with the traditional formal work groups that existed in the press shop and other local factories where formal and informal groupings of workers

centred around the job or craft that they were working on. With the introduction of multi-tasking further to the compression of the grade structure,
this sense of identity with task work groups was being threatened.

Following the Japanese take-over in the organization the nature of the
grading structure is being further reshaped so as to reduce the grades from
four to three. This has involved the servicemen and fork lift truck drivers
being merged into the grade C category of general operator as shown in
Table 9.1. The revision of the grading structure can be seen as part of the
organization's strategy of developing a flexible workforce capable of rotating between jobs according to fluctuations in work loads. The new grading
structure is significant in its attempts to break down traditional demarcation barriers existing on the shop-floor. These barriers were particularly
strong during the period of unionization in the organization prior to the
Japanese investment where a conflict about the time allowed for a job or
job manning would often lead to a direct confrontation between management and worker representatives rather than informal discussion between
the foreman and the workers.

As discussed above, workers in the press shop identified with the craft or
job they were working on. Informal work groups in the press shop could be
identified by the nature of the job that the worker was doing. The press
operators formed one group, joined together by sharing the same job
demands and pressures. Similarly there were the setters, the servicemen,

TABLE 9.1.   Job Evaluated Grade Structure amended 1st January 1995

Grade I	Grade II	Grade III
Electrician	Airway Setter Operator	*Cut to Length*
Fitter	Brazer	*FLT Driver*
Toolmaker	Auto Builder Setter Operator	Furnace Assistant
Prototype Fitter	Driver	*General Operator*
Skilled Inspector	Fin Coil Setter Operator	*Guillotine Setter Operator*
	Fitter (trainee)	Machine Adjuster
	FMC Setter Operator	Painter
	Furnaceman	Quality Facilitator
	NC Press Setter Operator	Stainless Steel Tester
	Press Brake Setter Operator	Storesperson
	Press Setter Operator	Facilitator
	Stainless Steel Setter Operator	
	Goods Inward Inspector	
	Special Unit Builder	
	Tube Mill Operator	
	Welder	

Note: Jobs existing in the press shop are in italic.

and the CNC/press brake operators. During the course of the shift the setters, press operators, and servicemen had to work together in carrying out the work process and keeping the shop running. The jobs of the setter, serviceman, and press operator can be outlined through a description of the work process.

Work starts on a press with the setter 'setting up' a press ready for work. He will give a work docket to the serviceman, who will bring the appropriate tools and drawings for the job on the press. The setter will then prepare the tools for the press, load the tools onto the press, set the press and run the 'first off'. The setter then compares the first off against the drawings and takes it to inspection, a small office at the side of the shop for checking. The inspector is an hourly paid worker reporting to the quality control department. A 'skilled' inspector, as was present in the press shop was considered a Grade I operator (see Table 9.1). If the 'first off' is approved the setter then demonstrates to the press operator the procedure to follow on the press for that particular job pointing out the checks to be made on the component.

From discussions on the shop-floor between the workers it was clear that the setters identified with the role of the setter first rather than with the press shop team. This was also the case for the servicemen and press operators. Workers tended to interact from the position of being an individual in a specific job carrying specific responsibilities rather than as a member of a group that had collectively certain responsibilities. This can be seen through the following example taken from my fieldnotes that highlights conflict between informal work groups relating to changing role expectations.

We gathered around for a team meeting. Greg our team leader took the meeting. He told us that efficiency had gone down in the last few weeks and was now around 70% in the press shop.

Greg. There are a couple of people I will ask to come into the office this afternoon.

Sharon (a press operator getting very worked up). So it's us to blame again. We are not working hard enough. What about the setters. They just stand around. Do you ask them to fill in a work record card? No. It's always the press operators that are to blame. If you call me into the office you are not going to get anything from me I will do bugger all after that if you call me in.

Greg. I am not going to call you in.

Sharon. It's always the operators you tell off . . .

A discussion began about performance times. Press operators clock on and off each job they do. The jobs have an expected work time and the operator's performance is then calculated against this.

Paula. Some people clock off for cleaning. Who is supposed to clean? The setters are supposed to do that. That was part of the agreement when they got their last pay rise, but they don't do anything. . . .

Sharon. So what are you going to say to the setters? Are you going to call them into the office?

Greg. You can tell them to clean up.

Sharon. It's your job to tell the setters to get some work done. They sit on their backside while we do all the work. . . .

Later Sharon continued:

And what about the servicemen. Do they fill in a works record card? It's only us. No other department has to.

The conflict between the press operators, setters, and servicemen can be understood by looking at the established demarcation lines that have existed in the UK manufacturing sector and particularly in engineering. Traditionally the industry was heavily unionized with strong unions protecting the interests of their craft members through operating 'closed shop' agreements. As Lane (1989) has outlined, in Britain the unions have been traditionally prominent in the training and accreditation process for skilled workers. The granting of skilled status to craft apprentices meant that at the same time a job territory was being claimed and defended for those possessing the skills through exclusion practices. Similarly semi-skilled workers, like their craft counterparts, have been committed to the practice of demarcation in British industry, defending their job territory by refusing to move to another machine (cf. Kristensen in this volume).

Further to de-unionization in the organization and the Japanese presence, the press shop has felt the impact of management strategies that are encouraging a move towards a breakdown of traditional demarcation lines on the shop-floor and a move towards multi-tasking. The reduction in job grades and the push towards multi-tasking were interconnected in their impact on social relations and social processes in the press shop. The reduction in job grades had meant that the press operators were no longer formally graded on a higher level than the servicemen, who traditionally had the role of cleaning on the shop-floor and moving materials to where they were needed. Both groups now received the same pay. This change in hierarchical 'status' on the shop-floor complemented the push towards increased flexibility of workers through multi-tasking where servicemen and press operators became interchangeable general operators. In this way there is a separation of formal status and pay from the actual job done.

5. MULTI-TASKING: THE EMERGENCE OF DEMARCATION
BATTLES BETWEEN WORK GROUPS

Large Japanese organizations are frequently characterized in the literature as having more ambiguous and fluid job definitions than in Western organizations. At the same time more *de facto* responsibility is delegated to the lower tiers of hierarchy in Japan (see for example Dore 1973; Cole 1979;

Jurgens 1989; Itoh 1994; Lincoln and Kalleberg 1985). Itoh argues that Japanese firms tend not to use detailed job classifications or to offer a clear job description to each individual worker. Jobs are assigned to groups of workers who closely collaborate to perform them, via mutual help and information-sharing. Workers perform multiple tasks via intragroup job rotation.

The following analysis of a demarcation battle between work groups in the press shop provides an example of how the traditional group norms and values in the British engineering industry made it quite difficult to transfer such a system of reduced job grades and increased flexibility across jobs. The push towards increased flexibility across tasks was challenging work group identity. This example of conflict between work group identities in the press shop occurred when the teamleader realized that four servicemen had turned in for work one morning.

I was standing by the teamleader and he told me that there was 'going to be a bit of a fight now' as he was going to ask one of the servicemen to work on the presses because there couldn't be four servicemen on the shop-floor together. Greg, the teamleader, proceeded to speak to the serviceman, who then stormed away.

Greg. I knew he wouldn't be happy. The servicemen don't like being asked to work the presses. I will have to call him into the office.

After having a word with him the serviceman went over to the press but stood with arms folded. Greg mentioned to me that if the man didn't work after the break then he would have to call him into Personnel. The man did work after the break.

Greg complained about the workers in the press shop being 'really bolshy' and 'the worst in the factory'.

Greg explained:

Greg. We've got a totally different way of doing things than what we used to. I mean like in the past it was one man for one job. Like if there was a spot welder, that would be all that he would do. But sometimes he might not have any work to do but he wouldn't be put doing something else. And then there were the unions until the big strike about eight years ago. Ray would you have moved onto a press if the supervisor had asked you in those days?

Ray. It would have depended on how the supervisor had asked me. If he had said 'oy you get over on to there', then no I wouldn't have.

Greg said that this was Yorkshire and that the unions were traditionally strong here.

Another example concerned the issue of cleaning in the press shop which often provoked workers to defend their perceived role and privileges on the shop-floor. An example of this was when Ray my trainer told me to clean around because there was no work to do. It was during my first week on the job and I started emptying the waste bins on the shop-floor.

Peter a setter who I had not spoken to before came up.

Peter. What are you cleaning around for?

DS. There is no work to do.

Peter. Who told you that? If you clean round they will expect everyone to clean round.

DS. Ray my trainer.

Peter. Tell him you're fed up of cleaning round. Tell him to get you some work to do.

DS. I don't think there is any work.

Peter. No work? There is. There's this one for starts. That's [cleaning round] for the servicemen to do.

In another incident Roger and Heather, two press operators discussed the implications of the new grading structure which redefined work roles and challenged work group identities.

Roger said that he was not going to sweep round if there was no work and that sweeping was not his job.

Heather. You have to do whatever they ask you to do in this company now.

Roger. You don't.

Heather. So what is your job?

Roger. I am a general operator.

Heather. So?

Roger. Anyway I will tell them.

Heather. You won't say anything to Clive [the section leader] because he will tell you what for.

Cleaning was a very important element of the Japanese management system of seeking to create order on the shop-floor. The system was known by everyone in the factory as 5S. It was met with some resistance at Maynard by the press shop operators and setters who were used to the cleaning role being reserved for the servicemen previously working on a grade below them. The press shop manager outlined how attempts were being made to get the skilled workers to do 5S. As he explained, it was difficult at first because they were used to having others clean up for them. He went on to say how it was difficult to get the grades down to three, to get everyone to accept that they were on the same salary scale as someone else. It may be argued therefore that the 5S system implemented in the press shop from the Japanese parent met the local governance system operating on the shop-floor and led to compromise solutions shaped by a process of renegotiation of work roles and expectations amongst workers and between workers and their superiors during daily social interaction on the shop-floor.

The greenfield site studied provided an interesting contrast in the way that the shop-floor workforce reacted to management initiatives to implement multi-tasking and a broad banded grading structure. At the greenfield site the strategic selection of workers with comparatively less experience in traditional UK industry, combined with an induction programme and more directly 'managed' organizational culture emphasizing co-operation, team-work, and single status, facilitated the implementation of management initiatives with less resistance than in the press shop. Nippon shop-floor workers were more responsive than the brownfield site workers to expectations placed on them to do 5S and cleaning.

A further example of work group identity and conflict between work groups is provided through a discussion by the press shop workers further to negotiations for a pay increase for hourly paid workers. The works committee served as the elected representatives of the employees in discussions with the organization.

A team meeting was held for the press shop workers. This took place in the canteen. Most people welcomed it as a chance for a coffee, a sit down, and a smoke. After running through our performance on due date delivery, efficiency, and scrap our teamleader Greg moved on to the pay proposal put forward to the works committee by management. Our representative from the press shop was at his side. The shop-floor through the works committee had asked for a £20 a week increase across the board covering all grades on the shop-floor.

Graham. There used to be a lot more grades, in the offices as well. They are trying to do away with the number of grades. That is why they are offering an across the board amount of £7.61. So the maintenance [skilled grade A workers] will get less of an increase than we would. It would bring us closer together. Graham said there should be a show of hands for who was in favour of the proposal.

All (about twenty) except one raised their hand. The one who didn't was a grade A CNC operator. He said he was not proud. I raised the point that maintenance would not be happy with the offer. The representative told me that there were not many maintenance people though. In practice each department was represented on the committee. Maintenance would be out voted if a ballot of representatives was made.

That was what in fact happened. One press shop operator's comment seems to reflect the general feeling of the operators and setters to maintenance workers: 'they just sit on their arse all day'.

6. DISCUSSION AND CONCLUSIONS

The chapter has discussed significant changes in shop-floor practices and work organization implemented in Maynard since the Japanese take-over. However, whilst the organization was trying to implement significant changes in practices, the infrastructure which supported these practices in the parent organization was not transferred. For example, the incentive payment system linked to long-term employment (Okuno 1984) found in many large organizations in Japan contrasts sharply with the history of a 'minimum involvement' philosophy in UK manufacturing (Whitley 1992*b*) and status–wage differentiation based on job classification. This 'minimum involvement' philosophy now stands in contradiction to the level of commitment and long-term thinking that the new management practices in

Maynard are requiring of the workforce. The antagonism of the workers towards the changing grade structure and multi-tasking can readily be understood given the wider context of the external labour market where firm-specific skills were not emphasized.

The extent to which, and the way in which, formal management practices were implemented in the press shop was crucially dependent on the team-leader who had the task of seeking to manage the shop-floor culture, as was discussed earlier in the chapter. The orientation to work of the press shop operators, embedded in the local working-class culture and the tradition in the region, proved very difficult to change and the interaction of parent organization management initiatives with local conventions led to compromise solutions on the shop-floor in which a hybrid culture emerged. In this hybrid culture the significant normative changes that were required to support the new management practices did not take place. Thus many workers would refer to the importance of quality and safety first, but in day-to-day work on the shop-floor the pressure to reach output expectations and not be cautioned for low productivity took priority. The notion of an individual bonus for output was not part of the new managerial control system. Rather the worker was expected to achieve an output efficiency target each day as a matter of course. The display of individual performance records is an example of attempts to apply informal social means of control through peer comparisons and team reinforcement. In the press shop, however, the display of performance records went largely unnoticed by the workers, who gave little attention to the 'paperwork' on the walls.

Whilst the formal structural dimensions of the change programme, including the changes in work organization, were potentially able to be introduced, their effective implementation and translation into day-to-day shop-floor practices was dependent on significant normative and behavioural changes amongst the press shop workers. The teamleader appeared to be the important link-pin between management and the workers in implementing these social dimensions of the change programme. However, the press shop culture was grounded in a historical legacy of confrontation, individualism, and contractual relations between the hourly paid workers and the organization. This culture proved too much of an obstacle for the newly appointed teamleaders in the press shop who themselves had been working in this culture. The comparative analysis with the second site of the Japanese subsidiary in the UK, which was a greenfield site, highlighted the effects of context, including established shop-floor tradition, organizational customs and conventions, and the composition of the workforce, on the way in which new managerial initiatives are received. On the greenfield site the possibility of starting with a new workforce, with comparatively less experience of factory work including middle-aged women and young workers recently out of school, with fewer preconceptions, has allowed the introduction of initiatives with comparatively less resistance and fear by the workers.

The press shop was an example of a traditional British engineering shop that had a long history of working in a market-based employment system. As Whitley (1992*b* and in this volume) outlines, characteristics of this system include amongst other features short-term and specific employer –employee commitments, considerable mobility between firms but limited mobility within them, standardized payment norms for standard skills set by labour markets, and the segmentation of jobs and skills by publicly certified competencies and sometimes by craft unions. These traditional features of the British employment system have significantly influenced the orientation and expectations of the local shop-floor workers and managers to the planned change initiatives in the press shop.

Changes in the institutional environment in the UK have, though, been significant in influencing the orientation of the workers to the organization and the ability of groups to compete for their own interests in the organization. The rise in unemployment in the UK through the last decade and the decline in the power of unions has reduced the bargaining power of workers in the organization. As one press operator put it: 'There will always be others queuing up at the factory gates if we don't want to work.' With the bargaining power of workers reduced, many organizations were also able to push through temporary contracts as a strategy to obtain increased flexibility in manpower numbers. Within Maynard temporary contracts were also used in this way. When employment prospects in the local area had been better, turnover from the organization had been higher. Now as one press operator mentioned: 'there isn't anywhere else to go. A few years ago there were jobs going and a lot of people left. But now, they know that they have got you because if you have worked here for a few years you don't want to go somewhere else on a temporary contract.'

As a result, changes in the local labour market and government employment initiatives favouring such employment practices as temporary work have provided a climate within the workplace that has allowed new work practices to be introduced relatively more easily than arguably would have been the case in the 1970s in the UK when trade unions were powerfully fighting for the protection of the interests of the groups they represented. However, even though these changes have taken place and the local environment has become more flexible (cf. Hibino in this volume), the case-study presented of the press shop has demonstrated how the local socially embedded traditions and conventions of work groups and authority relations are not easily changed. Rather the press shop may be viewed as a microcosm of competing and contrasting business systems. Compromise solutions are continually renegotiated and redefined in the day-to-day shop-floor interaction within and between work groups.

REFERENCES

Aoki, M. (1984) (ed.), *The Economic Analysis of the Japanese Firm* (Amsterdam: Elsevier Science Publishers BV).

——(1994), 'The Japanese Firm as a System of Attributes: A Survey and Research Agenda', in Aoki and Dore 1994: 11–40.

——and Dore, R. (1994) (eds.), *The Japanese Firm: Sources of Competitive Strength* (Oxford: Clarendon Press).

Botti, H. F. (1995), 'Going Local: The Hybridization Process as Organisational Learning', Paper presented at the workshop on The Production, Diffusion and Consumption of Management Knowledge in Europe, EMOT workshop, European Science Foundation programme, Barcelona, January.

Burawoy, M. (1979), *Manufacturing Consent: Changes in the Labour Process under Monopoly Capitalism* (London: University of Chicago Press).

Burns Morton, F. J. (1945), *The New Foremanship* (London: Chapman and Hall).

Clark, R. (1979), *The Japanese Company* (New Haven: Yale University Press).

Cole, R. E. (1979), *Work Mobility and Participation: A Comparative Study of American and Japanese Industry* (Berkeley: University of California Press).

Delbridge, R. (1995), 'Surviving JIT: Control and Resistance in a Japanese Transplant', *Journal of Management Studies*, 32/6: 803–17.

Dore, R. (1973), *British Factory, Japanese Factory: The Origins of National Diversity in Industrial Relations* (Berkeley: University of California Press).

——(1994), 'Equality–Efficiency Trade Offs: Japanese Perceptions and Choices', in Aoki and Dore 1994: 379–91.

Gottfried, H., and Graham, L. (1993), 'Constructing Difference: The Making of Gendered Subcultures in a Japanese Assembly Plant', *Sociology*, 27/4 (Nov.), 611–28.

Graham, L. (1993), 'Inside a Japanese Transplant: A Critical Perspective', *Work and Occupations*, 20/2 (May), 147–73.

Itoh, H. (1994), 'Japanese Human Resource Management Theory from the Viewpoint of Incentive Theory', in Aoki and Dore 1994: 233–64.

Jurgens, U. (1989), 'The Transfer of Japanese Management Concepts in the International Automobile Industry', in Wood 1989: 204–18.

Kleinberg, J. (1994), 'The Crazy Group: Emergent Culture in a Japanese-American Binational Workgroup', *Research in International Business and International Relations*, 6: 1–45.

Kristensen, P. H. (1994), 'Strategies in a Volatile World', *Economy and Society*, 23/3: 305–34.

——(1996), 'On the Constitution of Economic Actors in Denmark', in Whitley and Kristensen 1996: 118–58.

Kumazawa, M. and Yamada, J. (1989), 'Jobs and Skills under the Lifelong Nenko Employment Practice', in Wood 1989: 102–26.

Lane, C. (1989), *Management and Labour in Europe* (Aldershot: Edward Elgar).

——(1992), 'European Business Systems: Britain and Germany compared', in Whitley 1992c: 64–97.

Leibenstein, H. (1984), 'The Japanese Management System: An X-Efficiency-Game Theory Analysis', in Aoki 1984: 331–57.

Lincoln, J. R., and Kalleberg, A. L. (1985), 'Work Organization and Workforce Commitment: A Study of Plants and Employees in the U.S. and Japan', *American Sociological Review*, 50 (Dec.), 738–60.

Maurice, M., Sorge, A., and Warner, M. (1980), 'Societal Differences in Organising Manufacturing Units', *Organisation Studies*, 1/1: 59–86.

Okuno, M. (1984), 'Corporate Loyalty and Bonus Payments: An Analysis of Work Incentives in Japan', in Aoki 1984: 387–411.

Whitley, R. (1992*a*), *Business Systems in East Asia: Firms, Markets and Societies* (London: Sage).

——(1992*b*), 'Societies, Firms and Markets: The Social Structuring of Business Systems', in Whitley 1992*c*: 5–45.

——(1992*c*) (ed.), *European Business Systems: Firms and Markets in their National Contexts* (London: Sage Publications).

——and Kristensen, P. H. (1996) (eds.), *The Changing European Firm* (London: Routledge).

Wood, S. (1989) (ed.), *The Transformation of Work? Skill, Flexibility and the Labour Process*, London: Unwin Hyman.

10

The Transformation of Regional Governance
Institutional Lock-ins and the Development of Lean Production in Baden-Württemberg[1]

GERD SCHIENSTOCK

1. INTRODUCTION

Baden-Württemberg was long reckoned among the fastest-growing regions in Europe, and it still is one of the most prosperous regions on the Continent. However, the economic crisis of the early 1990s has hit the region's industry quite severely, further adding to the problems caused by deep-seated structural difficulties. Since the majority of companies in Baden-Württemberg represent traditional industries such as mechanical engineering, electronics, and car production, they are particularly exposed to increasing global competition. The fact that they were not prepared for the stiffening price, time, and quality competition that came with globalizing markets must be seen as the core of the crisis (Naschold 1996). To retain their competitiveness in the global market, companies in Baden-Württemberg can no longer rely on traditional, limited rationalization strategies. Instead, they have to restructure their entire business organization.

The first condition for regional recovery is a successful restructuration of the local companies. Having said that, it is clear that without major institutional adjustments, the companies of the region will not be able to achieve substantial productivity improvements.[2] Therefore the whole economic order of Baden-Württemberg and its governance mechanisms will be put to the test.[3]

[1] This article is based on a research project in the machinery and car industry which was carried out at the Center for Technology Assessment in Baden-Württemberg at Stuttgart between 1993 and 1995.

[2] This conclusion is in line with the widely accepted argument that for companies to be successful, some kind of fit is needed between their business organization and the institutional setting (see Whitley and Kristensen in this volume).

[3] For a definition of governance, see Lindberg *et al.* (1991).

The discussion below sets out to develop a theoretical concept for the analysis of economic transformation processes. Then, on the basis of this concept, we will proceed to analyse in detail the ongoing renewal of economic governance structures in Baden-Württemberg. This requires some background in the form of a brief description of the traditional production model. The next step is to outline some major trends of business restructuration and institutional renewal. Finally, a few examples are given of institutional adjustment—although as yet one cannot speak of the establishment of a new stable economic governance regime in the region.

2. THE THEORETICAL APPROACH

For the purpose of developing the theoretical approach that we need for an analysis of economic transformation processes, it seems useful to turn to evolutionary economics. In particular, the distinction between a technological or techno-economic paradigm and specific trajectories is relevant (Dosi 1982). However, the concept employed in the discussion below is the broader term of 'production paradigm'. This can be characterized as a model or *Leitbild* which opens up a new field of ideas as to how to resolve problems of production and economic development (Marz and Dierkes 1994). A development path or trajectory can be described as the dynamic aspect of a production paradigm. A governance structure which makes full use of the productivity and growth potential of a specific paradigm will be developed step by step through adaptive learning processes. A production paradigm, of course, can be translated into practice in different ways, depending on the existing governance regime. Therefore there are only limited options for transforming a production paradigm into a trajectory in each economy.

The production paradigm of Fordism has influenced existing forms of economic governance for quite a long time. However, as Boyer (1989) has demonstrated, a distinction can be made between a variety of national Fordist governance regimes. Through adaptive learning processes, economic actors were able to improve Fordist production systems and fully exploit their productivity and growth potential.

At the same time, adaptive learning can also foster so-called 'lock-ins' (Johnson 1992; Grabher 1993*a*). In this respect it is useful to make a distinction between 'structural', 'political', and 'cognitive lock-ins'. One can refer to a 'structural lock-in' when most of the resources of an economy are bound to only one or a few industries, leaving no space for industrial diversification, and when the institutional setting is mainly tied to this economic structure. A 'political lock-in' may be characterized by the existence of a firmly established power structure between the dominant economic actors. Finally, we can speak of a 'cognitive lock-in' if economic actors, possibly because of earlier successes, continue to adhere to the dominant governance mechanisms even if they have become economically inefficient.

Because of these 'lock-ins', actors often fail to realize economic threats and capitalize on chances of innovative learning. They may not be aware of new competitors, the development of major technological innovations, or the use of more efficient organizational models in other economies. 'Lock-ins' may therefore become a hindrance for early industrial adjustment. If economic actors react too late to changes within the global market, an economy may face severe structural problems and lose its global competitiveness.[4]

A deepening economic crisis may also have certain advantages, helping to break open existing lock-ins. An economic crisis can trigger a process of unlearning (Johnson 1992). Economic actors may become more insecure about the efficiency of the existing governance structure; they may perceive pressure for change and realize that the risks of staying put are greater than the risks of following the wrong path of development. However, to be able to initiate a fundamental transformation process of economic governance, actors need a *Leitbild* which generates a new field of ideas of how to organize business and develop industry. Economic actors can then start to search for a specific development path; the search process becomes an interorganizational exercise (Lindberg *et al.* 1991). It will be the aim of this chapter to show how the process of 'bootstrapping reforms' (Sabel 1994) proceeds in Baden-Württemberg. Before that, however, a brief description will be given of the traditional production model in this region.

3. THE TRADITIONAL ECONOMIC ORDER IN BADEN-WÜRTTEMBERG

The search for more flexible alternatives to the existing production model in the core sectors of the German economy and particularly in the companies of Baden-Württemberg got under way as early as the 1970s. Expectations that full automation of the production process would give complete independence of the 'human risk factor' did not materialize. Companies had realized the need for a more flexible production model that would have an important impact on the work organization and skill requirements. This led to attempts to restructure the work organization by relying more heavily on the productivity potential of human labour (Kern and Schumann 1984). On the one hand, standardized work processes and the demand for un- or semi-skilled workers were reduced; but on the other hand, production became more dependent on the competence and capa-

---

[4] Lane has a similar argument. Pointing at the importance of societal effects, she says that it is only in a second step that one has to consider how and to what extent global economic pressures and dominance effects interact with societal effects. See Lane in this volume.

bilities of skilled workers who had to operate and control the automated plants.

Although companies began to introduce new production concepts (new market orientation, automation of production, etc.), the social consequences of the restructuring processes in general were clearly overestimated. From a present-day perspective, one must doubt whether companies at that time really were intent on orientating themselves to a new production paradigm, or whether the companies of Baden-Württemberg really played a leading role in this transformation process.

It may be argued that in Germany, and in Baden-Württemberg in particular, a specific type of the Fordist production model was developed: flexi-Fordism (Boyer 1989) contained a broader range of options for designing production processes than was the case in other countries, such as France or the USA (Braczyk and Schienstock 1996*a*). We may assume that the intention of the restructuring projects during the 1980s was to exploit the full productivity potential of this specific type of Fordist development path rather than to completely restructure the production process on the basis of a new paradigm. That a specific Fordist development path came into being in Germany and in Baden-Württemberg can be explained by the institutional set-up in this country; the vocational training system which supports the industry with qualified craft-workers and the industrial relations system in which unions have a strong say may be mentioned as particularly important factors (Maurice *et al.* 1980).

The loss of global competitiveness in many companies of Baden-Württemberg in the early 1990s suggests that the restructuration of production during the 1980s did not go deep enough (see also Mueller and Loveridge in this volume). Naschold (1996) speaks of the 'lost 1980s': companies lost their chance for a substantive renewal of their business organization. The restructuring exercise was restricted to manufacturing and assembly, while processes before, parallel to, and after manufacturing such as construction, design, maintenance, quality control, and marketing have seldom been integrated. Hardly any attempt was made to integrate production and management, not to mention the restructuring of interorganizational cooperation.

As regards manufacturing, the integration of indirect functions got off to a very slow start. Functions such as maintenance, quality control, machine setting, or operations scheduling were organized separately and left to technical specialists. Therefore group work, if introduced at all, led to a reduced integration of functions; the skills and qualifications of the highly educated employees were still not put to full use. Nor was the right of the foreman and the technical specialist to issue orders and to control the production process called into question; hierarchies were left untouched. When the production model in Baden-Württemberg is characterized as post-Fordist, this applies to the market side only, where many companies followed a niche strategy. On the production side, the very reduced approach to restructuring indicates that companies still followed the Fordist logic of organization. It therefore seems to be more accurate to interpret the new production concepts introduced in the 1980s as a more flexible variation of the Fordist model than to assume that they were based on a new production paradigm (Braczyk and Schienstock 1996*a*).

Why is it only quite recently that companies in Baden-Württemberg have started to restructure their business, while their US competitors, for instance, began to readjust their business organization during the 1980s? One consideration is that companies in the USA were faced with Japanese competition earlier than companies in Baden-Württemberg: it was in the field of mass production that Japanese firms started to compete globally. In addition, a cognitive lock-in stopped companies from making organizational adjustments earlier. The more flexible German variant of the Fordist production model was seen as the number one explanation for economic success. Therefore, companies in Baden-Württemberg felt no pressure to fundamentally change their business organization. From a present-day perspective it seems to be more adequate to relate the success of Baden-Württemberg's companies primarily to the technological excellence of the products and to the well-protected niche markets than to organizational and institutional factors (Herrigel 1990).

In addition to this cognitive lock-in, we can also identify a 'structural' and a 'political lock-in'. Although this region is well known for its strong *Mittelstand*, major companies have had an important influence on the regional economy as many of the small and medium-sized firms were and are suppliers for the big companies, particularly in the car industry. The fact that the majority of the small and medium-sized firms are dependent on the major car producers can be seen as a 'structural lock-in'. Many of the supporting institutions are also closely related to the car industry cluster. This kind of mono-structure (Iver 1994) has a major impact on the regional power structure. The big car producers not only dominated the industrial relations system, but also had a significant influence on the industrial policy of the regional government.

Because of these lock-ins, companies and other economic and political actors did not take the first signs of crisis very seriously. The situation changed drastically when for the first time companies in Baden-Württemberg faced bigger losses as a result of intensified global competition. Since they had concentrated on the niche markets of high-quality production, companies were able to sell their products at whatever price they wanted. However, the fact that Japanese firms in particular have managed to penetrate these niche markets or at least compress the size of these niches, has changed the situation quite dramatically. The change from seller to buyer market reinstalled price as the main criterion of market success. However, companies in Baden-Württemberg not only had difficulty in holding their own in the price competition; they also had difficulty in meeting other criteria of competitiveness within the global market, such as advanced technology, short delivery times, comprehensive services, and sometimes even high quality.

These changes did not of course occur all of a sudden, but it was only with the economic downswing that companies in this region realized that they had lost their global competitiveness. The discussion on ways of regaining competitiveness first concentrated on site factors such as high wages, high taxation, bureaucratic control, etc., but soon a more critical view was taken on the dominant production model (Zukunftskommission Wirtschaft 2000 1993). Companies have now started to search for new ways of organizing their business. This of course has not been a strategic procedure; it has more or less been a kind of bootstrapping.

4. THE RESTRUCTURING PROCESS

There is no doubt that Lean Production has become the new *Leitbild* which guides the restructuring processes in Baden-Württemberg's companies (Schienstock and Steffensen 1995; Schumann *et al*. 1994).[5] An enquiry shows that a broad majority of companies from different industries are interested in adopting the principles of Lean Production. Surprisingly, not only mass and large batch producers but also small batch and single-part producers regard this production model as a chance to regain competitiveness (Wasserloos 1996). However, different companies have interpreted the concept of Lean Production very differently. Some use the term to justify staff lay-offs, others are merely experimenting with certain tools of the Lean Production model, such as 'Total Quality Management' or 'Just in Time', albeit with little success. In many cases companies use the term quite simply to legitimize ongoing restructuring projects, without any deeper knowledge of the concept at all.

Two approaches to Lean Production

Companies in Baden-Württemberg that started to move towards the production paradigm of Lean Production did so in two different ways. One may refer to a 'top-down' and a 'bottom-up' approach. This distinction highlights the fact that some companies started the restructuring process by changing their internal governance structure, while others set out by introducing new forms of cooperation on the shop-floor level. The two approaches are not of course mutually exclusive.

[5] Contrary to this assessment Lane, referring to findings by Cooke, argues that Lean Production has not fundamentally altered the German production system, as it still demands technological ingenuity, skills, and high quality. See Lane in this volume.

The top-down approach

The core element of the top-down approach, which is mainly applied in big companies, is the establishment of a centre concept; this means that more autonomy is given to the single factory within the company. At the same time factories are given full responsibility for costs and profits. The tasks and responsibilities of headquarters, on the other hand, are reduced quite considerably. The traditional relationships of bureaucratic control between headquarters and profit centres are transformed into contractual relationships. Agreements are signed in which output, the quality of the products, and the time of delivery as well as costs and profits are fixed. The head of the centre is responsible for the unit's adherence to the agreement, but he is free to choose the way in which he wants to organize the production process to achieve the targets set.

This process of target fixing takes place on different levels; sometimes it goes all the way down to the shop-floor. However, target fixing is not always an open bargaining process; not least because of the fierce price competition it is necessary continuously to cut costs, which means that there are constant pressures towards permanently reducing cost limits.

It would be consistent with the logic of the model if the autonomous centres also had the right to choose their own suppliers and to find their own customers, whether within or outside the company. This, of course, would imply a change in the mechanisms of governance; the tight hierarchic coupling between subunits through headquarters would have to be transformed into loosely associated market-like exchange relations. One consequence of such a change could be that subunits which are unable to compete against suppliers from outside the company would have to cut back operations or even close down. Most companies, however, flinch from a consequent introduction of market relationships, not least because this can lead to the loss of important production knowledge and to fierce competition between different subunits. Also, many customers would no longer associate specific products or services with the company as a whole, which is increasingly important as customers often call for systemic solutions. More and more, however, functions become the object of 'make or buy' decisions, which often leads to the outsourcing of peripheral subunits. Not only such functions or subunits as cleaning or foundry but also design and construction and sometimes even accounting are outsourced.

The restructuring of service functions is also part of the organizational renewal process. Finance, purchasing, personnel, accounting, long-term planning, controlling, and logistics are integrated into service and advice centres, which are to deliver the necessary services within the company and for external agencies, to take responsibility for corporate development, and to ensure the organization's goals are attained. Such service and advice centres have primarily a supportive function; this clearly demonstrates the new appreciation of production within companies. These centres are responsible for costs, time, and the quality of their services; but again companies hesitate to introduce a pure market system in which the centres would have to sell their services to internal and external customers.

As was pointed out earlier, it is not possible for headquarters within an intra-organizational network structure to rely on traditional control mechanisms. To get the management of subunits to accept and comply with their decisions, headquarters have to rely primarily on mechanisms of normative integration rather than on coercive mechanisms. In the centre model headquarters often turn to what may be called 'context control' or 'discursive coordination'. Organizing meetings to harmonize specific strategies of different subunits or to bring production policies in line with each other, the exchange of managers or specific incentives to support cooperation between centres can be seen as part of the discursive coordination strategy. Most companies introduce a comprehensive system of reference numbers and a detailed report system. In this case a network structure still exists within firms, but the subunits have only 'controlled autonomy'. These report systems often become the basis for internal 'benchmaking'. Subunits are informed about their position within the company, and they can compare their results with those of other subunits. It is expected that this kind of benchmaking will encourage centres to look for organizational strategies to improve their performance.

The reduction of hierarchical levels is an important element of the top-down approach. As soon as production and service centres are introduced, hierarchical levels between headquarters and the centres become obsolete, for the latter have gained more autonomy in decision-making and assumed responsibility for adherence to the targets and cost limits agreed upon. At least one or two hierarchical levels are eliminated. Flat hierarchies in medium-sized companies often mean that there are no more than three hierarchical levels on top of the shop-floor: headquarters, centre management, and chief of production islands. Companies realize that hierarchies have major disadvantages such as lengthy decision-making and loss of information; the whole bureaucratic apparatus is too costly and too inflexible to adapt to rapid market changes. Function-based hierarchies are very often the cause of power games and status conflicts. Middle management in particular is seen as an obstacle to organizational restructuration. Managers at intermediate levels of the hierarchy have good reasons to boycott organizational renewal, of course, because at the very least they will lose power, possibly even their job.

Decentralization on the company level does not automatically lead to decentralization on lower levels as well. Often the process of decentralization gets bogged down on the centre level, as middle management in particular will be trying to block the process. We therefore may find both centralized and decentralized decision-making within one company, which means that there are different social practices and specific organizational subcultures and that cooperation between subunits is often very difficult. There is always the risk that the top-down approach of restructuring does not lead to a radical renewal of the organization but results instead in a situation of blocked interaction and severe conflicts between the different production and service centres.

The process of organizational renewal also extends to interfirm relationships. Large companies completely restructure their supplier chain by drastically reducing the number of suppliers. Medium-sized firms, on the other hand, will try very hard to become system suppliers; failing to do so, their very survival will be at stake. It is quite clear that the number of firms in the supplier industry in Baden-Württemberg will be drastically reduced over the next few years. The fact that the core companies are restructuring their supplier chain indicates that spatial closeness does not always mean organizational closeness. Although core companies have had long-standing exchange with their suppliers, these were more or less contractual relationships within which there rarely was any cooperation in a broader sense; exchange and interaction was limited to the bare necessities.

The reshaping of supplier relationships is aimed primarily at reducing costs. Reducing the price of parts delivered by supplier firms is an integral part of the cost reduction programmes of major companies. Instead of simply accepting a price quoted by the supplying company, core firms will themselves pin their suppliers down to a specific price. Suppliers either have to take the price or they will be out of business. Demonstration of one's ability to increase efficiency and flexibility is also a precondition for becoming a system supplier.

Fixed prices put the supplier firms under pressure to increase productivity by restructuring their production process as well. They can be assisted in this by their customers, which broadens the range of cooperation; at the same time, however, it also means that they have to open their books. Many suppliers still hesitate to accept such an offer to cooperate; they are used to the traditional market model in which they had to fake their costs. There is good reason to do so as sometimes large companies, under the pretext of encouraging renewal processes, will try to shift the costs of adjustment to their suppliers. For example, supplier firms often have to take over research and development activities that core firms consider too costly for themselves.

Medium-sized firms often realize that the reshaping of supplier relationships may also have certain advantages for them. They can establish long-standing cooperation with their customers, they can make use of their experiences in the field of organizational restructuring, and they may even stand to gain from reductions by core firms in the depth of their production. To make use of such advantages, they will start an 'offensive of openness' to demonstrate their strength and to build up trust relations with their customers.

In general, however, interfirm networking faces certain major obstacles. Distrust continues to characterize the relationships between supplying firms and their major customers. Suppliers often complain that their customers are trying to squeeze them out as far as possible, leaving them to struggle for survival. Cooperation between supplier firms, which would be necessary in order to detect and counter such behaviour, is not very common.

The bottom-up approach

While the top-down approach starts from the restructuring of the internal governance regime, the focus in the bottom-up approach is on the shop-floor. This means that the traditional workshop principle is replaced by a process-oriented work organization. Self-contained processes are formed as a basis for organizational renewal, including not only direct manufacturing activities and the corresponding technologies, but also more and more indirect functions, such as quality testing, repair work, machine-setting, maintenance, and even production-planning and serial optimization.

Group work can be seen as the core element of a production island. Each group produces a major part of the whole product manufactured within the production island. Groups become responsible for quality, time, full use of production capacity, and costs. In these work groups there is no fixed division of work, but the work organization is flexibly adapted to the group's respective development stage. The ultimate aim is that most group members are capable of performing all the tasks of the integrated production process. Group work is completed by the introduction of quality circles. The aim of this kind of organizational decentralization is to mobilize production knowledge in an unconventional manner; groups are expected to continuously optimize their work organization.

With the introduction of self-organizing groups the foreman—traditionally a key figure in the production process—very often loses his dominant position. Many of his tasks and duties are now taken over by work group coordinators who become responsible not only for the smooth functioning of the group process but also for the outward representation of the group. They are often chosen by group members, but can also be appointed by the foreman. Working with their group members, the coordinators fix working hours, arrange the distribution of tasks, and organize shift work; but they also negotiate with management for non-contractual wages, output norms, and personnel. However, the role of the group coordinator does not represent a specific hierarchical level—the coordinator is a normal group member.

Work groups are often conceptualized in a dynamic way. Ideally, the self-organizing work group should be able continuously to extend its scope of activities by integrating more and more indirect functions. However, such a process would also threaten the hierarchy of technical experts; they, too, would have to become group members and would thereby lose their prestigious status position. Therefore technical experts have often tried to block the process of extending the tasks of the work group. Paralysing conflicts have occurred because technical experts have refused to cooperate with the work group, arguing that their members are not sufficiently experienced to carry out indirect tasks such as repair work or quality control. Such conflicts are sometimes solved by an agreement that specifies the tasks and responsibilities of technical experts and those of the work groups. This, of course, effectively undermines the dynamic development of the work group.

In the bottom-up approach the foreman's role has to be changed completely as many of his tasks are transferred to the group coordinator. From the disciplinary point of view he is still responsible for the workers; in their daily work, however, groups gain much more independence from the foreman. The idea is that the foreman takes on the role of a coach who supports the group in its development process and in dealing with more complex group tasks. The group's performance goals and its actual goal attainment also become a major concern of the foreman. Other tasks include the provision of technical, methodological, and social competencies for group work, guaranteeing an uninterrupted information flow within and between groups, determining training needs within groups, facilitating cooperation between groups, developing investment plans, and stimulating organizational development processes as well as assessing the performance, attitudes, and behaviour of individual members. However, many foremen fail to get to grips with such a new role but try instead to hold on to their former position, which gives them more power to control the shop-floor. Therefore the restructuring of business organizations from bottom up involves even more paralysing conflicts.

Rather than simply copying the Japanese model, companies in Baden-Württemberg are trying to find their own independent solutions for the organization of group work, leaning on experiences of the humanization of work in the 1970s and 1980s. There is as yet no single, homogeneous understanding of group work. Companies are still experimenting with different models, some of the more advanced of which have already been rejected. In terms of group work companies in Baden-Württemberg still lag far behind their Japanese competitors. Only about 5 per cent of all workplaces in production are integrated in group work.

In some cases the group approach has not only been applied in manufacturing and assembly but also in the design process. A new style of innovation management reintegrates research and development with engineering, design, procurement, production, and even marketing. The development of new products, market assessment, and price calculation—all these activities are performed within a cross-functional team consisting of members from various departments. The idea of such teams is that all products are designed with manufacturing in mind, which helps to trim down the expensive processes of redesign and also speeds up product marketing. Some companies have been able to cut back the time required to develop a new product by about 50 per cent. In general, however, cross-functional development teams have not been set up very often. Many companies are still concentrating on cutting costs and therefore on restructuring the production process; they have not yet realized that product innovations are crucial to retaining competitiveness.

Today, companies in Baden-Württemberg are trying to put the Lean Production paradigm into practice, in one way or another. As yet, however, there are no signs of a clear and consistent development towards organizing business and the production process on the basis of this paradigm. Only a few companies have realized that restructuring according to the Lean Production paradigm does not mean that they can simply put a number of well-known organizational elements into practice. They have understood that organizational solutions cannot successfully be copied or implanted, but the individual company has to interpret the Lean Production paradigm in its own way and proceed with restructuring at its own pace. However, even in this case the companies have failed to follow a holistic approach, but have adopted either the bottom-up or the top-down approach, usually leading to a dead end sooner or later. The bottom-up approach has met with fierce resistance on the part of technical experts as soon as the work groups have started to integrate indirect functions into their responsibilities. Therefore this approach often leads to paralysing conflicts between technical experts and work groups.

There have also been frequent problems with the top-down approach. As decision-making authority has been decentralized to the heads of the production and service centres, companies have rarely had a common approach to organizational renewal. Very often one centre will have applied a certain decentralization strategy, while others have continued with bureaucratic structures of decision-making. And even where group work has become an adopted part of organizational restructuring for the whole company, concrete practices on the shop-floor have still developed quite differently. The fact that various structures and local cultures have developed within the centre has emerged as a major obstacle to efficient cooperation within companies. Successes in restructuring have been greatest in companies pursuing both a bottom-up and a top-down process at the same time. In these cases the work groups have had the backing of headquarters to extend their field of activities, while at the same time the work groups have managed to induce the head of the centres to proceed with the decentralization of decision-making, affording the momentum of organizational restructuring a specific dynamic.

5. THE INSTITUTIONAL ENVIRONMENT

The problem of regaining competitiveness cannot be resolved on the level of individual companies. Companies are always embedded in a regional institutional set-up and depend on its supportive inputs (see Whitley and Lane in this volume). However, during the restructuring process many firms have realized that existing institutions are unable to provide the knowledge and resources they require and in this sense actually turned into obstacles to organizational renewal. It has become clear that in order to regain competitiveness within a global market, not only the companies but also the supportive institutional set-up need to go through major changes. There are some signs that such institutional adjustment is now under way in Baden-Württemberg. The following discussion describes such changes in the context of different institutions.

The regional government

Most economic actors in Baden-Württemberg agree that, in order to overcome the current economic crisis, an intensive, concerted effort is needed. A heightened consciousness of the current crisis is manifested in a joint attempt to develop new innovation strategies and new avenues for economic growth. The regional government often takes a leading role in the process of industrial renewal, but it no longer assumes the role of a 'doer'; instead it defines itself as an 'organizer' and 'moderator' of a dialogue on future developments (Zukunftskommission Wirtschaft 2000 1993; Schienstock 1994). The regional government has set a commission to analyse the facts and circumstances challenging the international competitiveness of local firms and to suggest ways to resolve the problem. One of the commission's recommendations was that the regional government should provide the necessary legal and institutional framework for increased flexibility in work organization and to support local firms in restructuring their work organization on the basis of the Lean Production model.

Other activities aimed at helping companies regain their competitiveness were carried out by the Ministry of Economics under the slogan 'dialogue-oriented economic policy'. Industry-wide dialogues bring employers of the region, representatives of economic associations, and unionists together to discuss strategies with which regional enterprises can attain this goal. So far there have been dialogues on the car industry, the machine-building industry, the supplier industry, and the environmental industry. The partners involved in these dialogues have made some suggestions which have become part of the industry and technology policy of the regional government.

In the meantime, employment initiatives have also been made on the sub-regional level, involving members of local government, firms, associations, unions, and the labour office. The aim of these initiatives is to stimulate economic growth and to generate new employment opportunities. In the region of Heilbronn/Neckarsulm, for instance, such initiatives have been made in the field of environmental technology.

The new role of the unions

These new institutional arrangements act to strengthen the position of the unions within the socio-economic modernization process (Kern 1994). Unions are seen as a partner (albeit sometimes as a junior partner) who can contribute to the analysis of current economic problems; and when it comes to the implementation of certain problem-solving steps, it is impossible to try and manage without this partner.

Participation in these cooperative forms of coping with the economic crisis implies a new strategic orientation on the part of the unions. So far unions have hardly had what can be called an 'industrial policy'. The new orientation results from the recognition that the very legitimacy of the unions is seriously questioned by increasing mass unemployment. It is obvious that the unions have to demonstrate their willingness to actively cooperate in the solution of this most pressing problem in society. 'Intelligent regulation' is seen as an answer to all three problems: regional competitiveness, unemployment, and the unions' legitimacy; the latter has already become apparent in declining membership numbers. The unions' main aim in this transformation process is to stimulate product innovations in new fields of social demand, as well as to promote an environmentally conscious use of natural resources. This can be done by developing organizational concepts which make good use of the creativity and productivity potential of workers. When unions adopt such a modernization strategy, it is more important for them to start an offensive in the field of education and vocational training than to continue to concentrate on traditional bargaining fields (Riester 1994).

It has to be questioned, however, whether the unions' strategy of cooperation really can and will be successful at the end of the day. The 'pact for work' they have suggested has been rejected by the employers' association 'Metall', which is particularly strong in Baden-Württemberg. The unions were prepared to accept real wage decreases in exchange for serious attempts by the companies to create new jobs.

The training system

It is often argued that the training system in Germany lends strong support to the organizational renewal process within companies through apprenticeship schemes—a combination of theoretical education and practical experience—which provide trainees with craft skills that allow them to solve problems independently, following only indicative instructions. This advantage, the argument continues, has not been put to good use within the flexi-Fordist model. However, the situation has changed with the introduction of group work, and employees' craft skills are no longer underutilized.

There is also a more critical line of argumentation on the German training system. That is, while craft skills allow employees to perform certain specialized tasks, group work requires process knowledge, which on the one hand is much broader than the expert knowledge of a single craft but on the other hand less fundamental. The expertise required for process-based group work has to bring together knowledge from different crafts, while the training system is still based on clearly demarcated crafts. It follows that the training system is largely responsible for the current adjustment difficulties of companies in Baden-Württemberg. There is some evidence that the acquisition of skills by way of apprenticeship can impede restructuring because it creates obstacles of cooperation within and between work groups as well as between them and various technical experts, who are trained in different crafts (Kern and Sabel 1994).

Sometimes the question is raised as to whether it still makes sense to train employees within a three- or four-year apprenticeship scheme for a specific craft. Some argue that the Japanese system of training on the job and rotating training is better suited to the needs of the future work organization. Training schemes have also been suggested whereby demand-specific modules are taught and where trainees get certificates for completing each training unit. However, there are also those who warn against underestimation of apprenticeship. Apart from the fact that training in a specific craft may increase self-confidence, a craft can also open the way to long-life learning. It is important that what can be called 'just-in-time training' has a solid training basis.

A combination of both training systems might provide the best solution. This would imply, on the one hand, a shorter period of apprenticeship, while at the same time training according to demand during one's working career would become more important. There is no doubt that with the establishment of dynamic self-organizing work groups, further training has become more important compared with initial training. The dynamic process of integrating more and more indirect work functions into group work will not take place if members of work groups do not acquire new technological competencies and social skills at the same time. The process of continuously extending the tasks of work groups needs to be supported by some kind of permanent further training.

Companies in Baden-Württemberg have realized the importance of further training. Many of them have increased their spending on further training quite significantly, but often at the expense of initial training. However, companies put special emphasis on the training of their middle and upper management, while at the same time retraining of the workers is reduced to training on the job. This means that the knowledge gap between management and workers is widening.

Technology transfer institutions

The strong market position of companies in Baden-Württemberg is often related to the high technological standards of their products. This advantage could only have been achieved, it is argued, because of the dense network of research, technology transfer, and consultancy institutions. In particular, reference can be made here to the technical college centres at the Fachhochschulen, related to the Steinbeiss Stiftung, which are spread across all of Baden-Württemberg to support local companies. The centres offer specific technological knowledge to help develop new products or improve the production process. In most cases they work on a short or medium-term contract. Although the technical college centres are founded to support the SMEs, they are not very well known within this group of firms. Only about 30 per cent of the region's SMEs had contact with these centres. Other technology transfer institutes, such as those from the Frauenhofer Gesellschaft, have closer links with the major companies.

One can assume that the strong technical orientation of the transfer institutions in Baden-Württemberg may become a hindrance to support companies in the current transformation process. What is needed today is not—at least not in the first place—specific technological knowledge but managerial knowledge, knowledge how to stimulate and control organizational renewal processes and how to motivate employees to actively engage and to support those processes. Many of the traditional consultancy organizations are also reluctant to help companies find their own individual way of organizing business, often selling only abstract organizational models without practical advice as to how to stimulate organizational learning.

There is increasing distrust nowadays among the most advanced companies in the direct approach, which suggests a specific organizational model to be implemented by management, sometimes with the assistance of workers. They have realized that the transformation process is too complex for it to be possible to suggest a structural model at the very outset of the renewal process. Companies need advice on how the process of self-organization can be started and monitored. Given these new demands of knowledge, new relationships are needed between companies and transfer institutions: the short-term, market-like relationships have to be transformed into long-term cooperation. However, the problem is that

SMEs cannot afford to pay for such long-term assistance. Therefore more financial support is required from governmental resources.

There are some signs that the demand for this new type of support cannot be met by the existing technology transfer institutions and consultancy organizations, although some of them are starting to respond to the new demands. Managers of certain companies have started to organize informal meetings to inform each other about their attempts to restructure business. Pioneering companies become a place of pilgrimage for potential emulators. The fact that companies talk to each other about their successes but also about the problems they are experiencing with their organizational renewal strategies may also indicate that companies today are very uncertain about the proper approach to organizational adjustment. One can imagine that such discussion forums may lead to the emergence of a new type of consultancy, as here the kind of process knowledge is available that the traditional transfer institutions can rarely offer.

6. CONCLUSION

The experience from Baden-Württemberg indicates that a new governance regime has not, as yet, emerged in the region that would be better adapted to the developing global markets. It can be seen that a few regional actors have taken steps towards economic adaptation, but it is difficult to say whether these steps will lead to a new 'position of equilibrium' of the regional economy. It is much more likely that at least for the foreseeable future, dynamic processes of organizational and industrial adaptation will dominate the scene, without leading to any stable situation.

What can be said is that the Fordist production paradigm is being called into question in the region: Lean Production has now taken over as a *Leitbild* that generates a new field of organizational tools. This paradigm now serves as a model for the current restructuring processes. Companies and other economic actors in Baden-Württemberg are working to transfer this paradigm into practice and to find a development path for future economic growth and competitiveness.

However, these efforts are still very cautious and surrounded by great uncertainty. Some companies are pushing forward with the restructuring process, while most institutions are lagging behind. Pioneering companies are already complaining about the backwardness of economic institutions, saying that they are an obstacle to the successful economic adjustment of the region. Therefore it remains open whether the current attempts to restructure companies and the whole regional governance system will end in a self-stabilizing process that will develop a dynamic of its own.

REFERENCES

Boyer, R. (1989), 'New Directions in Management Practices and Work Organisation'. Paper presented at the International OECD Conference in Helsinki, 11–13 Dec. 1989.

Braczyk, H.-J., and Schienstock, G. (1996*a*), 'Im Lean Express zum neuen Produktionsmodell', in Braczyk and Schienstock 1996*b*: 269–329.

——(1996*b*) (eds.), *Kurswechsel in der Industrie: Lean Production in Baden-Württemberg* (Stuttgart: W. Kohlhammer).

Dosi, G. (1982), 'Technological Paradigms and Technological Trajectories: A Suggested Interpretation of the Determinants and Directions of Technical Change', *Research Policy*, 11: 147–62.

Grabher, G. (1993*a*), 'The Weakness of Strong Ties: The Lock-in of Regional Development in the Ruhr Area', in Grabher 1993*b*: 255–77.

——(ed.) (1993*b*), *The Embedded Firm: On the Socioeconomics of Industrial Networks* (London: Routledge), 255–77.

Herrigel, G. B. (1990), *Industrial Organization and the Politics of Industry: Centralized and Decentralized Production in Germany* (Boston).

Iver, F. (1994), *Industriestandort Stuttgart 1994: Beschäftigungspolitik in der Region. Zur Lage und den Perspektiven in der Metallindustrie* (Munich: IMU-Informationsdienst No. 2).

Johnson, B. (1992), 'Institutional Learning', in B.-A. Lundvall (ed.), *National Systems of Innovation and Interactive Learning* (London: Pinter Publisher), 23–44.

Kern, H. (1994), 'Intelligente Regulierung: Gewerkschaftliche Beiträge in Ost und West zur Erneuerung des deutschen Produktionsmodells', *Soziale Welt*, 45: 33–59.

——and Sabel, C. (1994), 'Verblassende Tugenden: Zur Krise des deutschen Produktionsmodells', in N. Beckenbach and W. van Treeck (eds.), *Umbrueche gesellschaftlicher Arbeit*, in *Soziale Welt*, special vol. 9: 605–24.

——and Schumann, M. (1984), *Das Ende der Arbeitsteilung? Rationalisierung in der industriellen Produktion: Bestandsaufnahmen Trendbestimmung* (Munich: C. H. Beck).

Lane, C. (1989), *Management and Labour in Europe: The Industrial Enterprise in Germany, Britain and France* (Aldershot: Edward Elgar).

Lindberg, L. N., Campbell, J. L., and Hollingworth, J. R. (1991), 'Economic Governance and the Analysis of Structural Change in the American Economy', in J. L. Campbell, J. R. Hollingworth, and L. N. Lindberg (eds.), *Governance of the American Economy* (Cambridge: Cambridge University Press).

Marz, L., and Dierkes, M. (1994), 'Leitbildprägung und Leitbildgestaltung: Zum Beitrag der Technikgenese-Forschung fuer eine prospektive Technikfolgen-Regulierung', in G. Bechmann and T. Petermann (eds.), *Interdisziplinäre Technikforschung: Genese, Folgen, Diskurs* (Frankfurt: Campus Verlag), 35–72.

Maurice, M., Sorge, A., and Warner, M. (1980), 'Societal Differences in Organising Manufacturing Units', *Organization Studies*, 1: 59–86.

Naschold, F. (1996), 'Jenseits des baden-württembergischen "Exceptionalism": Strukturprobleme der deutschen Industrie', in Braczyk and Schienstock 1996*b*: 184–212.

Riester, W. (1994), 'Unsere Tarifverträge sind ein Spiegelbild der tayloristischen Arbeitsorganisation (Das MB Gespräch)', *Die Mitbestimmung*, 4: 16–20.

Sabel, C. (1994), 'Bootstrapping Reform: Rebuilding Firms, the Welfare State and Unions'. Revised version of an Address to the Confederation des Syndicats Nationaux, Montreal, 15–16 Nov. 1993. MIT mimeo.

Schienstock, G. (1994), 'Technology Policy in the Process of Change: Changing Paradigms in Research and Technology Policy', in G. Aichholzer and G. Schienstock (eds.), *Technology Policy: Towards an Integration of Social and Ecological Concerns* (Berlin: Walter de Gruyter), 1–23.

——and Steffensen, B. (1995), '"Lean Production" als Leitbild der Restrukturierung einer Region: Die Wirtschaft Baden-Württembergs im Wandel', in J. Fischer and S. Gensior (eds.), *Netzspannungen: Trends in der sozialen und technischen Vernetzung von Arbeit* (Berlin: Edition Sigma), 347–83.

Schumann, M., Baethge-Kinsky, V., Kuhlmann, M., Kunz, C., and Neumann, U. (1994), 'Rationalisierung im Uebergang: Neue Befunde der Industriesoziologie zum Wandel der Produktionskonzepte und Arbeitsstrukturen', *WSI-Mitteilungen*, 47: 405–14.

Wasserloos, G. (1996), 'Sind wir "lean-fähig"?', in H.-J. Braczyk and G. Schienstock (eds.), *Kurswechsel in der Industrie: Lean Production in Baden-Württemberg* (Stuttgart: W. Kohlhammer), 232–44.

Zukunftskommission Wirtschaft 2000 (1993), *Aufbruch aus der Krise: Bericht der Zukunftskommission 'Wirtschaft 2000 des Landes Baden-Württemberg.* Staatsministerium Baden-Württemberg, Stuttgart.

11

Changing Governance Structures and Work Organization in Slovenia

MARKO JAKLIC

1. INTRODUCTION

Changes in both the economic and political fields since 1989 have been witnessed in all of the former socialist countries in Eastern Europe. Although the process of transformation has commonly focused on achieving market-oriented economies similar to those of western Europe, the transition has varied among the countries according to their specific historical past. Slovenia in particular is quite distinct in its relatively high level of industrial development and orientation to Western markets at the start of the transformation process, as well as the legacy of the Yugoslav 'self-management' system which resulted in much greater decentralization of economic decision-making than elsewhere in eastern Europe.

This chapter contrasts the former and present governance structures in Slovenia, and their linkages with patterns of work organization. It shows how the legacies of the Yugoslav form of socialism, together with earlier developments, have become modified since Slovenia became independent in 1991. Through the discussions of the changing macro socio-economic environment, the transformation of social groups and their interests, and the organization of the relations in the workplace in Slovenian companies, this chapter shows that changes are not as radical as seen from the surface. Slovenian governance structures are very much rooted in the historical and institutional context of Slovenian society.

2. THE CHANGING MACRO SOCIO-ECONOMIC ENVIRONMENT

The Yugoslav self-management system

In 1952 the Yugoslav model of socialism softened drastically as it separated from the eastern one.[1] Although the state still played an important role

[1] For more on the economic characteristics of the Yugoslav socialist system see Prasnikar and Prasnikar 1986.

and owned companies' fixed and working capital, decision-making processes were largely decentralized. This period lasted until 1960 and was
characterized by the introduction of self-management, typical of
Yugoslavia. The next period is referred to as the period of market socialism (1961–70). As opposed to previous systems which were based on plans,
the concept of market was emphasized in this term. Companies thus became
more independent and responsible for their own business results.

In 1971 an integrated self-management system was established which
encouraged companies to become financially and organizationally integrated so that some became powerful giants employing more than 10,000
workers. The ideal of the free market was pushed aside and an important
role was again attributed to planning. However, because of complicated
procedures there was more formal administration than real planning. A new
social equilibrium was now sought in a system of 'free associated labour'.
Workers were supposed to make decisions about income distribution,
investments, and foreign trade within their Basic Organization of
Associated Labour (BOAL). Various BOALs were linked into the bigger
Work Organization (WO) and Composite Organization of Associated
Labour (COAL) where the interests of workers were to be coordinated.
This system was implemented in order to improve workers' self-
management (Prasnikar and Svejnar 1988). Direct workers' management,
in a form of workers' participation, encompassed the activities and interests of workers in BOALs. Their indirect management, through delegates,
concerned the coordination of BOALs, the interests of workers from
various BOALs, and the operations of the WO or COAL. Similar to the
previous period, direct self-management included Workers' Assemblies, ref-
erenda, and individual commitments. Indirect involvement was still
managed via Workers' Councils which appointed the Board of Directors
that was responsible for the execution of tasks assigned by either the
Workers' Assembly or Workers' Council.

Serious macro-economic problems accumulated during this period which
resulted in hyperinflation at the end of the 1980s.[2] The need for a fundamental change in the system arose and at the end of 1989 shock therapy
was implemented to stop the hyperinflation which was primarily a result of
an expansive monetary policy combined with a 'soft-budget' constraint.
However, the policy was not strictly implemented: wages increased, public
spending remained unchanged, the banking system reform failed, and
industrial production further decreased. The main goal of eliminating inflation was not achieved.

---

[2] It is true that in the last period Yugoslavia reached high rates of economic growth, but it
was mostly due to increases in external debt (Prasnikar and Pregl 1991).

Post-independence developments

The economic arguments for independence were linked to the prospects of transition to a normal market economy, which had become unrealistic in the Yugoslav environment. The political and social differences between various parts of Yugoslavia were a serious barrier to the introduction and implementation of the systematic changes required. When it became clear that the constituent republics of the former Yugoslavia would be unable to agree on a rational solution, Slovenia declared its independence in June 1991. The loss of strategic southern and east European markets resulted in a decline in production and employment.

Key structural reforms in both the financial and enterprise sectors became critical as increasing losses and insolvency problems developed in the enterprise sector, unemployment rose, inflation soared, and industrial production fell. To address these issues, basic legislation concerning corporatization, privatization, bank rehabilitation, enterprise restructuring, and a market-oriented legal framework has been adopted. The government launched a special programme, consisting of several projects to reform the enterprise sector by linking restructuring with privatization and rehabilitation of the banking system.

Privatization and restructuring of enterprises

Following an initial focus on macro-economic stabilization, attention was shifted to the *privatization and restructuring* of large enterprises with social capital (equity that formally belonged to all citizens and was managed on behalf of the community by the employees of the company). By December 1990, two governmental institutions were founded to build, supervise, and assist the privatization process in Slovenia. The Agency for Privatization serves a monitoring and control function, prepares guidelines, and approves privatization programmes, while the Development Fund acts as the owner of the social equity and has the right to negotiate transactions and sign sales contracts. The fund is also authorized to invest the proceeds from the sales of companies.

The Law on Ownership Transformation of Companies was finally passed by the Parliament in November 1992, after long political discussions, with issues of justice and fairness having priority over economic efficiency. It took two years of very intensive public debate, the resignation of several ministers, and, eventually, the fall of the whole government over the issue, to find a privatization concept that was finally acceptable to the major political parties (Korze and Simoneti 1993: 212).

A combination of free distribution of shares and commercial privatization of companies has been introduced, thus including various methods of privatization. Typically, 10 per cent of shares of a company are transferred to the Compensation/Restitution Fund, 10 per cent to the Pension Fund, 20 per cent to the special Privatization Investment Funds for free distribution to all Slovenian citizens via ownership certificates. The remaining 60 per cent is available for internal free distribution to employees via ownership certificates, for selling on preferential terms to insiders under a special internal buy-out scheme, and/or for selling on commercial terms through the public offering of shares, public tender, or public auction.

The law is quite flexible as it allows for the modification of the basic transformation scheme, and therefore various combinations of methods can be used. Companies may well be transformed by raising new private equity on commercial terms and transferring the existing shares representing social capital to different financial institutions.

Real privatization in the economic sense is expected to be achieved gradually since after the initial distribution (dispersion) of shares, there is no group of active private owners able and willing to make changes within the enterprise. To avoid a sharp drop in the value of shares on the capital market, which could happen because of widespread ownership, and to diminish the risk of such negative effects on interest rates and economic growth, shares from internal distribution cannot, by law, be transferred at least for two years. Shares acquired through internal buy-outs are transferable only between participants of the internal buy-out until the programme is concluded. It is thus expected that a real privatization will take place only gradually through the resale of shares by their initial owners.

3. TRANSFORMATION OF SOCIAL GROUPS AND THEIR INTERESTS

Characteristics of the self-management system

The Yugoslav system of self-management bequeathed numerous problems within enterprises, especially in the area of management where there was an inadequate understanding of and ability to combine leadership, management, and governance functions. In particular, the interference of central bureaucratic and administrative structures made the Yugoslav enterprise resemble more closely the term 'public enterprise' than its given name of 'self-managed' firm (Prasnikar 1989: 97). Thus, the dominance of political structures over the entire economy logically put ownership and entrepreneurial functions into the hands of political authorities. Ownership rights and functions were exercised in a way that when a company was dealing with large red numbers, top management was replaced with a new board from the Communist party milieu. Entrepreneurship functions more formally, but also informally, also bonded the leading manager of a company to centralized Communist political structures. Top managers, party members themselves, adhered to the concept of democratic centralism, an organizational principle which meant that in practice the fulfilment of decisions and orders at the firm level were made by the party's leaders (Jerovsek and Rus 1989: 27). Consequently, managers found themselves in a very difficult position as they were faced with a problem of double loyalty: a loyalty to the party and a loyalty to all the employees within their firm.

Leading positions in legal entities within the economy and the society in general were either very much influenced or completely in the hands of political elites at different levels: in municipalities, regions, or even on the national and federal level when and if there was a matter of greater importance. A consensus among the three main institutions, the Self-Management, Operational Management, and Sociopolitical Organizations, represented a basis for formal implementation of a 'pluralistic management of enterprises' (Prasnikar and Svejnar 1988). Sociopolitical Communities (local, republican, and federal government units) were legally entitled to enter the decision-making process when such a consensus could not be achieved. In practice, government officials had informal channels of influencing enterprise behaviour as well.

In such circumstances, Yugoslav firms had a sophisticated formal framework in which the participation of workers should have developed at a very high level. Some surveys on the distribution of power in Yugoslav enterprises show that there was rather a great deal of dissatisfaction between workers regarding their actual level of participation in the decision-making process (Prasnikar 1989: 103–9). Another survey (Rus 1986) shows that workers' councils failed to represent workers' interests, although formally they were the most powerful body within a firm. The actual distribution of power in Yugoslav enterprises was much more hierarchical than would be suggested by a pure workers' self-management model (Prasnikar and Svejnar 1988). Numerous sociological studies have found that the actual distribution of power among different interest groups in the enterprise deviated considerably from the distribution of power anticipated by constitutional, legal, and statutory norms. Analyses of relative power show that enterprise directors (operating in the so-called collegium[3]) wielded the most power, followed by decision-makers in the technical departments, supervisors of economic units, the management board, and the workers' councils. Semi-skilled and unskilled workers were found to have the least power (Rus 1986). This relative distribution of power is reported to have existed for decades. In addition, observers agree that the main external institutions, the League of Communists, trade unions, and government authorities exerted significant external influence. However, some

---

[3] Apart from the general manager of the enterprise and the president of the enterprise workers' council, the collegium membership was composed of the enterprise president of the League of Communists, the president of the local trade union, and external experts.

information from that period suggests that the independent power of some managers of large companies increased to the level which caused some fear and caution among politicians.

The hypothesis that the economic performance of Yugoslav enterprises is attributable primarily to the system of workers' self-management becomes questionable as numerous studies have found semi-skilled and unskilled workers to have very little influence and power. The acknowledged influence of external institutions and the fact that the most powerful internal body, the collegium, included external political and social decision-makers also suggests that the behaviour of Yugoslav companies may have been guided more by political and social objectives then by the self-interest of workers-insiders. It is very difficult to draw a single conclusion about the dominant goals and strategies of enterprises in this period. However, evidence from interviews suggests that high and equitably distributed personal incomes and collective consumption, employment generation, and enterprise growth were the most important goals of Yugoslav firms.

Towards a capitalist socio-economic orientation

Following the first democratic elections in April 1990, the new political structures and coalition started to interfere in the decision-making process of large socially owned enterprises, which were previously led by 'red directors' (members of the Communist party), by appointing new management teams from their milieu. Attempts to interfere in the personnel policies of media, university, and socially owned companies were exactly the same as those which caused de-professionalism and negative attitudes towards promotion mechanisms in the past.

Today, as during the Second World War, confrontation exists between two political elites: the clergy and the Communists (Rus 1991: 51).[4] Both sides mobilize various organizations and their members' power to pursue their intended political goals and to accumulate enough political power to dominate over the opposing side. It is possible that these tendencies of political interference represent a continuity of the former system and have only been a natural reaction to the absence of professional associations in public, business, professional, and working activities, such as those discussed by Kristensen, Whitley, and others in this volume.

---

[4] The Catholic Church is also playing an important role in the denationalization process currently on its way. The idea of the law on returning the property to former owners has divided the public opinion. The Church represents one of the main candidates with restitution claims, demanding its property, especially land and forests, to be returned to it as the former owner.

Managers and external owners

In these new circumstances, the position of managers in society did not change a great deal. Despite the impression of significant political interference, the position of managers remains quite independent. In particular, the privatization process has not yet resulted in any significant direct pressure on managers to be accountable to the owners. When a company is privatized, according to statute, managers are accountable to the shareholders and Advisory Boards. The most common privatization outcome is that 60 per cent of the ownership is represented by internal owners, 10 per cent is represented by the Pension Fund, 10 per cent by the Compensation Fund, and 20 per cent by the Privatization Investment Fund(s).[5] This dispersed structure and the power position allows managers to retain a large degree of freedom with respect to the governance of firms. This may change when, after two to three years, the shares become tradable on capital markets.

In this respect, the role of Privatization Investment Funds should be mentioned, as they represent an instrument for the fund to collect ownership certificates from the population to buy packages of shares previously transferred to the Development Fund. Consequently, the main founders of Investment Funds are brokerage houses, banks, and insurance companies. Many believe that the Privatization Investment Funds will not have sufficient knowledge to participate in the companies as active owners in the future.

Another complicating issue arises when describing the position of managers in the transformation. This so-called 'wild privatization', where a great number of managers of socially owned companies took advantage of a very liberal Federal company law that was valid until the new Law on Ownership Transformation of Companies was passed in 1992, allowed managers of public enterprises to create new companies by underestimating the value of their assets and later at least partially privatizing these newly established companies without much supervision (Korze and Simoneti 1993: 213). It was not an unusual procedure for managers of socially owned companies to simply sign commercial contracts favourable to private companies (often owned by the same managers or their relatives) and in this way transfer business activity and bypass companies without proper compensation. Unregulated privatization of single vital parts of a company, market, and business connections as well as technological knowledge through transfers of capital, hire, and leasing arrangements, or simply a departure of main people into the private sector caused the destruction of many firms. Indeed,

[5] We are describing a predominant form of enterprises and their privatization. There are of course also companies that were in private hands since the time of establishing. Corporate governance issues are also much clearer in companies with foreign ownership.

'wild privatization' created a negative public opinion towards managers in general.

A growing privatization issue affecting the position of managers is the initiative for a legislative framework concerning the hostile take-overs of newly privatized companies in the near future, when current non-tradable securities will become available on capital markets. The Slovenian capital market belongs to the group of developing markets. There is a relatively small number of corporations (joint-stock companies) whose shares can be publicly and unlimitedly traded, with low liquidity levels and market capitalization additionally affecting the stability of this market. After the programme of privatization is finished, there will presumably be some 100 companies with shares freely transferable on secondary security markets. In addition to potential domestic investors, foreign legal and physical entities, with much more experience on the field of take-overs from their own environment, will also appear as possible investors. However, it could happen that because of the fear of foreign hostile take-overs, legislation could enable managers to retain even more freedom and control over the companies and thus diminish the already low level of contestability among managers.

Workers as workers and internal owners

The workers' position in Slovenian companies is special because they are usually also co-owners of the companies in which they work and form a coalition of internal owners with managers. The current experience of some privatized companies is rather painful, with some disputes between internal and external owners already in court. The basis of conflict is usually the fact that Private Investment Funds require a higher return on equity (and higher dividends) than managers (and workers) are willing to give. In many cases, managers prepare the strategic schemes which retain the majority internal-ownership structure in the future which, they believe, will allow them to retain their same current level of independence. The union usually plays a major role in educating and informing the workers on ownership. A close relationship between managers and workers is essential in these cases. One of the unfortunate consequences of this development is that managers spend too much time on these issues. Another one is that in these fragile relationships, managers are not willing to take risks that would be necessary in the process of real restructuring of firms. The status quo is thus retained.

An important reason for delays in restructuring and the late actions of managers is the power and capability of workers and trade unions to obstruct any suggestions on modification of a firm. Experience from Slovenia and other eastern countries shows that privatization leads to a radical decrease in employment, on average 25–30 per cent (Korze 1996).

Workers and trade unions therefore often resist privatization, especially in a form which would bring into firms owners with enough power to begin the restructuring. Worker resistance depends upon the number of workers who would be better off if the restructuring takes place, relative to those who would lose their privileges during the process.

Another reason for slow restructuring is the high cost of dismissing employees, since part of cost of dismissal has been transferred to employers. The cost of six to nine monthly wages (plus the time when negotiating with trade unions) and payments of very high indemnities represent a serious burden even for a successful enterprise (Korze 1996). The ones with difficulties could only deal with such costs if facing bankruptcy. Obviously it has been in the interest of politicians to prevent employers firing workers. The problems are also aggravated by the low mobility of workers, an often abused welfare system, a lack of available qualitative information on employment possibilities, and an incompatibility between the knowledge and skills base of redundant workers and the requirements or needs of a company.

Local communities

Governance structures show different levels of flexibility depending upon the location of the firm. In smaller towns located outside central Slovenia, localization is an important factor in decision-making, especially regarding employment, educational, and environmental issues. The main reason for such influence is the fact that, in local areas, people usually know each other well, and therefore those who do not follow or accept 'social' wishes and values are quickly excluded or disrespected by the society. This socio-cultural situation represents a heavy burden for managers and supervisors within a company. Local people's attitude towards specific issues forces management to behave according to the rules and expectations of the public. An important issue in this respect is the influence of global competitive pressures on these small communities. There are many towns and regions in Slovenia where one company is the sole employer for the area. The problems are very difficult, especially if the company is in a labour-intensive industry which is subject to notable cost pressures from global competition.

Other interest groups and elites

Other interest groups, such as lawyers, farmer unions, and business unions are also present, but to date, they have not been given much attention as far as the governance system is concerned. Doctors and teachers have a slightly different status due to the larger size and power of their trade unions.

Together with the reforms of the Slovene economic system, the perception of elites in Slovenia has changed during the last few years. Radical egalitarianism, which appeared during the decades following the Second World War, has caused a demolition of any elite structure based on origin, power, personality, or expertise. All groups were considered more or less equal and no special rewards were allowed for individual achievement within a company. In such a passive atmosphere, a lack of innovations resulted (Kos 1990: 217–22).

A very interesting example of elite groups in the past and present is the 'engineering' community. Some authors have stated that if more power had been attributed to the engineering community in the past, its motivation would have increased and today probably provided industry with new ideas and their implementations (Jerovsek and Rus 1989: 42). The engineering community today feels that it has lost even its small power (on the political as well as firm level) which existed in the past. They claim that because of lower costs, higher short-term profits, and lower risks, management often prefers involvement in subcontracting activities and licensing agreements with foreigners to in-house new product development. On the other hand, the managerial elite, which is more and more visible through professional associations and their changing life-style, claims that the engineering community is not capable of developing new products and that its power in the firms is sometimes even too strong. The conflict between the two elite groups, engineers and managers, will most probably remain until social agreement on development issues is reached and institutionalized.

4. WORK ORGANIZATION

If we examine the organizational structure of Yugoslav firms, we can identify some clear characteristics: (1) a distinctive hierarchical structure, (2) dependence upon bureaucratic models, (3) low levels of sub-unit autonomy within the macro system of companies, and consequently (4) low levels of any socio-organizational group autonomy within a company, (5) rigid leadership, (6) and personnel promotion policies which generally ignored skills, talents, and work results (Jerovsek and Rus 1989: 17). In the four decades of Yugoslav self-management, which tended to develop as a (re)distributive system on a company level, Yugoslav workers were only involved in profit-sharing activities. Meanwhile in other, primarily Western countries, various forms of production worker involvement, from autonomous working groups and quality control formations to movements for higher working standards emerged. Another characteristic of Yugoslav self-management was that neither syndicate (labour union) nor economic democracy developed (Rus 1991: 209). Negotiations on collective agreements and job security are two issues that mark the syndicate democracy. The wider the field of negotiating, the more developed becomes the syndicate democracy. With self-management and social agreements Yugoslavia formally introduced this idea, but the role of trade unions was anything but active, and due to its dependence on specific political structures, also irrelevant.

Work organization in firms was never an object of serious political interference and was also not directly affected by the introduction of the self-management system. The characteristics of work organization in general followed old traditions and norms, perhaps best illustrated by the German *Meister* system. However, the position of a supervisor has traditionally been more equal to that of the other workers. Usually their influence was somewhere between middle management and workers, which means that in some fields they had even more power and influence than representative bodies and external structures. Their influence on decision-making process could be described as neither large nor small, but somewhere in between (Rus 1986: 69). In most cases concerning decision-making on various levels, supervisors were either able to express their own opinion on certain decisions, where their contributions were sometimes taken into account, or they were just informed in advance. Our research shows that a supervisor could usually build his reputation and authority among workers only through his superior professional knowledge.

The fact is that in the past, the educated workers did not have many possibilities for their own participation. Enterprises fostered a passive environment where workers could not take advantage of their own knowledge and in many cases used it only as a negative power or resistance, instead of as an instrument for better cooperation. Conclusions of a survey revealed that workers with higher qualifications did not have any stronger influence on decision-making, and higher levels of education did not correspond with a more equal distribution of influence. If an employee did not have a suitable position within an organization, his education could not help him in obtaining greater influence inside a firm (Rus 1986: 55). The results further more revealed that the influence of workers was much stronger in bigger rather than in smaller companies. It also seemed that in the cases where there was more equality in power, it led to a much better usage of knowledge. A survey on the real distribution of influence stressed the following characteristics (Rus 1986: 76):

1. Workers' participation in the real decision-making process is almost irrelevant, while middle management shows the highest forms of participation. The same is true for aspirations on participation.
2. Aspirations of workers regarding the participation of representative bodies are very high, while the opposite goes for middle management.

3. The distribution of influence depends primarily upon organizational structure and environment, while forms of real participation correspond with technology and personal characteristics of participants.
4. Correlations of the quantity of influence between various organizational groups are mostly positive with only one exception: the influence of management is in a negative relationship to the influence of mostly every other organizational group.

The role of a technical manager was predominant in the factory in the past. He was/is usually also the second man in a firm. His role has been changing since the introduction of profit and cost centres and a new species of technical managers is emerging. The role of engineers in firms was in general quite important. Slovenian firms always based their competitive advantages on 'craftsmanship', but they were usually lagging behind in R&D and especially (international) marketing. However, the role of engineers is substantially diminished in firms where the R&D function performs poorly and there is no longer much demand for their outdated products or services. In these cases, the economists in the firms usually prevailed with their short-term solutions to problems by engaging in subcontracting operations or licensing agreements. Our research shows that there is very little rotation of engineers between firms and within firms as well. Local peculiarities and the relatively low mobility of Slovenian people to move or commute explains this. Many firms practise lifetime employment. Because of strong local community ties of both workers and management, it is also very difficult for managers to lay off workers. As already explained, the current ownership structure additionally makes the displacement of workers much more difficult.

In general, there have been very low levels of job rotation among factories. However, the Slovenian case shows many changes in the top management of the firms. In the last three years, 40.7 per cent of firms have hired new managing directors. In the last four years, nearly two-thirds of the companies have been given new managing directors. But there are still 23.7 per cent of companies with managing directors who have been holding their position for at least six years, and retaining their power within an enterprise also during the period of transition. The share of firms with a new managing director in the last three years is larger than the share of firms in need of a revitalization or turnaround (as 36 per cent of companies are in crisis or latent crisis). It seems that replacement in the top managing position in Slovenia is as regular as in other developed or undeveloped regions of the world (Pucko 1994).

In the former system, the hiring of people with special qualifications and education was also very difficult. A need for such workers appeared at specific periods of time, but due to the fact that firms could not offer them better conditions and alternative payment schemes, those workers were very difficult to acquire. Furthermore, the system allowed workers of special education and skills to refuse being removed or shifted to lower positions of work. On the other hand, the system permitted overmanning, especially of people who proved to be a technological surplus. The mobility of workers inside a company was possible only with additional preparations and new qualifications, which, in this way, is similar to Japanese corporations with lifetime employment and flexible reallocation of workers within an enterprise (Prasnikar 1989: 135).

Workers have usually not been very flexible and have had little discretion over task performance. In the past, and even at the present time, management was/are not able to lay off workers apart from due to serious violations of work discipline. If market circumstances demanded increased production, the company would hire some workers temporarily or instead increase the work obligations of workers already employed. When there had been a lack of demand for their products, firms simply launched the idea of collective holidays for all employees or decreased the number of workers by retiring or by voluntary departures. In case of a short-term disturbance in the market, firms did not fire workers, as job security is one of the most important values of employees.

According to our interviews with managers, there were some attempts by political officials to interfere more directly in work organization issues, especially in the 1970s. The quality of these 'directives' was so poor that they did not receive much attention from managers in companies. An important influence on the work organization came indirectly through the reform of the educational system in 1963 which interrupted the tradition, similar to that in German-speaking countries, where a special exam was required for a worker to be promoted to a supervisor position in a firm. Those people who qualified worked as experts in their vocations, teaching and supervising the others in the different departments of firms. Now, the Chamber of Craft of Slovenia is lobbying to restore some of this traditional knowledge by appointing multiplicators (mentors), individuals who would transfer vocational knowledge through different school programmes.

Work organization issues are now gaining in importance. We can say that cost management is important only in the last few years. Previous inflationary, soft-budget constraints and the relatively large and closed Yugoslav market conditions allowed firms levels of inefficiency which are no longer tolerable in international competition and the more settled macroeconomic conditions of today. A trend towards team-work and global quality procedures is becoming evident. The role of supervisors is also changing. Demands which were before oriented towards a supervisor's technical knowledge are now more concentrated on his or her ability to manage people. A lack of this ability has become evident. Different modes of production cells are being introduced into manufacturing firms in order to improve quality and productivity. Our research and that of other researchers shows very good results with these newly introduced methods, which can be partly attributed to previously held negative attitudes towards excessively hierarchical structures and the strong cultural value of equality in Slovenian society.[6]

A primary constraint with respect to the developments in work organization is the lack of knowledge at the top management level which has critical consequences for the successful application of knowledge, innovations, and work experience to the lower levels of a corporate hierarchy. The data show that top management in the Slovenian economy has the lowest formal education within Europe (Jerovsek and Rus 1989: 140). The self-management system also worked against the possibility of selecting 'core' workers within a company. In companies where a form of management buy-out privatization scheme (as opposed to an employee buy-out programme) dominated, the establishment of 'core' employees is already evident. This is also the only case where owners currently have influence on work organization issues.

5. CONCLUSION

It was the intention of this chapter to demonstrate, through the case of Slovenia as one of the richest and most successful of the former east European socialist economies, how complicated reality is with respect to governance structures of transforming economies. The underlying continuities of the past must be considered side by side with the initiation of complementary change mechanisms to promote market development.

Macro-institutional changes have initiated some change in governance structures, but in general very little has changed at the work system level. In this respect, the current transformation process parallels the situation under the former socialist system. This fact can, in general, be attributed to the specifics of the socialist system in Yugoslavia, where the competitive questions of efficiency and effectiveness were not important enough to encourage internal efforts by companies to change work systems. External political (ideological) influences were oriented primarily to areas where some results were more easily visible (e.g. organizational structures of firms) and did not address more complicated issues of inter-worker relationships which can usually not be resolved by a decree approach. The

---

[6] It is interesting to note that some foreign MNCs are at the forefront of introduction of new organizational principles on the working place. See for example the case of Revoz (Renault's company in Slovenia) where they discovered greater similarities between Slovenian and Japanese workers than between French and Japanese workers (Globokar 1995). Some other large Slovenian companies (e.g. Gorenje, Iskra Emeco) are already introducing these concepts and are building on the experience of this case.

specifics of the socialist system, supported by the deeply rooted local peculiarities and historical context of Slovenian society, developed fragile relationships among different social actors, which are to a great extent preserved in the transformation period.

In addition to this, the transformation period thus far has preoccupied firms with privatization leaving little space to tackle issues such as business strategy and work organization. It is expected that global competitiveness pressures will have the biggest effect on the developments of the work systems in Slovenia in the future. It is yet to be seen how these pressures will be accommodated in the Slovenian context. Deeper knowledge and understanding about the nature of global changes as well as the understanding of Slovenian specifics is needed among all social actors in Slovenia in order to achieve a more natural and thus more successful response to these challenges.

REFERENCES

Globokar, T. (1995), 'Eastern Europe Meets Ouest', An Empirical Study on French Management in a Slovenian Plant, paper delivered to the 12th EGOS Colloquium (Turkey).

Jerovsek, J., and Rus, V. (1989), *Inovativno podjetje* (Ljubljana).

Korze, U. (1996), 'Prestrukturiranje podjetij v Sloveniji v devetdesetih' in *Zbornik referatov*: 28. simpozij o sodobnih metodah v racunovodstvu in poslovnih financah, Zveza ekonomistov Slovenije and Zveza racunovodij, financnikov in revizorjev Slovenije, 9–24 (Portoroz).

——and Simoneti, M. (1993), 'Privatization in Slovenia—1992', in CEEPN Annual Conference Series, *Privatization in Central & Eastern Europe 1992*, 208–35.

Kos, M. (1990), 'Slovenski inzenirji in mit izdelka', *RR* 7: 36–7 (Ljubljana).

Prasnikar, J. (1989), *Delavska participacija in samoupravljanje v dezelah v razvoju* (Ljubljana).

——and Prasnikar, V. (1986), 'The Yugoslav Self-Managed Firm in Historical Perspective', *Economic and Industrial Democracy*, 7: 167–90.

——and Pregl, Z. (1991), 'Economic Development in Yugoslavia in 1990 and Prospects for the Future', in *AEA Papers and Proceedings*, 81/2: 191–5.

——and Svejnar, J. (1988), 'Economic behaviour of Yugoslav enterprises', in *Advances in the Economic Analysis of Participatory and Labour Managed Firms*, 3: 237 311.

Pucko, D. (1994), 'Restructuring Strategies in the Slovenian Firms', paper delivered to the European International Business Association, 20th Annual Conference (Warsaw).

Rus, V. (1986), *Odlocanje in moc* (Maribor).

——(1991), 'Kvaliteta zivljenja', *Nova proizvodnja*, 6: 302–5.

PART 4

Concluding Overview

12

The Social Regulation of Work Systems
Institutions, Interest Groups, and Varieties of Work Organization in Capitalist Societies

RICHARD WHITLEY

1. INTRODUCTION

As the chapters in this book demonstrate, the organization and control of work processes and of workplace relations in capitalist societies are complex, systemic phenomena which vary substantially between institutional contexts (cf. Boyer 1990, 1991; Lane 1989). While Taylorism or scientific management principles were once thought to represent the only efficient way of structuring work activities, they are now seen to be historically and societally contingent patterns of work organization which depended on a number of circumstantial factors to become established in the USA, and which by no means dominated industrial organizations in Europe or Japan (Guillén 1994; Merkle 1980). As Kristensen emphasizes, it is also apparent that Fordist production systems have had many variants and have not always proved as cost effective as some adherents claimed (Boyer 1988, 1991; Wood 1989).

Equally, the idea that these sorts of work system are being replaced by a single standardized form of work organization and control in the more 'advanced' capitalist economies, whether summarized as flexible specialization, neo- or post-Fordism, or diversified quality production, is increasingly discredited. Rather, the prevalent ways in which work is organized and controlled, and connected to more general labour management policies, in different sectors, regions, and countries vary considerably and there is no reason to expect any particular pattern to become dominant across institutional contexts on the grounds of economic efficiency or through 'globalization' by multinational companies. Instead of hypostatizing particular modes of structuring work processes as exemplifications of different stages of capitalist development which inexorably succeed each other according to some economic functionalist logic, it is more fruitful to examine how and why distinctive patterns of work organization and control have become established and changed in different capitalist societies.

To do this requires clarification of their essential characteristics and how these vary between market economies to constitute distinctive work systems. Such systems combine particular ways of structuring tasks and the division of labour, controlling how work is allocated, performed, and rewarded as well as certain employment practices. As Kristensen, Iterson, Lane, and other contributors have shown, these systems are linked to the nature of firms, interest groups, and dominant governance principles or 'rules of the game' in different societies, which in turn often stem from particular patterns of industrialization. The comparative analysis of work systems therefore necessitates both the identification of the processes by which major work-related interest groups are constituted in different societies and the associated conventions governing how they compete and cooperate in workplaces.

Just as the rules of electoral politics affect the nature and structure of political parties and how they compete in liberal democracies, so too the institutions governing the organization of, and access to, capital and labour power in market economies affect the nature of owners' interest groups, managers, and various labour groupings, as well as the ways in which they compete and cooperate. Such norms and conventions also lead these groups to invest in particular kinds of skills and knowledge which, in turn, influence the ways they deal with each other and eventually reflects back on dominant institutional conventions (North 1993). Differences between British and German managerial identities, skills, and practices, for instance, reflect variations in labour market institutions and educational systems, as well as general conceptions of professional expertise and status which stem partly from different industrialization patterns (Lane in this volume; Stewart *et al.* 1994). The sorts of prevalent work organization patterns that have become established in different capitalist societies, then, reflect both the nature of interest groupings and the governance principles underlying their formation and interaction.

Drawing on the contributions to this book and other recent analyses, I here outline a framework for comparing and contrasting the key differences in these phenomena across capitalist societies, and for explaining the prevalence—or relative absence—of particular kinds of work system such as the ideal types of Taylorism and delegated responsibility. For ease of exposition, work systems will be presented in this chapter largely as the direct and indirect outcome of both particular kinds of interest groups and of certain institutions, but institutions are not, of course, immutable and do develop over time, as Morgan shows in his analysis of welfare regimes. Equally, system contradictions do occur and are often critical sources of system change, but the emphasis here is on how particular institutions and types of social groups tend to encourage the development and reproduction of distinctive kinds of work organization and control and, perhaps more directly, discourage antithetical ones.

Initially, I shall suggest how we might develop a small set of dimensions for distinguishing major kinds of work systems as distinctive ways of structuring work relations and labour management. Second, I consider how we could differentiate between the organization of interest groups in various capitalist societies and how these variations are connected to the development of different work systems. Third, the key institutions affecting both phenomena will be analysed, together with their most significant linkages to work system characteristics, and the conditions encouraging and discouraging the adoption of contrasting patterns of work organization and control identified.

2. CHARACTERISTICS AND TYPES OF WORK SYSTEMS

Key Characteristics of Work Systems

Most comparative analyses of systems of work organization and control in capitalist societies implicitly or explicitly rely on an ideal type of Taylorism as the key reference point for contrasting types of task control and labour management (cf. Wood 1989). In discussions of 'genuine', 'flawed', or 'hybrid' Fordism, this focus on task control has been extended to broader organizational characteristics, such as the stratification of skills and statuses and the nature of reward systems, and to more macro-societal phenomena such as the welfare state and the 'social wage' (e.g. Boyer 1990, 1994; cf. Morgan in this volume).

In seeking to understand why different kinds of work system have become established in different societies, and the roles of various groups in these institutionalization processes, it is difficult to isolate the work process control practices from more general employment and labour management strategies since these are often mutually implicative, as the examples of scientific management and responsible autonomy illustrate (Friedman 1977). How tasks are structured and task performance controlled are usually quite closely interlinked with recruitment, training, and reward strategies, as well as to bargaining practices, and these in turn are often connected to firms' overall product and market strategies as the contrast of British, French, and German practices shows (Lane 1989 and in this volume; Sorge 1991, 1996). Work systems, then, are constituted by interconnected aspects of task organization and control, workplace relations between social groups, and employment practices and policies. Their key characteristics will now be identified.

Work processes are typically analysed in terms of task specialization or fragmentation, on the one hand, and worker discretion over task performance, on the other hand (e.g. Lane 1989: 139). 'Taylorized' tasks are usually portrayed as highly standardized by external agents, highly simplified, and narrowly specialized with little or no scope for individuals to influence how tasks are executed—summarized as the separation of conception from execution (Guillén 1994: 42). Responsible autonomy or delegated responsibility task systems, on the other hand, allocate much greater independence to individuals or work groups as to how work is to be conducted, and tasks are usually more broadly defined and complex. However, it is worth noting that specialization and fragmentation of tasks is not always the corollary of simplification, as Kuhn (1989) points out, and that low discretion can accompany considerable task variety, as in the Chinese family business (Redding 1990). Thus, the first characteristic of work systems to be identified here, task fragmentation and specialization, should be distinguished from the second one, the degree of worker discretion over how tasks are performed and involvement in problem solving.

A further aspect of work processes which differentiates many continental European work systems from some North American and East Asian ones, is the extent of worker influence over task allocation and definition, worker deployment, and work organization more generally. As Kumazawa and Yamada (1989) have emphasized, Japanese workers in large firms may have some discretion over task performance, and are involved in problem solving, but have very little say in what tasks they do or the conditions under which they do them. In contrast, German and Scandinavian workers since the war have considerable collective influence over task allocation and worker deployment (Jurgens 1989; Kristensen 1996 and in this volume). This characteristic of work systems can be termed the degree of managerial control over work organization and allocation.

Related aspects of labour management strategies and employment policies concern management–worker relations and the ways that rewards are allocated. The Taylorist emphasis on separating task execution from conception according to 'scientific' work study and measurement, for example, was intended to facilitate job standardization and simplification so that skilled workers could be replaced by unskilled and cheaper ones who were in principle easily replaced. This standardization of jobs and organizational roles enabled rewards to be based on the amount of standard outputs produced by each role incumbent, as distinct from their specific skills or personal capacities, and did not reward—or seek to elicit—workers' initiatives in solving problems. Most employees were expected to perform highly standardized tasks and paid according to their success in meeting the demands of the predetermined and narrowly defined role. Managers in scientific management work systems, on the other hand, were seen as knowledgeable and highly skilled—at least those that formulated, standardized, and controlled work processes, i.e. Mintzberg's technostructure—and so were quite remote and separate from the bulk of the workforce in terms of their expected commitment, competencies, and substitutability.

In contrast, the various responsible or delegated autonomy work systems tie rewards more to skills and/or individual capabilities which are often quite broadly conceived and assessed over substantial periods of time. Here, workers' involvement in problem diagnosis and solving is seen as crucial to the organization's success and their skills need to be broader to deal with complex tasks. The core workforce is not, then, easily disposable or replaceable and their knowledge is usually continuous with that of management rather than being qualitatively different and very much inferior. Typically, reward differentials are lower in these work systems than in more 'Taylorized' ones and less tied to job definitions (Lane 1989).

Types of Work Systems

This comparison reveals a further three important characteristics of work systems: the extent to which managers and workers are separated and opposed in their backgrounds and skills, the degree of employer commitment to retaining their core workforce, as manifested in efforts to provide employment security for them, and the basis of reward allocation and differentiation. Significant variations in these occur across Europe and elsewhere, as Kristensen has shown in his analysis of Britain, Germany, and Denmark. Together with the three aspects of work processes identified above, they constitute the key dimensions for comparing and contrasting work systems in capitalist societies. At least five distinct kinds of work system can be identified in terms of these six characteristics and are summarized in Table 12.1. These types are relatively internally consistent and develop interdependently with particular kinds of interest groups and rules of the game governing their interaction and control over resources. 'Taylorism' for instance combines high levels of job fragmentation, managerial control over task performance and work organization, strong manager–worker separation, low employer commitment to employment security, and job-based reward systems. It is unlikely to become widely implemented as a work system where unions are strongly organized on a skill basis, and/or managers share many of the experiences and skills of the workforce, and/or labour organizations are incorporated into state mechanisms for regulating conflicts between interest groups (Guillén 1994; Lazonick 1991).

In contrast, delegated responsibility work systems emphasize worker involvement in problem diagnosis and solution in dealing with complex tasks, and so require greater levels of mutual dependence and commitment between employers and their core workforce. This is difficult to develop where managers and workers have quite distinct identities and

TABLE 12.1. Types of Work Systems

Characteristics	Taylorist	Delegated responsibility		Flexible specialization	
		Negotiated	Paternalist	Artisanal	Patriarchal
Job fragmentation	High	Low	Low	Low	Low
Worker discretion and involvement	Low	High	Considerable	High	Limited
Managerial control of work organization	High	Medium	High	Medium	High
Separation of managers from workers	High	Low	High	Low	High
Employer commitment to employment security for core workforce	Low	Considerable	Limited	Limited	Limited
Rewards tied to	Standardized jobs	Skills	Personal performance and abilities	Skills and personal evaluation	Personal evaluation of performance

backgrounds, are mobile between firms and industries, and owners do not share long-term risks with particular firms. A major difference between many work systems of this kind that have developed in continental Europe and in Japan and elsewhere concerns the degree of worker influence on work organization and allocation. Strong industrial or craft unions in much of post-war Europe have limited managerial control over work organization, and generated what are termed 'negotiated' work systems here, in contrast to the enterprise-based unions in Japan and the relatively weak occupational associations there and in other countries. Relatedly, while rewards are usually linked to formally certified skills in negotiated systems, they are more based on personal performance and capacities as assessed by supervisors and managers over some time in more 'paternalist' work systems.

The third general type of work system discussed here is labelled flexible specialization because of its emphasis on flexibility of work processes and products and the typical small size of organizations. They combine fluid job categories and flexible employees, in terms of tasks undertaken and skills developed, with a high level of specialization on particular outputs and processes, and reliance on various forms of market contracting to coordinate inputs and outputs across the production chain. This emphasis on organizational flexibility typically implies much lower levels of mutual commitment between employers and employees than in most delegated responsibility work systems, and a corresponding high level of interfirm mobility—and indeed of firm birth and death.

The two distinct forms of flexible specialization identified in Table 12.1 differ mostly in their authority relationships and the significance of formally certified skills. The artisanal form is typified by many European variants of industrial districts, whether Marshallian, Italian, or Danish, in which small firms compete and cooperate on the basis of workers' skills, flexibility, and innovativeness (Kristensen 1996; Langlois and Robertson 1995). Jobs and tasks are varied and wide ranging, with considerable worker discretion—sometimes buttressed by strong unions (Trigilia 1990)—and owner-managers and workers usually share a common skill base. Managerial control over work organization is limited by the need to maintain skilled workers' commitment, as is managers' ability to allocate rewards personally and differentially. In contrast, the patriarchal form combines much greater levels of managerial control over work organization, and sometimes over task performance, with a considerable separation of the owner-manager from the bulk of the workforce. Typified by the Chinese family business, it reflects many aspects of pre-industrial authority relations in newly industrialized countries in which patriarchal family authority patterns mirror, at least ideologically, those institutionalized in the state (Pye 1985). The lack of strong intermediary organizations between the family and the state in many of these societies, and usually of a strong public training system, encourage highly personal and direct control over work processes and limited employer–employee trust (Redding 1990; Whitley 1992a).

These characteristics of work systems, and their varying establishment in capitalist societies in the twentieth century, reflect the sorts of interest groups and collective actors that have developed in these societies and the dominant ways in which they compete for resources and control over juris-dictions as the result of variations in political, financial, labour, and cultur-al systems. In the next section I outline the crucial ways in which interest groups are differently constituted across market economies in relation to their impact on work system characteristics.

3. THE ORGANIZATION OF INTEREST GROUPS AND WORK SYSTEM CHARACTERISTICS

Key Features of Interest Groups

Interest groups are seen here as organized collective actors representing particular social interests which compete for control over resources and socially valued activities. They differ in the extent to which they mobilize and represent particular kinds of interests in a market economy, how they do so, and on what basis they compete with each other. The most signifi-cant differentiating feature of such groups across countries is the overall extent to which they mobilize interests throughout society and function as intermediary organizations between families and the state. Generally, industrializing societies are relatively weak in such forms of interest repre-sentation compared to most European countries, such as Finland, Germany, and the Netherlands as discussed by Lilja, Lane, and Iterson. Relatedly, the importance of 'horizontal' forms of affiliation and collective action, such as unions and professional associations, clearly differs between, say, France and Germany, let alone between the Scandinavian countries and Pacific-Asian ones.

Further differences occur with respect to the scope of interests repre-sented in dominant organizations—from narrow crafts and professional skills to broad categories of manual workers throughout a sector—the degree of mobilization and organization of specific interest groups, and prevalent modes of competition and cooperation. These last vary from largely adversarial, zero-sum conflicts over distributional issues in which market power is the determining factor, to more formally regulated disputes over a range of issues where groups combine collaboration over, say, train-ing, with competition and conflicts on a continuing basis. Competition between interest groups can, then, vary in terms of: (a) the stability and formal recognition of the parties concerned, (b) the regularity and conti-nuity of their interactions, (c) the formal regulation of conflicts, (d) the extent and scope of any cooperation between groups, and (*e*) the systematic structuring and integration of conflicts at different levels of the bargaining system and across industries and sectors in various forms of corporatism.

From this broad set of characteristics of collective actors and interest groups, three major ones can be identified which are particularly relevant to the analysis of work systems. First, there is the overall extent to which employees are in general mobilized around horizontal forms of interest representation. One of the most striking differences in the organization of work groups and collective actors within organizations between European countries and, *a fortiori* between Europe, North America, and Pacific Asia, is the varied extent to which these are based on extra-organizational ties and identities which are more or less formally structured. Interest groups based on certified skills and union membership are clearly much more important in the German and Scandinavian economies than they are in Mediterranean Europe or Pacific Asia. Collective action by employees in the former societies is therefore structured more around extra-organizational identities and commitments than it is in the latter. Of course, family, kinship, locality, and schools/university-based cliques and factions can and do function as the basis for collective identities within and between work organizations in many countries, but these personal and particularistic groupings rarely form stable and systematically organized interest groups which compete for control over resources and rewards in an institutionalized framework. An important distinguishing characteristic of interest groups, then, is their strength in mobilizing horizontal interests across organizations and sectors.

Second, where horizontally based interest groups are significant collective actors, the extent to which they are segmented and fragmented into a number of distinct strongly bounded and rather narrow groupings can vary considerably. Britain and Denmark, for example, seem to share a quite strong distinction between skilled workers' and 'general' unskilled workers' unions, whereas post-war Germany, Finland, and Sweden have more sector-based forms of labour mobilization and representation, as reported by Kristensen and Lilja in this book. Additionally, Britain has a much more fragmented organization of high-level white-collar expertise in engineering, accounting, etc. than most European countries (Campagnac and Winch, and Lane, in this volume; Geddes 1995). This segmentation and stratification of skill-based interest groups can have quite marked effects on the organization of work, particularly its specialization, as the separation of skilled maintenance workers from semi-skilled operators and of different professional groups in Britain indicates (Child *et al.* 1983; Maurice *et al.* 1980). This characteristic of interest groups can be described as the degree of segmentation.

Third, interest groups vary in their legitimacy and prevalent mode of competing with each other. Unions, for example, have widely contrasting legal rights and duties, and quite different roles in conflict resolution, training, and general policy-making across Europe, let alone elsewhere. Relatedly, states have differed in their attempts to regulate industrial conflicts formally, and to specify the role of different groups. This aspect of interest group structure and behaviour combines the recognition and regulation of them as appropriate collective actors with their involvement in a range of activities which typically require cooperation as well as competition. At one extreme they may be only quasi-legalized and interact as essentially oppositional agents not only to employers but also to the state as a whole, while at the other they are highly institutionalized as full partners in a wide range of regulated activities in corporatist states such as Austria, the Netherlands, and Finland (Katzenstein 1985). This characteristic can be summarized as the degree of incorporation of horizontal interest groups as legitimate and formally regulated social partners.

Further aspects of collective actors and interest groups in capitalist societies concern, of course, the organization of ownership and control of economic activities. There are a number of aspects to be considered here, such as the fragmentation of owners, the significance of family and broader kinship-based owning groups, the power of financial intermediaries and the development of a distinct socio-economic stratum of senior managers separate from property rights holders, but three interrelated ones are particularly important in the context of work systems. These concern the dependence of owners and managers on the success and growth of particular firms and/or sectors and their associated interests, including, of course, their mutual interdependence or separation.

Considering first the organization and roles of property rights holders, there are two characteristics of these which affect work organization and control patterns, partly directly and partly through the interdependence of managerial careers with the fate of particular firms as opposed to a separation of senior managers' interests from those of specific companies. First of all, there is the strong difference between market economies in which owners typically are directly involved in the management of economic activities and those in which they delegate control to non-owning managers. This obviously affects the extent to which ownership-based collective actors develop separately from those organizing senior managers' interests.

Secondly, amongst this latter group there are significant variations in the scope of their interests in the firms in which they invest. In particular, the extent to which share ownership overlaps with other business relationships between companies differs greatly between capital market-based financial systems such as the Anglo-American economies and bank-dominated ones such as Japan and Germany. In those latter societies, owners are more often 'locked in' to the fate and success of the firms they invest in, and so have much greater interest in their long-term growth, as well as having a variety of business ties and links with them so that share ownership is just one aspect of complex and extensive interdependences. These two characteristics can be summarized in a single dimension as the range and strength of owners' interests in the activities and success of particular firms.

The third aspect of owners and managers which affects the organization of collective actors and work systems is the dependence of senior managers on the fate of particular companies and/or sectors. This affects the extent to which they see themselves as a distinct social group or identify themselves more with specific organizations and industries. The obvious contrast here is between the post-war Japanese economic system where managers in the large-firm sector typically spend nearly all their working life in the same corporation, and so depend very largely on its growth and success for their own career, and the common Anglo-Saxon pattern of high rates of interfirm mobility, and often intersectoral mobility, frequently based upon the possession of a general management credential such as the MBA degree. In these latter cultures, 'management' is seen more as a generalizable set of skills and competences than as industry-specific functions linked to more technical competences. Where access to elite managerial posts is tied to academic success in a small number of higher education organizations, such as the *grandes écoles* in France, careers at the top of organizational hierarchies are also more governed by general credentials than by individual firm performance but interfirm and intersectoral mobility at lower levels is often more limited than in the Anglo-Saxon labour markets (Boyer 1990; Lane 1989). The interests of elite managers in this situation are thus more general across the economy than are those of more junior staff.

These aspects of ownership and management are interconnected. Low levels of direct owner involvement coupled with purely financial interests, for instance, probably limit the dependence of managerial careers and interests on particular firms and sectors because risk sharing and mutual commitment between shareholders and managers is restricted in this situation, and the market for corporate control is likely to be mirrored by considerable managerial mobility as elite managers seek to reduce their 'exposure' to individual organizations. As owners treat their holdings in individual firms more as elements of a liquid portfolio, in other words, so too can we expect managers to 'diversify' their career risks by developing general skills which can be applied across a range of organizations and sectors, although this obviously also depends on labour market conditions and the education and training system.

High levels of direct owner involvement and broad interests in particular businesses, however, are consonant with varying degrees of managerial dependence on individual firms and sectors. While this combination is often associated with considerable managerial stability and an emphasis on the firm and industry specificity of valued managerial skills—as in Germany and Japan—it is not always so. This link is especially weak when strong and direct owner control limits opportunities for managerial autonomy and entrepreneurial skills are more highly valued than technical ones, as in economies dominated by Chinese family businesses. Here, as in many economies and/or sectors dominated by small firms, managers without strong family-like ties to owners frequently leave employers when they have learnt enough about the business to start their own firms, sometimes with the supports of their previous employer (Wong 1988).

Connections between interest group features and work systems

Considering next the linkages between these five features of interest groups and work systems in market economies, it is clear that many characteristics of these systems depend on more general contextual arrangements, such as those governing labour markets and the development, certification, and organization of skills than just on the nature of collective actors. There are, however, a number of direct connections that can be identified and these are summarized in Table 12.2. Considering first the degree of job fragmentation and managerial control of task performance, these are limited by strong horizontal groupings, especially skill-based ones, as Kristensen emphasizes is the case in much of Danish industry. Additionally, strong and direct owner involvement in management will often limit job fragmentation because most owner-managed firms are small and flexible, and do not have large production planning departments to Taylorize work practices.

Managerial discretion over work organization and allocation is also likely to be restricted by strong horizontal groupings, whether based on skills or sectors. It is additionally limited by highly corporatist arrangements because these often grant unions some negotiating rights over the power of managers to restructure organizations and transfer workers between jobs and plants. On the other hand, strong owner control is likely to encourage managerial insistence on the right to determine how work is to be organized and allocated because of the personal involvement of owners in day-to-day managements, subject to the power of the unions.

High levels of manager–worker separation as implied in Taylorist systems are limited by corporatist regulation of interest groups since this implies mutual recognition of employers and employees as partners across a range of activities and goes well beyond purely market relations. They are additionally restricted by high levels of owner and manager dependence on the success of individual firms since this encourages belief in a common destiny and commitment to the same organization. On the other hand, they are likely to be enhanced where managers are clearly much better and differently educated from the bulk of the workforce, and have high level credentials, such as the MBA, which enable them to transfer easily between firms and sectors.

TABLE 12.2. Linkages between Characteristics of Interest Groups and Work Systems

Characteristics of interest groups	Work system characteristics					
	Job fragmentation	Worker discretion	Managerial control over work organization	Manager–worker separation	Employer commitment to employment security	Rewards basis
Strength of horizontal interest groups	Limited	Considerable for skilled workers	Limited		Considerable	
Specialization of interest groups		Considerable over specialized tasks				Skills where interest groups are based on skills
Incorporation of interest groups			Limited	Limited	Considerable	
Involvement of owners in management of specific firms	Limited		High except where unions are strong		Limited to personal commitments	Personal evaluation except where unions are strong
Managers' dependence on specific firm and/or sector growth				Limited	Medium	

Similarly, employer commitment to the core workforce is encouraged when organizational dependence of managers is high, corporatist arrangements are strong, and horizontal associations are powerful because of the difficulties of disposing of workers in this situation and the greater significance of firm specific competences for senior managers. Strong owner control, in contrast, may well limit such commitment where flexibility is at a premium, and trust is overwhelmingly based on personal, rather than organizational commitments. Finally, rewards will be based more on skills where these are strongly entrenched as the foundation of specialist groups, but more on personal qualities and performance where owners are in direct control of relatively small organizations.

4. SOCIAL INSTITUTIONS, INTEREST GROUPS AND WORK SYSTEMS

Institutions and interest groups

Many of these connections are highly dependent on the broader institutional contexts in which they develop, particularly the institutions governing the development and organization of skills, the availability of capital and trust, and authority relations. In this section I summarize the key relationships between particular institutional features of market economies, the characteristics of interest groups just discussed, and their joint structuring of work systems. First, I discuss how the central institutions governing skills, capital, trust, and authority relations are related to the organization of collective actors and then I will consider how they combine to affect patterns of work organization and control.

The major institutions governing the organization of work-related interests in market economies concern the development and control of skills, the ways in which the state regulated workplace relations during and after industrialization, including systems of financial security as discussed by Morgan, and the nature of the financial system, as well as prevalent trust and authority relations. In particular, the strength and organization of the public training system have substantial consequences for the sorts of skills that are developed and their connections to interest groupings. Work by Maurice *et al.* (1980, 1986), for instance, has shown the importance of a strong, widely accepted, and far-reaching public training system for work organization patterns in Germany and it obviously also affects the development of occupational skill-based groupings, and their significance throughout the workforce, as well.

Relatedly, the more unions and employers are jointly involved with state agencies in its direction and operation, the more likely the skills it produces will be regarded as useful by firms. Where, on the other hand, the public training system is weak, and formal educational achievements regarded as crucial indicators of competence and ability, it is likely that the verdicts of the various levels of the academic educational system will stratify entry to— and perhaps limit movement between—labour markets, especially at elite levels. This academic stratification of labour markets limits the development of common identities within organizations and encourages the separation of status groups based on success in the formal educational system.

Also crucial to the establishment of strong occupational groupings are the strength and policies of the state during and after industrialization and, in particular, the extent to which pre-industrial forms of skill development and control have been reinforced and reproduced by the state, as Campagnac and Winch demonstrate in their comparison of Britain and France. The major contrast here is between societies where the state has supported the establishment of intermediary associations between itself and families which mobilize commitments and generate distinct collective identities, and those where it has destroyed pre-industrial associational forms and/or actively discouraged the development of horizontal interest groups mediating citizen–state relations. A third situation occurs in those countries, typically Anglo-Saxon ones, where the state has delegated substantial control over skill development to practitioner associations and educational organizations, but without formally integrating these processes or developing systematic procedures for organizing relations between associations and the state. Especially in Europe, these differences are quite strong and have had major consequences for interest groups and work systems, as Lane, van Iterson, Kristensen, and others demonstrate in this book

Two key features of institutions governing ownership relations concern the extent to which owners are locked into the fates of the firms they invest in, and, relatedly, their trust in the formal institutions governing property rights, control over economic activities and economic exchanges in general, what has been termed systemic trust or 'confidence' (Luhmann 1979, 1988). The former is linked to the existence of large liquid secondary financial markets, upon which financial claims can easily be traded between anonymous actors, in capital market-based financial systems. This enables owners to treat equity holdings as components of portfolios whose overall financial performance is to be maximized, and so reduces the risks attached to any single shareholding and owners' commitment to it. Capital market financial systems, then, reduce the scope of owners' interests in particular firms' activities and, by enabling a market for corporate control to develop, also limit managers' dependence on the fortunes of any specific organization. Relatedly, because such financial systems presuppose considerable trust in formal institutions governing exchange relations, the degree of systemic trust affects owner behaviour, especially the lack of it. The less trust that private property owners have in formal institutional procedures and in the good faith of their agents—what Barber (1983) terms fiduciary trust—

the more direct will be their involvement in management and the broader will be their concerns.

The final institutional feature to be considered here is the nature of authority relations. A key aspect of subordination in market economies is the extent to which authority is linked to paternalism because this affects the scope of connections between managers and workers as well as the legitimate ability of superiors to require compliance with a wide range of orders. As Beetham (1991) points out, paternalism implies parent–child authority relations in which the parties are inherently unequal and superiors are therefore expected to act in the interests of subordinates—since the latter are incapable of recognizing their true interests and acting appropriately. Paternalist authority relations thus encourage close owner involvement in management and broad owner interests. These connections are summarized in Table 12.3 and the effects of combining these features will now be discussed in a little more detail.

Considering first the contrast of societies which combine a strong public training system with joint employer/union involvement in its control and operation against those without such a system, it is clear that the former are much more likely to generate distinctive occupational interests around certified expertise than are the latter. This is especially so when skill-based unions are strongly entrenched—as in Denmark. The combination of strong skill-based unions with a highly developed technical training system—partly controlled by the unions—seems here to have led to work groups being predominantly organized around externally certified skills and their interests focused on the control of tasks and technologies through continued skill enhancement in Danish firms, to the extent that managerial integration and control of work processes is limited (Kristensen 1992, 1996). Where, on the other hand, unions are more sector based—as in Germany and other Scandinavian countries—this high degree of skill identification and competition seems less marked and managerial coordination correspondingly greater.

A well-funded and highly regarded training system which incorporates a wide range of skills for different sectors jointly controlled through standardized structures by unions, employers, and the state also implies the development of expertise-based identities and interests among a large part of the working population, as opposed to these being restricted to elite groups or a limited number of roles such as maintenance workers. As a result, the majority of people in societies with such training systems expect to gain a certified skill and invest accordingly. In contrast, training systems for many skills in the Anglo-Saxon economies combine strong practitioner control over their definition, assessment, and certification with the bulk of the workforce being excluded from the system altogether or else limited to low-status, narrowly defined skills. The delegation of responsibility for skill development and control by the state to unions, professional associations,

TABLE 12.3. Social Institutions and the Organization of Interest Groups

Institutional Features	Characteristics of the organization of collective actors				
	Specialization of interest groupings	Strength of horizontal associations	Incorporation of interest groups	Strength and scope of owner involvement in firms	Managerial dependence on firms & sectors
Historical continuity and priority of skill-based groups	+	+			
State support for intermediary organizations	+	+	+		+
Scope and strength of public training system	–	+	+		
Employer/union involvement in public training system			+		
Academic stratification of labour markets	–		–		–
Capital market based financial system				–	–
Degree of systemic trust			–	–	
Paternalist authority relations		–		+	–

and similar groups has led to a highly varied, weakly standardized system which covers only a minority of employees in some of these societies and, as a result, specialization of interest groups is high.

At least in the UK, the combination of practitioner elite control of the more prestigious 'professional' skills, and the limited or non-existent cooperation between professional associations, the education system, and employers in defining, developing, and assessing such skills, has led to an emphasis on controlling the numbers of newly qualified practitioners—and so maintaining incomes—and reproducing existing professional practices, most notably in accountancy (Geddes 1995). Because technical societies also function, in effect, as trade unions in many Anglo-Saxon countries, and originally controlled training through personal apprenticeships in many instances, they tend to concentrate on monopolizing particular work jurisdictions (Abbott 1988) and develop skills for carrying out existing tasks in the current 'best practice' mode for those jurisdictions. Competition between these occupational groups for control over problem-solving tasks encourages rather a narrow identification of particular skills with particular jobs and roles as they seek to maintain their distinctive social identity and privileged position in the labour market. The high degree of professional specialization in the British construction industry stems partly from this competition between occupational associations (Winch 1996, and Campagnac and Winch in this volume).

Where, on the other hand, skill definition, development, and assessment are carried out in more standardized ways involving state agencies and educational organizations, and prestigious qualifications are not so directly linked to specific roles and problem-solving tasks through professional associations' control of work jurisdictions, skills tend to be less tied to current professional practices and social identities less dependent on particular skill-based roles. Competences in these sorts of societies are more broadly based and not so tightly connected to specific jobs. However, since employers are involved in their definition, development, and evaluation, at least in the 'German' type of training system, they remain organizationally useful. In leading to distinctive occupational 'interests', then, such skills do not limit these to particular, narrowly defined roles. Because they are not so tied to specific jobs and tasks, these interest groups compete more broadly over a wider range of competences than do the Anglo-Saxon professional associations and skilled workers' unions, and seek to control areas of organizational activity rather than protect particular positions. Collective actors in these countries are unlikely to be so self-conscious of their distinctive 'professional' identity and interests as they are in societies where practitioner elites dominate skill definition, development, and certification.

In contrast, countries where public training systems are only weakly developed, have low status, and/or have little impact on the organization of labour markets and the organization of work in firms, certified skills are unlikely to form the basis of interest groups or to structure organizational roles. Instead, a combination of informal, personal groups and networks and the hierarchy of the general education system become key influences on group organization within and across firms. The role of kinship links, common geographical origins, and shared educational experiences in generating personal networks and common identities in and between organizations is well known in Pacific Asia, most notably perhaps among the expatriate Chinese (Limlingham 1986; Redding 1990), but also occurs in Europe and elsewhere. However, they rarely structure labour markets or organizational roles in a comparable manner to formally certified skills in societies with strong public training systems. On the other hand, the selection processes of the general education system can play a significant role in organizing careers and collective actors which transcend organizations and, sometimes, sectors.

The most notable example of educational stratification of labour markets and organizational hierarchies is perhaps the elaborate grading of *grandes écoles* in France, which strongly influences the careers of graduates and provides distinctive elite identities that are reinforced through the *grands corps*. Here, relative success in the formal public educational system has a strong, not to say the strongest, influence on individuals' life chances and differentiates access to jobs in large organizations. At the apex of the system, the small technically focused schools, including now the Parisian Commerce schools, provide high-status identities and organized networks which control—or at least strongly influence—access to top posts in the state bureaucracy and in the private sector (Bauer 1987). The *grands corps*, and arguably the *grandes écoles* in general, constitute important collective actors in France which transcend firm, sector, and ownership boundaries. It is less clear, however, that the universities or the *lycées* perform similar roles, not least because of their much greater size.

The education system in France, then, filters and grades people in ways that structure their future careers, but perhaps only generates organized collective actors at the elite level and so limits the scope of formally structured horizontal interest groups to elite groups. Similarly the Japanese education system organizes life chances and access to hierarchical positions in firms of different sizes, but does not itself generate distinctive, formally organized, interest groups which transcend organizational boundaries. While university attendance may structure factions and allegiances inside ministries and large firms in Japan, collective interests are typically based around employing organizations rather than horizontal identities derived from the educational system.

These general points also apply to managerial groups in that a strong and pervasive public training system will structure their identities and organization as well as those of manual and clerical workers, technicians, etc. Indeed, many continental European societies have not institutionalized distinctive managerial identities because of the strength of traditional apprenticeship and functional careers based on expertise in engineering, law, and other fields. As Stewart *et al.* (1994) have pointed out, a major difference between British and German managers lies in the formers' separation of their managerial role from technical proficiency and involvement in task performance, while the latter conflate their managerial identity with their technical competence. This partly reflects the much more systematic, prestigious, and far-reaching training system in Germany in which technical qualifications are cumulative and careers are what Offe (1976) calls 'task continuous'. Managerial skills and activities are viewed as building on existing technical competences because these are widespread and highly regarded rather than being detached from them as a separate set of capabilities. These characteristics also affect the ways that firms organize transactions between themselves, as Lane shows in her contribution.

Additionally, however, the development of distinctive managerial identities and collective interests, separate both from other occupational roles and from the success of individual employers and industries, reflects general arrangements governing access to capital and the organization of markets through their impact on managerial mobility and organizational change. The more managerial elites move between firms and sectors, the less committed they will be to any one organization and industry and the less they will view their particular expertise as being closely dependent on knowledge and experience of specific sectors. This is especially likely when, as in many post-war Anglo-Saxon economies, firms are often seen as diversified businesses which can be run as a portfolio of separate units, to be bought and sold as their financial performance dictates. In such companies, managerial expertise and interests are clearly less identified with those of particular divisions and industries than when senior managers spend most of their working lives in the same firm and/or sector and their careers depend on their success within it. A general set of managerial skills which are transferable across industries, such as those institutionalized in the MBA degree, is much more likely to be regarded as the basis for a distinctive identity and collective interest in the former societies than in the latter ones.

High rates of managerial mobility and discontinuous organizational change are more likely in economies where the financial system is dominated by capital markets and the state is essentially regulatory and remote from firms and markets. Capital markets in the post-war period have become dominated by institutional investors and fund managers who compete for investment returns on diversified portfolios of shareholdings and remain distant from the fortunes and activities of any one firm they invest in. Because investors are not committed to the future of any one company, they do not develop much expertise in its products, technologies, or markets and generally prefer to sell their shares than intervene when problems arise. Thus, capital market financial systems generate strong markets for corporate control in which ownership can change quite rapidly and businesses are bought and sold in the same way as commodities in general. Any one company can, then, radically alter its subsidiaries and its ownership. Managerial skills and interests in these economies are clearly not so closely dependent on specific industries and activities since the nature of firms can change quickly.

Additionally, such change is also facilitated by 'regulatory' states which stand aloof from economic processes and actors (Johnson 1982). They tend to outlaw cartels and similar forms of market collaboration as being 'anti-competitive', do not encourage strong sectoral trade associations and do not attempt to limit industry entry and exit. Here, firms are free to move into, and out of, any business sector and so industry membership is fluctuating with little collaboration between companies and weak institutionalization of industrial norms and regulatory conventions. The overall level of firm mobility in and out of industries, and their cooperation in training, bargaining, and other areas, are, then, additional factors affecting managers' dependence on the success of particular firms.

Similar factors affect the strength and scope of owner involvement in firms' affairs. Where shareholders treat their property rights as a diversified portfolio of assets to be bought and sold on liquid secondary markets solely as their financial performance dictates, clearly their interest in the activities and capabilities of any individual firm they invest in is quite limited and narrow. Conversely, where banks and other investors are effectively 'locked in' to shareownership and/or share trusteeship of specific businesses, they have to develop longer-term and broader interests in their growth and development, both to provide other services and business relationships as firms expand, and to ensure their investments pay off in the medium term. Investors here develop more elaborate monitoring skills and knowledge about specific clients' products, technologies, and markets so that they can evaluate particular risks more effectively and, over time, offer informed advice about opportunities and strategic choices. Credit-based financial systems in general develop broad owner interests because they, and/or their agents such as banks, trustees, and other intermediaries, cannot easily sell their shares on large, liquid, and anonymous capital markets and so are exposed to higher levels of risk for individual investments than owners in capital market-based financial systems.

A further factor encouraging close and wide ranging owner interest in particular firms' activities is the lack of trust in formal institutions for resolving disputes and ensuring contractual compliance. Clearly, remote owner–manager relations are more risky for investors when there is no well-established and functioning regulatory system and information asymmetries are considerable. The less reliable are the institutions governing property rights, the flow of information about firms' activities and control procedures, the more owners are likely to become closely involved in the affairs of their companies and be concerned with a wide range of issues. Whether in newly industrializing countries or in the former state socialist societies, this lack of institutional reliability limits owner delegation of control to managers and generally restricts the development of separate managerial roles and identities. Even where owners do not themselves manage operations in these circumstances, they will develop much more detailed understandings of their firms' activities and capabilities than those in societies where formal institutions are regarded as being more reliable, in order to manage the greater risks more effectively. This need to be personally fully informed about particular firms' products, technologies, and markets—or to be limited to relying only on those partners with whom strong levels of personal trust have been established—limits owners' abilities to diversify widely and/or to manage complex businesses which require much specialist technical knowledge to be successful. Thus, many Chinese family businesses diversify only into fields, such as property development, where dealing skills are more important than detailed technical knowledge of products and processes (Redding 1990). As Jaklic shows, however, these points do not apply where managers are effectively able to act as owners because a separate and distinct group of property rights holder has not yet become established as a powerful interest group, as in many former state socialist societies such as Slovenia.

Connection between institutions, interest groups, and work systems

Turning now to consider how these institutional features and characteristics of collective actors are connected to work patterns, I shall briefly discuss some of the key direct linkages between institutional arrangements and prevalent forms of work organization and control, before summarizing the ways in which particular combinations of these factors encourage and inhibit establishment of different work systems in different economies. In Table 12.4 I suggest that a strong and broadly based public training system in which employers and unions jointly play an important role will limit job fragmentation and manager–worker separation, and will probably encourage managers to rely on skilled workers for firm growth, effective task performance and problem solving, where firm, owner, and managerial mobility is limited. This is because certified skills are widely available, broadly based, and employers have confidence in their utility and flexibility. Together with strong state support for intermediary associations, these phenomena are also likely to restrict managerial control over work organization somewhat.

On the other hand, a high level of academic stratification of labour markets—which usually implies the absence of a strong, highly regarded, training system—limits employers' willingness to depend on skilled workers and increases manager–worker separation because of the lack of broad,

TABLE 12.4. Direct Linkages between Institutional Features and Work System Characteristics

Institutional Features	Work system characteristics					
	Job fragmentation	Workers' discretion	Managerial control over work organization	Manager–worker separation	Employer commitment to employment security	Reward basis
Strong continuity of skill-based groupings			−			skills
State support for intermediate organizations						
Strong and broad public training system	−	+	−	−	+	skills
High level of joint employer and union involvement in public training system	−	+	−	−	+	skills
Strong academic stratification			+	+	−	jobs
Capital market based financial system			+		−	
Low trust in formal institutions		−				personal evaluation
Paternalist authority relations	−	−	+			personal evaluation

publicly certified skills on which employers have had some influence, and the tendency for elite groups to regard those filtered out by the general education system as less worthy and competent overall than themselves. Skills are less likely to become the basis for reward allocation and differentials than organizational roles in this situation. Capital market-based financial systems additionally inhibit such dependence because of the strong market for corporate control and limited amount of owner risk sharing.

Low levels of contractual and fiduciary trust in business partners—including employees—encourage direct supervision of work processes and an unwillingness to delegate control to managers through formal procedures. Thus, fully-fledged Taylorist work systems which rely on impersonal and formalized control processes are unlikely to become established in societies where systemic trust is very limited. Relatedly, paternalist authority relations will also inhibit the development of formal rule-governed systems of work control because of their emphasis on personal relationships between leaders and the led. Similarly, these personal connections will limit job fragmentation and rigidity because the scope of superiors' authority is not restricted by impersonal rules. While unskilled work in Korean *chaebol* may, for example, be quite narrowly focused, supervisors may also be able to require rapid change to a variety of new tasks because of the lack of formal procedures delimiting obligations and job characteristics (Janelli 1993).

Combining these linkages with those involving characteristics of collective actors to explain the establishment of different work system types, it is often easier to see how particular combinations restrict the development of particular kinds of work organizations and control, rather than how they actively generate specific forms to become prevalent in a society. For example, high levels of job fragmentation, separation of task conception from task execution, and managerial coordination of work activities in Taylorist work systems are unlikely to be prevalent in market economies with strong horizontal associations, skill-based unions and an extensive and highly regarded training system with strong practitioner influence. These negative relationships are summarized in Figure 12.1 which highlights the major connections between institutions, interest groups, and work systems, omitting some of the relationships identified in Table 12.4.

Such connections are often strongest between extreme values of the variables discussed here and it is important to note that reverse relations do not always obtain. In the case of Taylorism for instance, the lack of strong institutions governing skill production, certification, and control in most East Asian societies has not led to the widespread reliance on highly fragmented tasks and jobs and formalized, rule-governed managerial coordination and control systems. They do, though, often limit the level of worker discretion and tend to rely more on direct supervision of work processes than occurs in many European countries (Janelli 1993; Lincoln and Kalleberg 1990; Redding 1990).

Similarly, work systems that rely heavily on contractual obligations and elaborate managerial hierarchies to control and coordinate activities are not likely to develop in societies where authority is largely paternalist and formal institutions governing competence and contractual trust are regarded as unreliable—or simply non-existent. These conditions are, though

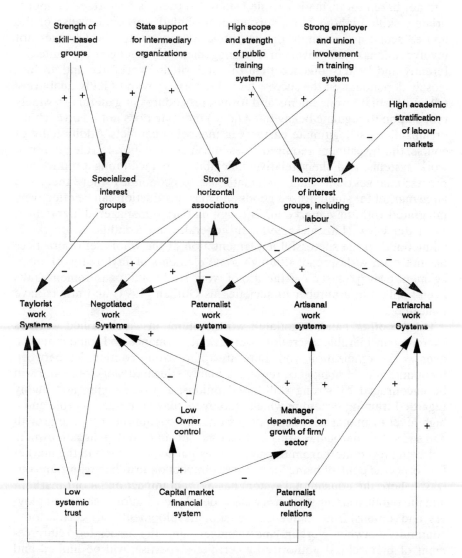

FIG. 12.1. Connections between institutional features, interest groups, and work system types (omitting some direct links between institutions and work systems)

likely to limit owners' willingness to delegate responsibility for controlling work to a managerial bureaucracy and/or to grant workers considerable discretion over task performance. Again, though, the reverse situation is by no means going to encourage Taylorism as many Central European countries demonstrate.

Overall, then, fully-fledged Taylorist work systems seem most likely to become widely established in a capitalist society when: (*a*) unions are weak and not based on formally certified skills, (*b*) there is a shortage of appropriately skilled labour but a surplus of unskilled workers because of the limited scope and strength of the public training system which does not involve unions or employers in its management, (*c*) managers are quite differently and better educated than the bulk of the workforce and are not closely dependent on the success and long-term growth of individual firms, (*d*) contractual arrangements and formal procedures in general are widely relied upon to regulate behaviour, and (*e*) the state does not involve labour organizations as legitimate partners in managing conflicts. Additionally, of course, the investment required to establish such elaborate rule-governed work systems, and their relative inflexibility in facilitating product and process changes, limit their systematic use to economies where there is a large market for standardized goods and mass production can be effectively integrated with mass marketing through elaborate managerial hierarchies, as in the USA (Lazonick 1991). In general, these conditions are rarely all met and so the successful implementation of the whole set of practices has not been widespread, although some elements of Taylorist work management principles, such as the use of work study and measurement, have been applied in a number of societies, as Guillén (1994) and others have indicated.

On the other hand, negotiated work systems in which skilled workers exercise considerable discretion over task performance and some influence over work organization, and there are quite strong continuities between them and middle managers, require a highly educated workforce and will be encouraged by strong skill-based unions, a wide ranging and highly regarded training system in which employers play an influential role and a high level of managerial dependence on, and commitment to, the growth and success of particular firms and sectors. This in turn depends on owners not being too remote from the activities of particular firms and the market for corporate control being limited in its impact on firm behaviour. In contrast, where the educational system has a direct impact on labour markets, and the public training system is weakly developed and/or excludes employers and unions from influence on skill development and certification, continuity between workers and managers, and the associated reinforcement of hierarchical authority by certified expertise, will be limited and managerial coordination of work processes more likely.

Given these points, it may be wondered how the post-war Japanese business system has developed such a considerable dependence on its core manual workforce with a high level of firm-specific skills being generated, or at least why the combination of academic stratification of labour markets, enterprise unions, and a weak public training system has not prevented the white collarization of the manual labour force. While it is not possible to provide a full answer here, I suggest that the high level of risk sharing between other economic groupings in the large-firm sector, particularly between banks, suppliers, customers, and trading companies, the coordinating role of state agencies in managing economic and industrial change and concomitant encouragement of interfirm cooperation, and the high dependence of managers on individual firm growth and success—together with substantial autonomy from passive shareholders—have all encouraged, or at least facilitated, the incorporation of the core, male workforce into the firms' long-term development (Whitley 1992).

Additionally, the shortage of skilled labour during the high-growth period and the strength of unions in the 1950s and 1960s further encouraged employers to invest in employees and develop mutual long-term commitments with them. It is particularly the lack of an effective external labour market for males over 30 years old in large firms which has made both managers and other groups of employees highly jointly dependent on the success of 'their' firm, thus weakening if not entirely negating the differentiating effects of the educational stratification of labour markets in Japan. Thus, paternalist work systems are encouraged by a high level of manager and large shareholder interdependence with firms, considerable risk sharing between organizations, their banks and—in the Japanese case—trading companies, together with a strong coordinating role by the state, and the absence of strong skill-based unions. Risk sharing and mutual dependence with the core workforce is helped here by the generally high level of cooperation in the economy and the close links between enterprise unions and employers in the large-firm sector.

Work systems that combine more personal management of work processes, considerable dependence on relatively autonomous skilled workers, and continuity between workers and owner-managers develop in a variety of circumstances, such as the industrial districts of north-east and central Italy and western Jutland, but share a common rejection of extensive managerial hierarchies and formal systems of coordinating work processes. In Denmark this seems to arise from the combination of strong skill-based unions which exert considerable influence over the extensive and highly regarded state-funded training system with considerable continuity between skilled workers and managers and a lack of influence from capital owners beyond the entrepreneurial groups of owner-managers (Kristensen 1996, and in this volume).

In Italy, unions are also influential, especially in the Emilia-Romagna, but do not seem to be so organized around skills or to exert such strong control over the training system. Here, the localization of work in specialized communities which have strong systems of reputational control and informal coordination processes, buttressed by municipal and allied organizations, that combine personal and formal means of facilitating internal cooperation and excluding outsiders enables small firms to integrate inputs and outputs without formal managerial procedures and ensure that both workers and owner-managers are jointly dependent on the success of the sector or part of the production chain. Effectively all the major groups in these industrial districts are locked in to each others' fate so that they have to collaborate as well as compete in the short to medium term and so risks are shared throughout particular geographical areas (Langlois and Robertson 1995; Lazerson 1988, 1995; cf. Friedman 1988).

In contrast, patriarchal work systems are the product of an insecure business environment in which trust and authority are highly personalized and formal procedures are rarely relied upon to control behaviour or resolve disputes. In societies where these are dominant forms of work organization and control, horizontal associations are weak and often based on kinship ties or similar ascriptive criteria so that workers have little collective influence. Given the overriding pursuit of flexibility and risk reduction by limiting commitments in many of the antagonistic and adversarial contexts where these work systems are widespread, for example among the overseas Chinese (Redding 1990), job and task fragmentation is usually limited. Paternalist political ideologies obviously reinforce these tendencies to highly personal and directive control over work processes by owner-managers (Deyo 1989).

5. CONCLUSIONS AND IMPLICATIONS

This analysis of the conditions encouraging and inhibiting the development and widespread adoption of different kinds of work systems emphasizes the importance of what Lane, following the Aix group, terms the societal effect, as opposed to the dominance effect, in explaining variations and changes in work organization and control across capitalist economies. The highly societally specific nature of many labour market institutions, education and training systems, state structures and policies, and the other institutions discussed above have generated quite varied forms of interest representation and capital–labour relations. As many of the chapters in this book show, these variations and historical continuities prevent the establishment of a single standard pattern of work organization throughout a sector across institutional boundaries and ensure that local conditions mediate the adoption of production systems from elsewhere, despite the efforts of managerial elites such as those described by Mueller and Loveridge.

In particular, the wholesale transfer of managerial practices without alteration from one context to another, such as those sometimes characterized as 'Japanization', is clearly impracticable, as the papers by Hibino and Sharpe indicate (cf. Abo 1994). Just as technological innovations change over the course of their development and adoption, so too do social innovations, whether transferred from abroad or developed domestically, alter as their context changes and different aspects are accepted in different situations. As long, then, as the organization of interest groups and prevalent rules of the game governing workplace relations vary significantly between societal contexts, the standardization of work systems around a single model of efficient production will remain limited. Rather, some features of work organization are being transferred across countries by some multinational firms, as Mueller and Loveridge discuss in this volume, but these typically vary between firms and contexts as interest group structures and institutional arrangements differ in nature and strength across contexts. Economic functionalist arguments which simply assume that competition will automatically standardize work systems are, then, inadequate.

This contextual interdependence of work organization and control patterns has a number of implications for the analysis of work system change. First, it is clear that widespread and radical transformation of the prevalent system in any society is highly dependent on related changes in the most closely linked rules of the game and organization of interest groups. Changing the basis of reward systems in German organizations, for example, away from skills towards more individual evaluations by supervisors and personnel departments is most unlikely to become widely implemented without quite major changes in union structures and powers, and in the organization and prestige of the public training systems. Similarly, institutionalizing 'Japanese' levels of mutual dependence between employers and employees in Anglo-Saxon societies without also limiting the market for corporate control—and hence altering the operation of the financial system—and increasing the 'stickiness' of external labour markets is likely to prove difficult, if not impossible in the short term. The more integrated the work system is with institutional arrangements that are standardized and firmly established throughout a society, the more difficult such change will be, as Schienstock's analysis of Baden-Württemberg implies.

Second, as the Fordism literature indicates, many work system characteristics are closely connected to other aspects of dominant business systems, particularly the nature of firms, and thereby further integrated with their institutional context. For example, the considerable employer commitment to employment security for their core workforce in large Japanese companies is linked to the general pattern of risk sharing between firms, banks, and other agencies in Japan, and to their relatively low degree of diversification, broad owner–management connections and focus on growth strategies (Whitley 1992). Changing this characteristic significantly would, then, involve changing a number of important aspects of Japanese large firms and their interrelated institutional contexts, which is why the recent major recession in Japan has not resulted in substantial alterations to these employment policies in most large companies.

Third, because the degree of institutional integration and mutual dependence in capitalist societies varies between, say, Britain and Japan, the variety of work systems and their susceptibility to change also differs substantially. Sectoral variations in how work is organized and controlled are more significant when labour market institutions and interest groups are not highly standardized throughout a society and differ between industries. Similarly, changing such practices will be easier, in principle, where it does not involve challenging the entire national pattern of labour market organization and highly institutionalized system of interest group organization. Altering some aspects of British patterns of work organization in some sectors is, then, more straightforward than it would be in Germany or some Scandinavian countries. The extent of societal regulation and standardization of interest groups and workplace relations, and their interdependence with other institutional features, thus affects the variability of work systems between industries and the ease of changing them, as the contributions of Kristensen, Sharpe, and Schienstock emphasize. The regulated and standardized nature of workplace relations and groups in state socialist societies helps to explain the limited extent of organizational change in many enterprises despite the institutional transformations of the late 1980s and early 1990s in these countries, as Jaklic suggests.

Fourth, just as the standardization and integration of key institutions affect the variability and susceptibility to change of work systems within societies, so too the varying strength and centrality of particular institutional arrangements and interest groups affect the likelihood that some characteristics of work systems can be altered more easily than others in different countries. The strength of the German public training system, for example, means that altering the basis of rewards is more difficult for firms operating in that country than it is in Britain where the training system is more weakly institutionalized and standardized across industrial sectors. This in turn affects the systemic nature of work systems in different countries. Because of the nationally regulated nature of many aspects of workplace relations, interest groups, and training systems in Germany and some other European countries, work system characteristics are more interconnected and standardized throughout the society than they tend to be in Anglo-Saxon countries where the state does not play such a strong role in coordinating activities and the formal system of regulation is less elaborate.

Work system change in the latter countries is usually more piecemeal than in the former ones as a result.

Finally, although the systemic and institutionally interlocked nature of many characteristics of work organization in capitalist economies, and the associated institutional 'lock-in' effect discussed by Schienstock in this volume (cf. Grabher 1993; Herrigel 1994), limits major changes to work systems in the short term throughout a number of societies, it is worth pointing out that some interest group structures and institutions are more established and unlikely to change than others. Most obviously, perhaps, the nature of many formal rules and procedures are more susceptible to reform and influence by collective actors than are the conventions by which they are generated and altered. The rules of the game are usually longer lived and more deeply entrenched than are the specific policies and outcomes of conflicts which they govern.

For example, labour law and training systems are typically more malleable than the structure of interest groups involved in battling over changes or the conventions according to which disputes are settled. Similarly, professional jurisdictions and expertise change more in Britain than the dominant conception of the profession as the primary mode of organizing high-level expertise and its practitioner-controlled training and certification system which has existed for over 500 years. New skills and occupational groups continue to follow similar patterns which retain considerable prestige (cf. Geddes 1995). To change the nature of skill-based groups and the ways they compete in the workplace in Britain, especially in non-manual areas of work, is a very slow process and would involve major shifts in the roles of professional associations, the state, and educational organizations. So too in Baden-Württemburg and other European regions, changing the policies of regional governments, developing new skills and technology institutes are relatively straightforward compared to altering the ways these activities are carried out and the nature of the groups involved. Where, then, particular rules of the game or background institutions are closely linked to patterns of work organization and control, these latter are unlikely to alter radically, but where in contrast the associated structures and conventions are more recently developed and linked to specific policies, such as the 1980s reforms of some Scandinavian financial systems, institutional lock-ins are less restricting.

REFERENCES

Abbott, A. (1988), *The System of Professions* (Chicago: University of Chicago Press).
Abo, T. (1994), *Hybrid Factory* (Oxford: Oxford University Press).

Barber, B. (1983), *The Logic and Limits of Trust* (New Brunswick, NJ: Rutgers University Press).

Bauer, M. (1987), *Les 200* (Paris: Seuil).

Beetham, D. (1991), *The Legitimation of Power* (London: Macmillan).

Boyer, R. (1988), 'Which Model Should Europe Follow?' in R. Boyer (ed.), *The Search for Labour Market Flexibility* (Oxford: Clarendon Press), 189–290.

——(1990), 'The Capital Labour Relations in OECD Countries', Paris: CEPREMAP Working Paper No. 9020.

——(1991), 'Capital Labor Relation and Wage Formation: Continuities and Changes of National Trajectories', in T. Mizoguchi (ed.), *Making Economies more Efficient and More Equitable* (Tokyo: Kinokuniya), 297–340.

——(1994), 'Do Labour Institutions Matter for Economic Development? A "Regulation" Approach for the OECD and Latin America, with an Extension to Asia', in G. Rodgers (ed.), *Workers, Institutions and Economic Growth in Asia* (Geneva: ILO), 25–112.

Child, J., Fores, M., Glover, I., and Lawrence, P. (1983), 'A Price to Pay? Professionalism and Work Organization in Britain and Germany', *Sociology*, 17: 63–78.

Deyo, F. C. (1989), *Beneath the Miracle: Labour Subordination in the New Asian Industrialism* (Berkeley: University of California Press).

Friedman, A. L. (1977), *Industry and Labour* (London: Macmillan).

Friedman, D. (1988), *The Misunderstood Miracle* (Ithaca, NY: Cornell University Press).

Geddes, B. (1995), 'The Development of Accountancy Education, Training and Research in England', unpublished Ph.D. thesis, University of Manchester.

Grabher, G. (1993), 'The Weakness of Strong Ties: The Lock-in of Regional Development in the Ruhr Area', in G. Grabher (ed.), *The Embedded Firm* (London: Routledge), 255–77.

Guillén, Mauro F. (1994), *Models of Management: Work, Authority and Organization in a Comparative Perspective* (Chicago: University of Chicago Press).

Herrigel, G. (1994), 'Industry as a Form of Order', in R. Hollingsworth, P. Schmitter, and W. Streeck (eds.), *Governing Capitalist Economies* (Oxford: Oxford University Press), 97–128.

Janelli, R. L. (1993), *Making Capitalism: the Social and Cultural Construction of a South Korean Conglomerate* (Stanford, Calif.: Stanford University Press).

Johnson, C. (1982), *MITI and the Japanese Miracle* (Stanford, Calif.: Stanford University Press).

Jürgens, U. (1989), 'The Transfer of Japanese Management Concepts in the International Automobile Industry', in S. Wood (ed.), *The Transformation of Work* (London: Allen and Unwin), 204–18.

Katzenstein, P. J. (1985), *Small States in World Markets* (Ithaca, NY: Cornell University Press).

Kristensen, P. H. (1992), 'Strategies against Structure: Institutions and Economic Organisation in Denmark', in R. D. Whitley (ed.), *European Business Systems* (London: Sage Publications).

——(1996), 'On the Constitution of Economic Actors in Denmark', in R. Whitley and P. H. Kristensen (eds.), *The Changing European Firm* (London: Routledge), 118–58.

Kuhn, S. (1989), 'The Limits to Industrialization: Computer Software Development in a Large Commercial Bank', in S. Wood (ed.), *The Transformation of Work?* (London: Unwin Hyman), 266–78.

Kumazawa, M., and Yamada, J. (1989), 'Jobs and Skills under the Lifelong *Nenko* Employment Practice', in S. Wood (ed.), *The Transformation of Work?* (London: Unwin Hyman), 102–26.

Lane, C. (1989), *Management and Labour in Europe* (Aldershot: Edward Elgar).

Langlois, R. N., and Robertson, P. L. (1995), *Firms, Markets and Economic Change* (London: Routledge).

Lazerson, M. H. (1988), 'Organisational Growth of Small Firms: An Outcome of Markets and Hierarchies', *American Sociological Review*, 53: 330–42.

——(1995), 'A New Phoenix? Modern Putting-out in the Modena Knitwear Industry', *Administrative Science Quarterly*, 40: 34–59.

Lazonick, W. (1991), *Business Organization and the Myth of the Market Economy* (Cambridge: Cambridge University Press).

Limlingan, V. S. (1986), *The Overseas Chinese in Asean: Business Strategies and Management Practices* (Pasig, Metro Manila: Vita Development Corporation).

Lincoln, J., and Kalleberg, A. (1990), *Culture, Control and Commitment* (Cambridge: Cambridge University Press).

Luhmann, N. (1979), *Trust and Power* (Chichester: John Wiley).

——(1988), 'Familiarity, Confidence, Trust: Problems and Alternatives', in D. Gambetta (ed.), *Trust* (Oxford: Blackwell), 94–107.

Maurice, M., Sellier, F., and Silvestre, J. J. (1986), *The Social Foundations of Industrial Power* (Cambridge, Mass.: MIT Press).

——Sorge, A., and Warner, M. (1980), 'Societal Differences in Organising Manufacturing Units', *Organisation Studies*, 1: 59–86.

Merkle, Judith A. (1980), *Management and Ideology* (Berkeley: University of California Press).

North, D. (1993), 'Institutions and Credible Commitment', *Journal of Institutional and Theoretical Economics*, 149: 11–23.

Offe, C. (1976), *Industry and Inequality* (London: Edward Arnold).

Pye, L. (1985), *Asian Power and Politics* (Cambridge, Mass.: Harvard University Press).

Redding, S. G. (1990), *The Spirit of Chinese Capitalism* (Berlin: de Gruyter).

Sorge, A. (1991), 'Strategic Fit and the Societal Effect: Interpreting Cross-National Comparisons of Technology, Organisations and Human Resources', *Organisation Studies*, 12: 161–90.

——(1996), 'Societal Effects in Cross-National Organization Studies', in R. Whitley and P. H. Kristensen (eds.), *The Changing European Firm* (London: Routledge), 67–86.

Stewart, R., Barsoux, J.-L., Kieser, A., Ganter, H.-D., and Walgenbach, P. (1994), *Managing in Britain and Germany* (London: Macmillan).

Trigilia, C. (1990), 'Work and Politics in the Third Italy's Industrial Politics', in F. Pyke *et al.* (eds.), *Industrial Districts and Inter-firm Cooperation in Italy* (Geneva: ILO), 160–84.

Whitley, R. (1992), *Business Systems in East Asia* (London: Sage).

Winch, G. (1996), 'Contracting Systems in the European Construction Industry', in R. Whitley and P. H. Kristensen (eds.), *The Changing European Firm* (London: Routledge).

Wong, S.-L. (1988), 'The Applicability of Asian Family Values to other Sociocultural Settings', in P. L. Berger and H.-H. M. Hsiao (eds.), *In Search of an East Asian Development Model* (New Brunswick, NJ: Transaction Books).

Wood, S. (1989), 'The Transformation of Work?', in S. Wood (ed.), *The Transformation of Work?* (London: Unwin Hyman), 1–45.

INDEX

Index